CRUISERS

OF THE ROYAL AND COMMONWEALTH NAVIES
SINCE 1879

DOUGLAS MORRIS

MARITIME
BOOKS

First published in Great Britain by
Maritime Books, Liskeard, Cornwall.

© *Douglas Morris 1987*

ISBN 0 907771 35 1

Design by Evan Jones

Typeset and printed in Great Britain by
Penwell Ltd., Parkwood, Callington, Cornwall.

ACKNOWLEDGEMENTS

Grateful thanks are due to the following for allowing their photographs to be used in this book:

Imperial War Museum
Wright and Logan
Husbands of Bristol
National Maritime Museum
Fleet Photographic Unit

Skyfotos
Beken of Cowes
Royal New Zealand Navy
Australian War Memorial

Without the encouragement of the publisher, Mike Critchley of Maritime Books, this book might well have remained a box of index cards. I am indebted to Lt. Cdr. B. Warlow R.N. for checking accuracy and for his most valuable advice in revising the original draft. Any errors that remain are my own.

Finally, I would like to thank my family, colleagues and friends for their interest and patience during the preparation of this work.

Douglas Morris

Tunbridge Wells
October 1987

CONTENTS

ABBREVIATIONS

AA	anti aircraft	LCS	Light Cruiser Squadron
AMC	Armed Merchant Cruiser	m	metres
ASW	anti submarine warfare	mm	millimetres
aw	above water	MG	machine gun
BLR	breech loading, rifled	MLS	Mine Layer Squadron
BS	Battle Squadron	NCACo	Naval Construction and
CS	Cruiser Squadron		Armament Company
cyl.	cylinders	oa	(length) over all
DF	Destroyer Flotilla	pdr	pounder
DNC	Director of Naval Constrution	pp	(length) between perpendiculars,
DP	dual purpose		i.e. from stempost to rudderpost.
Flot.	Flotilla	QF	quick firing
ft	feet	RAN	Royal Australian Navy
GWS	guided weapon system	RCN	Royal Canadian Navy
HA	high angle	RN	Royal Navy
HDAC	horizontal double-acting	RNZN	Royal New Zealand Navy
	compound	SHP	shaft horse power
HMAS	His (Her) Majesty's Australian	S/M	submarine
	Ship	SMS	Seine Majestats Schieffe (His
HMCS	His (Her) Majesty's Canadian		Majesty's Ship)
	Ship	SR	single reduction
HMNZS	His (Her) Majesty's New Zealand	TB	torpedo boat
	Ship	TC	torpedo carriage
HMS	His (Her) Majesty's Ship	TE	triple expansion
HP	horse power	TT	torpedo tubes
IHP	indicated horse power	USS	United States Ship
in	inch	VC	vertical compound
kts	knots		
LA	low angle		

METRIC EQUIVALENTS OF GUN AND TORPEDO SIZES

9.2in	234mm		3in	76mm
8in	203mm		13pdr	76.2mm
7.5in	191mm		3pdr	47mm
6in	152mm		2pdr	40mm
5.5in	140mm	Torpedo		
5.25in	133mm	tubes:	21in	533mm
5in	127mm		18in	457mm
4.7in	119mm		14in	256mm
4.5in	114mm			
4in	102mm			

INTRODUCTION

The cruiser was the heir, but not the descendant, of the frigates of Nelson's day, which during the Napoleonic wars were the 'eyes of the fleet', working with the battlefleet, scouting and shadowing. At the same time, in squadrons hugging the enemy coast, frigates pressed home a classic blockade of French arsenals. Blockade and counter blockade remained central to understanding the cruiser's role. In 1914 and again in 1939, British cruiser strategy was to enforce a blockade against Germany and round up her commerce raiders.

In the melting pot of warship evolution from 1860-80, the three decker 'wooden walls' went to extinction, and the frigate with its guns on a single deck became the progenitor of a new generation of battleships. The frigate's place was taken by a succession of fully rigged 'cruising ships', 'corvettes' or 'cruizers' of composite construction, the last of which were built in the 1880s. Their place was taken in turn by the burgeoning family of late Victorian cruisers, which were all-steel and fully fledged steamships. It is with these ships that our story begins.

Great endurance for independent operations was the cruiser's first requirement. She had to be faster than the generality of merchant ships—faster still if she was to work with the fleet, as most cruisers were expected to do. Size varied enormously, even among contemporary ships; some cruisers were almost second-class battleships, while others were little more than colonial gunboats. But great or small, their function was always bound up with command of the sea.

Admiral of the Fleet Lord Hill-Norton has expressed it well; 'The battle fleet guaranteed sea power: the cruisers put it into practice.' Britain's naval supremecy in the nineteenth century, guaranteed in the Channel and in the Mediterranean by the presence of her vast battle fleets, had to be made effective in every sea and ocean for her empire and commerce to be secure. Britain's majestic mastery of the seas for a century and a half was never malevolent or vainglorious: born of necessity, it was maintained as a defence posture as hard-headed as it was herculean. It sought to preserve the freedom of the seas because any threat to that freedom threatened to rob Britain of her possessions, her trade, and increasingly, her very livelihood. As the principal instrument of that policy, the cruiser was for Britain primarily a defensive weapon. In the hands of her rivals, the cruiser was a commerce raider and an inexpensive means of undermining the Royal Navy's supremecy.

To extend that supremecy throughout the globe, Britain built and maintained a prodigious number of cruisers. She had 132 of all types in 1897, 107 in 1907, 122 in 1914, 119 in 1918, 57 in 1939, 26 in 1950, and 13 in 1960. Normally in peacetime a little over half would be in full commission. On them the peace of the world depended in no small measure for eighty years and, in two world wars they battled for its destiny. Most of the ships now stand in the twilight of living memory, and a book like this, of its nature, can do no more than baldly record the past without doing justice to its drama or tale. Even so, this book is dedicated with respect and gratitude to the men who breathed life and soul into these artefacts of steel.

This volume began as a collection of brief ship histories, to which data and short notes have been added for each class. The intention was never to write a technical book, although care has been taken to ensure accuracy. Data refers to ships as built. Major changes in armament are recorded, but no attempt is made to note every minor alteration; where small variations arose within a class after completion, armament is given for a representative ship.

AUTHOR'S NOTES

Data on protection is confined to the principal protective features—the belt, the protective deck, and the box citadels. The reader can take it that protection was also applied gunshields, turrets, barbettes, ammunition hoists and conning towers. An explanation of the various patterns of protection is given in an Appendix.

British cruisers divide fairly naturally into eight waves of ships having contemporary spans of service. In the chapter titles 1879-1905, etc., the first date is the year in which the earliest ships in the group entered service, and the second is usually a watershed year by which the vast majority had been withdrawn. Each chapter is prefaced by a background to the factors which determined the building and service of the ships, and usually ends with cruiser dispositions just prior to the next generation entering service. Other background notes are interspersed in the text where they seem most appropriate. On the basis of their short service lives, the Bristol and Arethusa classes strictly belong in the 1901-19 section, but are included with the later 'Town' and 'C' classes in the following chapter so as not to artificially interrupt two lines of development.

Battle of Sirte—taken from the bridge of *Euryalus*.

1879-1905: THE FIRST GENERATION

Dispatch Vessels: Iris class

Cruisers: Leander, Mersey, Blake, Medea and Pallas classes

Belted Cruisers: Orlando and Imperieuse classes

Torpedo Cruisers: Scout, Archer, Barracouta and Barham classes

The Fleet which *Iris* and *Mercury* joined in 1879 was in a parlous state. Decades of peace had induced torpor and complacency. There was much drill and shining paintwork, but the arts of war were little practiced. The Navy had been neglected by Disraeli's government and starved of money. Its ships represented each phase of the immense evolution in warship design that had taken place over the previous twenty years: some were built of wood, some of wood and iron, others of iron or iron and steel, while the latest were all steel; most ships had both engines and a full sailing rig, but some were more true steamers than others; some had muzzle loading and others breach loading guns. From such a rag-bag it was impossible to form homogenous and efficient fighting squadrons, and the sheer pace of developments had rendered many quite new ships obsolete.

Surveying the scene in 1879, three ship designs stand out as embodying the latest and best in naval thinking, pointing the way forward: the battleship *Collingwood*, the despatch vessel *Iris*, and the torpedo boat *Lightning*. Each firmly belonging to the dawning age of steel and steam and became, respectively, the basis for most future battleship, cruiser, and torpedo boat developments.

Iris and *Mercury* were followed by the improved but similar Leanders, developed in turn into the Mersey class ordered in 1883, which became the genesis of the whole family of late Victorian cruisers. Quite outside this mainline of development, two armoured cruisers, *Imperieuse* and *Warspite* were laid down in the early 1880s, and also two little torpedo cruisers, *Scout* and *Fearless*.

Sailing corvettes, loosely described as 'cruising vessels', continued to be built into the 1880s, the last examples being the steel framed and iron plated Comus class (2,380 tons) of nine ships launched in 1878-81, and their near sisters, *Calypso* and *Calliope* (2,770 tons) launched in 1883-84. These, and three earlier armoured cruisers *Shannon*, *Nelson* and *Northampton* properly belong to the transitional era and are not included in this work.

Meanwhile, across the Channel, Britain was facing a growing threat from France. Throughout the 1880s there was an increasing awareness that 'something had to be done' about the Navy in terms both of efficiency and material. Naval shipbuilding gained new impetus in 1884 when the First Lord of the Admiralty, Lord Northbrook, unveiled a £3.1m five year plan of construction. The Northbrook programme, as it came to be called, provided for two battleships (*Sans Pareil* and *Victoria*), seven Orlando class armoured cruisers, six Archer class torpedo cruisers and 14 torpedo boats. On this occasion the Liberal government had been stung into action in an election year by the public outcry which followed a series of articles in the Pall Mall Gazette, showing the Navy to be deficient in men, organization, ships, stores and equipment. The magazine's editor, W. T. Stead, had been fed all the information he needed by the Hon. Reginald Brett and a rising Captain J. A. Fisher, then captain of the naval gunnery school, HMS *Excellent*. The same alliance between the journalist Stead and the then Admiral Fisher as First Sea Lord reappeared to help usher in the Dreadnought era twenty years later.

In 1885, William White (who designed the *Iris*) succeeded Nathaniel Barnaby as Director of Naval Construction. Later to be one of the principal authors of the Naval Defence Act, White put in hand many organization reforms, both in the Dockyards and at the Admiralty, which paved the way for the naval expansion to come. By the time this outstanding naval architect and public servant retired in 1902, he had been responsible for the designs of no fewer than 128 British cruisers, though his most celebrated designs were the Royal Sovereign and Majestic class battleships.

White's earliest cruiser designs as DNC foreshadowed the shape of things to come: the Blakes were prototype first class protected cruisers; the Medeas initiated a long cycle of second class protected cruisers, and the Pallases, five of which were built under the Imperial Defence Act of 1887, set the pattern for third class protected cruisers. The handsome two funnel profile, first seen in the Orlandos, was now firmly established and became typical of the late Victorian cruiser.

In 1887 the Colonial Conference made public some of the findings of the Carnarvon Commission concerning 'The Defence of British possessions and commerce abroad'. The Commission had found that overseas bases were practically undefended, and that the Navy in its present state was incapable of defending either the bases or the sea lanes. So the stage was set for a great naval resurgence.

All the ships in this section, except four Pallases, were authorised before the Naval Defence Act, and all were completed between 1879 and 1892. Most of them saw extensive service until the early 1900s, and nearly all met their end under Fisher's axe in 1905, when he scrawled across a list of 154 ships of the Royal Navy 'Scrap the lot!' A few went on to serve for many years as destroyer or submarine depot ships. Only one, *Philomel*, survived by fluke to serve as a cruiser in the First World War.

Mercury, 1890, prior to departure for China Station.

IRIS CLASS (2 ships)

Iris, Mercury

Displacement (tons):	3,730 load.
Dimensions (feet):	330pp, 333oa (*Mercury* 315oa) x 46 x 22
(metres):	91.4pp, 101.5oa, (96oa) x 14 x 6.7
Machinery:	2 shaft Maudslay 2 cyl. HDAC. 8 oval, 4 cylindrical boilers. 6,000 IHP = 17 knots. Forced draught: *Iris* 7,300 HP = 17¾ knots. *Mercury* 7,735 HP = 18½ knots.
Fuel:	Coal 780 tons.
Protection:	Nil.
Armament: as built;	10—64pdr MLR, 4—torpedo carriages.
Iris **1880;**	2—64pdr MLR, 4—6in BL, 4—5in BL, 4—torpedo carriages.
Both ships 1888;	13—5in BL, 4—torpedo carriages.
Complement:	275

Designed as Dispatch Vessels by William White under the direction of Nathaniel Barnaby, but later re-rated as Second Class Cruisers, *Irish* and *Mercury* were the Royal Navy's first all-steel ships. Within their long, slender hulls, an unprecedented amount of space was devoted to machinery, and powerful engines and fine lines made them the fastest ships of their day, *Mercury* attaining 18.6 knots. Genuine steamers, their light barque sailing rig was for tradition's sake only, and was in time reduced and eventually removed. Extensive internal subdivision gave their unarmoured hulls some protection against flooding.

Soon after completion, *Iris* had her main deck 64pdrs replaced by a mixture of 6in and 5in guns; she retained her forecastle and poop 64pdr mountings. Both ships were given a uniform 5in armament in 1887-88.

Mercury was distinguished from *Iris* by her straight bow, accounting for her shorter length.

IRIS

Built at Pembroke Dockyard. Laid down 10.11.1875. Launched 12.4.1877. Completed 4.1879 Mediterranean 1879-87. Portsmouth Reserve 1887-1903. Harbour service, Portsmouth as tender to *St Vincent* for Mechanical Training of Boys 1903-04. Sold 1905.

MERCURY

Built at Pembroke Dockyard. Laid down 16.3.1876. Launched 17.4.1878. Completed 9.1879 Portsmouth Reserve 1879-90. China 1890-95. Portsmouth Reserve 1895-1903. Navigation School Ship for Navigating Officers, Portsmouth (seagoing) 1903-05. Submarine Depot Ship, Portsmouth 1906-13. Hulked at Chatham, 1914, for service at Rosyth and renamed *Columbine*. Sold 1919, Forth S'breaking Co., Bo'ness.

Iris **showing fine lines—note different bow.**

LEANDER CLASS (4 ships), *1880 Programme*

Amphion, Arethusa, Leander, Phaeton

Displacement (tons):	4,300 load.
Dimensions (feet):	300pp, 315oa x 46 x 20½
(metres):	91.4pp, 96oa, 14 x 6.2
Machinery:	2 shaft, 2 cyl. HDAC. 12 cylindrical boilers. 5,500 IHP = 16½ knots.
Fuel:	Coal 1,016 tons.
Protection:	Deck over machinery, 1½in (38mm).
Armament:	10—6in BLR, 4—3pdr, 16 MGs. 4—TT above water.

Originally classed as Dispatch Vessels, but re-rated as Second Class Cruisers before completion. Similar to *Iris* and *Mercury*, but incorporating a short protective deck and improved armament and machinery. The light barque rig, identical to *Mercury's*, was more of a hindrance than a help and was reduced first to a barquentine and then to a schooner rig. In their last days, those in commission were stripped of spars altogether. Good steamers but disappointing seaboats, wet amidships and rolling heavily in some weather conditions.

Amphion with original sailing rig.

Arethusa, **1896, with spars removed.**

AMPHION

Built at Pembroke Dockyard. Laid down 25.4.1881. Launched 13.10.1883. Completed 1887. Held at Devonport 1887-88. Pacific 1888-90. Mediterranean 1890-95. Devonport 1895-97. Pacific 1897-1904 (refit 1900). At Devonport 1905. Sold 5.1906, King, Garston.

ARETHUSA

Built by Napier, Glasgow. Laid down 14.6.1880. Launched 23.12.1882. Completed 1886. Held at Chatham 1886-93. Mediterranean 1893-97. Chatham 1897-99. Pacific 1899-1903 (China, temp. 1900). At Chatham 1903-05. Sold 4.1905, Garnham.

Battle Honour: China 1900.

LEANDER

Built by Napier, Glasgow. Laid down 14.6.1880. Launched 28.10.1882. Completed 29.5.1885. Particular Service 1885. China 1886-96. Chatham 1896-97. Pacific 1897-1901. Converted to Destroyer Depot Ship 1902-04. Depot Ship, Mediterranean 1904-05, Atlantic 1905, Nore 1906, Devonport 1907-14, Grand Fleet 1914-19. Devonport, paid off 1919-20. Sold 1920, Castle, Plymouth.

PHAETON

Built by Napier, Glasgow. Laid down 14.6.1880. Launched 27.2.1883. Completed 20.4.1886. Mediterranean 1886-93. Devonport Reserve 1893-97. Pacific 1897-1903. Harbour service, Devonport 1904-   . Sold 1913, became *TS Indefatigable* (1.1914), renamed *Carrick II* 1941. Broken up, Ward, Preston, 1947.

MERSEY CLASS (4 ships), *1883 Programme*

Forth, Mersey, Severn, Thames

Displacement (tons):	4,050 load.
Dimensions (feet):	300pp, 315oa x 46 x 19½
(metres):	91.4pp, 96oa x 14 x 5.9
Machinery:	2 shaft, 2 cyl. HDAC. 12 boilers. 4,500/6,000 HP = 17/18 knots.
Fuel:	Coal, 900 tons.
Protection:	Full length deck 3in-2in (76mm-51mm).
Armament:	2—8in BLR, 10—6in BLR, 3—6pdr QF, TT: *Severn* 1 sub., 2aw; *Mersey* 2 sub., 2aw; *Forth, Thames* 2aw.
Complement:	300

The first cruisers without any sailing rig whatever. Otherwise similar to the Leanders but with a full length protective deck and much higher bulwarks to secure dryness amidships. In many ways the most successful cruisers so far; handy ships, steady gun platforms, and good seaboats. Unfortunately, the advent of the quick-firing gun soon rendered the Merseys obsolescent, and only *Severn* saw much active employment as a cruiser. After many years in reserve, however, *Forth* and *Thames* survived the 1905 axe to give long service as depot ships.

*Mersey,*1887, **on completion.**

IMPERIAL WAR MUSEUM

Severn, **1892, on China Station—the only one of her class to serve abroad as a cruiser.**

FORTH

Built at Pembroke Dockyard. Laid down 1.12.1884. Launched 23.10.1886. Completed 1889 Devonport Reserve 1889-1903. Submarine Depot Ship, Devonport 1904-14, Humber 1914-16, Harwich 1916-19. Portsmouth, paid off 1919. Sold 11.1921, Slough Trading Co., and broken up in Germany 1921.

MERSEY

Built at Chatham Dockyard. Laid down 9.7.1883. Launched 31.3.1885. Completed 1887. Chatham Reserve 1887-93. Coast Guard, Harwich 1893-98. Chatham Reserve 1898-1905. Sold 1905, Isaacs.

SEVERN

Built at Chatham Dockyard. Laid down 1.1.1884. Launched 29.9.1885. Completed 1888. Prepared for service at Portsmouth 1888-89. China 1889-95. Chatham Reserve 1895-98. Coast Guard, Harwich 1898-1904. Chatham 1904-05. Sold 1905, Isaacs.

THAMES

Built at Pembroke Dockyard. Laid down 14.4.1884. Launched 3.12.1885. Completed 1888. Devonport Reserve 1888-1903. Submarine Depot Ship, Portsmouth 1903-07, Sheerness 1907-14, Harwich 1914, Sheerness 1914-17, Portsmouth and Campbeltown 1917-19. Chatham, paid off 1919. Sold to South Africa, 1920, and renamed *General Botha* Training Ship at Cape. Scuttled in Simon's Bay 1947.

ORLANDO CLASS (7 ships), *Northbrook Programme 1884*

Aurora, Australia, Galatea, Immortalité, Narcissus, Orlando, Undaunted

Displacement (tons):	5,600 load.
Dimensions (feet):	300pp, x 56 x 22½
(metres):	91.4pp, 17.1 x 6.9
Machinery:	2 shaft 3 cyl. TE. 4 double ended boilers. 5,500/8,500 HP = 17/18 knots.
Fuel:	Coal.
Protection:	Midship belt 10in (254mm) — 200ft x 5½ft (61m x 1.7m) Bulkheads 16in (406mm). Deck (full length) 3in-2in (76mm-51mm).
Armament:	2—9.2in, 10—6in BL, 10—3pdr QF, 2—18in TT submerged.
Complement:	484

Enlarged Merseys, with 9.2in guns and a narrow midship belt. Though technically armoured cruisers, the Orlandos were built for trade protection rather than the fleet role (for which they were too slow), and are best considered as protected cruisers pure and simple. The belt was in any case too low in the water to be of much value, since a recasting of the design to incorporate heavier machinery and more bunkerage had raised the load waterline to the belt's top edge.

Funnels were raised after a few years to improve draught, and all the class were rearmed in the 1890s with 30 calibre 9.2in and quick-firing 6in guns.

Despite their useless belts and poor speed, the Orlandos were popular in service, reliable steamers and good seaboats. With a range of 8,000 miles at 10 knots, they were ideally suited for world-wide trade protection. However, the armoured cruiser type was not repeated in the Royal Navy until the Cressys, thirteen years later.

AURORA

Built at Pembroke Dockyard. Laid down 1.2.1886. Launched 28.10.1887. Completed 9.1889. Devonport 1889-90. Channel Squadron 1890-92. Devonport 1892-93. Coast Guard, Bantry 1893-95. Devonport 1895-99. China 1899-1902. Refit, Clydebank 1902-03. Devonport 1904. Laid up, Holy Loch 1905. Sold 10.1907, Payton, Milford Haven.

Battle Honour: China 1900.

AUSTRALIA

Built by Fairfield, Govan. Laid down 21.4.1885. Launched 25.11.1886. Completed 10.1888. Chatham 1888-89. Mediterranean 1889-93. Coast Guard, Southampton Water 1893-1903. Chatham 1904. Sold 1906, King, Troon.

Galatea. **Some of this class appeared at the 1889 review with dummy wooden guns.**

GALATEA

Built Napier, Glasgow. Laid down 21.4.1885. Launched 10.3.1887. Completed 3.1889. Portsmouth 1889-90. Channel Squadron 1890-92. Portsmouth 1892-93. Coast Guard, Queensferry 1893-95. Coast Guard, Hull 1895-1903. At Chatham 1904. Sold 1905.

IMMORTALITE

Built at Chatham Dockyard. Laid down 18.1.1886. Launched 7.6.1887. Completed 1.7.1890. Channel Squadron 1890-94. Chatham 1894-95. China 1895-99. Sheerness 1899-1901. Tender to *Wildfire* as Gunnery Training Ship, Sheerness 1901-05. Laid up in Holy Loch 1905-07. Sold 1907, Shipbreaking Co., Blackwell.

NARCISSUS

Built by Earle Hull. Laid down 27.4.1884. Launched 15.12.1886. Completed 7.1889. Chatham Reserve 1889-92. Channel Squadron 1892-94. Portsmouth 1895. China 1895-99. Portsmouth 1899-1901. Tender to *Excellent* as Gunnery Training Ship, Portsmouth 1901-05. Sold 1906.

ORLANDO

Built by Palmers, Jarrow. Laid down 23.4.1885. Launched 3.8.1886. Completed 6.1888. Flagship, Australia 1888-98. Portsmouth 1898-99. China 1899-1902. Portsmouth 1903-05. Sold 1905, Ward, Morecambe.

Battle Honour: China 1900.

UNDAUNTED

Built by Palmers, Jarrow. Laid down 23.4.1885. Launched 25.11.1886. Completed 7.1889. Devonport 1889-90. Mediterranean 1890-93. China 1893-1900. Tender to *Cambridge* as Gunnery Training Ship, Devonport 1901-04. Sold 1907, Harris, Bristol.

Battle Honour: China 1900.

Orlando, 1898, note lengthened funnels.

Narcissus, 1899, at **Portsmouth.**

BLAKE CLASS (2 ships), *1887 Programme*

Blake, Blenheim

Displacement (tons):	9,150 load.
Dimensions (feet):	375pp, 399¾oa x 65 x 24
(metres):	114.3pp, 121.8oa, 19.8 x 7.3
Machinery:	2 shaft, 3 cyl. TE. 6 double ended cylindrical boilers, 13,000/20,000 HP = 20/22 knots.
Fuel:	Coal 1,800 tons.
Protection:	Full length deck 6in-3in (152mm-76mm).
Armament:	2—9.2in, 10—6in QF, 16—3pdr, 4—14in. TT (2 submerged, 2 above water).
Complement:	570

Built as a response to France's *Dupuy de Lome*, the Blakes were the biggest cruisers yet and longer than the contemporary Royal Sovereign class battleships. Shipping the same armament as Barnaby's Orlandos, the Blakes illustrate White's radically different approach to ship design. Speed was raised to 22 knots by a vast increase in installed power, necessitating a much longer hull. Side armour was abandoned in favour of a thicker protective deck, some protection also being applied to gunshields, casemates, ammunition hoists etc.

The design speed of 22 knots presupposed an unrealistic degree of forced draught, and in practice the Blakes were 20 knot ships. Both became Destroyer Depot Ships after the 1905 axe ended their careers as cruisers.

BLAKE

Built at Chatham Dockyard. Laid down 7.1888. Launched 23.11.1889. Completed 1892. Flagship, N. America & W.I. 1892-95. Channel 1895-98. Devonport Reserve 1898-1907 (trooping to Mediterranean 1900-01). Converted to Destroyer Depot Ship 1907. Depot Ship, Nore 1908-09, Home 1909-14, 2 DF then 11DF Grand Fleet 1914-19. Sold 1922, Rees, Llanelli.

BLENHEIM

Built by Thames Iron Works. Laid down 10.1888. Launched 5.7.1890. Completed 26.5.1894. Held at Chatham 1891-94. Channel 1894-98. Reserve 1898-1901. China 1901-04. Converted to Destroyer Depot Ship 1905-06. Depot Ship, Home 1906-13, Mediterranean 1913-20. Depot for Reserve Minesweepers, Harwich and later, Sheerness 1921-25. Sold 1926, Ward, Pembroke Dock.

Blake, **1895.**

Blenheim **served for 30 years, the second half of her career as a depot ship.**

MEDEA CLASS (5 ships), *1886 Programme*

Magicienne, Marathon, Medea, Medusa, Melpomone

Displacement (tons):	2,800 load, *Medea & Medusa*, 2,950 others (sheathed).
Dimensions (feet):	265pp, 278oa x 41 (42 sheathed) x 16½
(metres):	80.8pp, 84.7oa, 12.5 (12.8) x 5
Machinery:	2 shaft, 2 cyl. VC in *Medea & Medusa*, HDAC others, 6 cylindrical boilers. 5,000/9,000 HP = 16/20 knots.
Fuel:	Coal 400 tons.
Protection:	Full length deck 2in (51mm) *Medea & Medusa*, 1½in (38mm) rest.
Armament:	6—6in BLR (eplaced by 6in QF in 1890s), 9-6pdr QF, 3 MGs, 4—18in TT above water.
Complement:	218

Reduced editions of the Merseys, and William White's first cruiser design on his return to the Admiralty. Powerful little ships on paper, in fact too much had been attempted on their modest dimensions. Overgunned and very cramped, space in the boiler rooms was too restricted for efficient stoking, and they were poor steamers, particularly in a seaway. They also proved bad seaboats, low freeboard making them very wet amidships.

Unlike their sisters, *Medea* and *Medusa* were not sheathed for foreign service and had vertical, rather than horizontal, engines. The cylinders, protruding above the protective deck, had to be enclosed in an armoured glacis.

Despite their shortcomings the Medeas were considered worth re-arming with quick-firing guns in the 1890s, and saw extensive service into the new century. They were re-rated third class cruisers in 1890.

MAGICIENNE

Built by Fairfield, Govan. Laid down 10.8.1887. Launched 12.5.1888. Complete 1889. Cape 1890-91. N. America & W.I. 1891-96. Devonport 1896-97. Cape 1897-1901 (Gambia 1901). Devonport, paid off 1901-04. Sold 1905.

Battle Honour: South Africa 1899-1900.

MARATHON

Built Fairfield, Govan. Laid down 10.8.1887. Launched 23.8.1888. Completed 1889. East Indies 1890-97. Refit, Portsmouth 1897-98. East Indies 1899-1901. Portsmouth, laid up 1901-04. Sold 1905, Ward, Preston.

Battle Honour: China 1900.

Marathon, 1898, with *Melpomme* and *Magicienne* **had a sheathed and copper bottom.**

Medea, 1903, in the new overall grey paint (known as crabfat).

MEDEA

Built at Chatham Dockyard. Laid down 25.4.1887. Launched 9.6.1888. Completed 4.1895.
RNR Drillship, Southampton 1895-1901. Refit, Jarrow 1901-02. Cruiser Training Squadron
1902-03. Seagoing Tender to TS *Impregnable* at Devonport 1904. Laid up, Sheerness 1904-09.
Attached Mediterranean BS 1909-13. Sold 1914.

MEDUSA

Built at Chatham Dockyard. Laid down 25.8.1887. Launched 11.8.1888. Completed 1895.
RNR Drill Ship, North Shields 1895-1901. Refit, Jarrow 1901-02. Cruiser Training Squadron
1902-03. Seagoing Tender to TS *Impregnable* at Devonport 1904. Laid up, Motherbank
1905-08. Sales list at Sheerness 1908. Refit, Pembroke Dock 1909. Towed to Bantry Bay for
use as calibrating vessel 1910. Harbour service, Queenstown 1917-18. Sold 1920, Stanlee.
Resold 1921, J. E. Thomas.

MELPOMONE

Built at Portsmouth Dockyard. Laid down 10.10.1887. Launched 20.9.1888. Completed 1890.
Pacific 1890-93. Portsmouth 1894-97. East Indies 1897-1900. Portsmouth, paid off 1901-05.
Sold 1905, Ward Preston.

PALLAS CLASS (9 ships)

Katoomba, Mildura, Ringarooma, Tauranga, Wallaroo (Imperial Defence Act 1887).
Pallas, Pearl, Philomel, Phoebe (Naval Defence Act 1889).

Displacement (tons):	2,575 load.
Dimensions (feet): **(metres):**	265pp, 278oa x 41 x 15½ 80.8pp, 84.7oa, 12.5 x 4.7
Machinery:	2 shaft 3 cyl. TE. 4 double ended cylindrical boilers. Australians 4,000/7,500 HP = 17/19 knots; British 4,500/7,500 = 17½/19 knots.
Fuel:	Coal, 440 tons..
Protection:	Full length deck 2in-1in (51mm-25mm).
Armament:	8—4.7in QF, 8—3pdr, 4—Nordenfelts, 4—14in TT above water.
Complement:	217

Third class cruiser editions of the Medeas, with 4.7in in place of 6in guns and reduced engine power. More balanced ships than the Medeas which were quarts in pint pots, but still indifferent seaboats.

The first five ships were built under the Imperial Defence Act 1887 to form an Australasian squadron. Following their launch they were renamed in 1890 after small towns in Australia and New Zealand (Tauranga). The four ships with 'P' names were built under the Naval Defence Act 1889 for general service in the Royal Navy, and had slightly more powerful machinery.

Speed and power dropped off after a few years, particularly in the less well maintained Australian ships, but all served until 1903-05. *Philomel* survived her sisters to become the first ship of the New Zealand Division of the Royal Navy in 1913, and went on to see active employment in the First World War. Later, as harbour training ship at Auckland, she came to be remembered as the cradle of the Royal New Zealand Navy.

KATOOMBA (ex Pandora)

Built by Armstrong, Elswick. Laid down 15.8.1888. Launched 27.8.1889. Completed 24.3.1891. Australia 1891-1905. *(Katoomba* and *Wallaroo* replaced by *Encounter*). Sold 1906.

MILDURA (ex Pelorus)

Built by Armstrong, Elswick. Laid down 15.8.1888. Launched 25.11.1889. Completed 18.3.1891. Australia 1891-1905. Sold 1906, Garnham.

Wallaroo, 1891, survived WW1 serving as a guard ship.

RINGAROOMA (ex *Psyche*)

Built by Thomson, Clydebank. Laid down 6.12.1888. Launched 10.12.1889. Completed 3.2.1891. Australia 1891-1904. Sold 1906, Forth S'breaking Co.

TAURANGA (ex *Phoenix*)

Built by Thomson, Clydebank. Laid down 1.12.1888. Launched 28.10.1889. Completed 27.1.1891. Australia 1891-1905. Sold 1906, Ward, Preston.

WALLAROO (ex *Persian*)

Built by Armstrong, Elswick. Laid down 16.8.1888. Launched 5.2.1890. Completed 31.3.1891. Australia 1891-1905 *(Wallaroo* and *Katoomba* replaced by *Encounter).* Harbour service 1906-   attached to *Indus,* TS for mechanicians. Rearmed 1914 for service as guardship at Chatham. Renamed *Wallington,* 3.1919. Sold 1920, G. Sharpe.

PALLAS

Built at Portsmouth Dockyard. Laid down 1.7.1889. Launched 30.6.1890. Completed 30.6.1891. China 1891-94. Portsmouth 1894-96. N. America & W.I. 1896-1900. Refit 1900. N. America & W.I. 1900-04. Sold at Bermuda, 1906.

PEARL

Built at Pembroke Dockyard. Laid down 1.4.1889. Launched 28.7.1890. Completed 10.1892. Devonport Reserve 1892-97. N. America & W.I. 1897-1901. Cape 1901-04. Sold at Simonstown 1906. Broken up by Cohen, Felixstowe.

Philomel, 1909, became the first ship of the New Zealand Division of the Royal Navy in 1914. Went on to survive World War 2.

PHILOMEL

Built at Devonport Dockyard. Laid down 8.5.1889. Launched 28.8.1890. Completed 10.11.1891. Cape 1891-98. (Benin River 1894). Refit, Devonport 1898. Cape 1898-1902. Refit, Haulbowline 1902. Non effective list 1904. Laid up, Firth of Forth 2.1905. Refit, Haulbowline 1906-08. Attached Mediterranean BS 1908. East Indies 1909-13. New Zealand Division from 1914. Pacific 1914. Mediterranean and Persian Gulf 1914-17. Paid off 1917. Training hulk at Auckland 1921, later Base Ship. For disposal 1946. Scuttled off Coromandel 1949.

Battle Honours: Benin 1897, South Africa 1899-1901.

PHOEBE

Built at Devonport Dockyard. Laid down 23.4.1889. Launched 1.7.1890. Completed 1.12.1892. Cape 1892-99 (Benin River 1894, M'wele 1895-96, Benin 1897). Devonport 1899-1901. Australia 1901-05. Paid off, Portsmouth 1905. Sold 1906. A. Anderson of Copenhagen.

Battle Honour: Benin 1897.

In the 1870s, Britain built the armoured cruiser *Shannon*, followed by the larger *Nelson* and *Northampton*. Truly transitional ships, steel framed and iron plated, steam powered and fully rigged, they were designed by Barnaby to serve as flagships on foreign stations. Almost battleships, with a main armament of 10in guns, they had a waterline belt with a full length protective deck above it. The all-steel *Imperieuse* and *Warspite* laid down in 1881 were their successors.

IMPERIEUSE CLASS (2 ships)

Imperieuse, Warspite

Displacement (tons):	8,500 load (8,400 after removal of rig.)
Dimensions (feet):	315pp, x 52 x 27¼
(metres):	96pp, 18.9 x 8.3
Machinery:	2 shaft Maudslay *(Warspite* Penn) 3 cyl. inverted compound engines, cylindrical, oval boilers. 8,000/10,000 IHP = 16/16¾ knots.
Fuel:	Coal 900 (max. 1,130) tons. Range 5,500 miles at 10 knots.
Protection:	Midship belt along boiler & machinery spaces 10in (254mm), 140ft (42.6m) long, closed by bulkheads 9in (228mm). Full length deck, 2in (51mm) over belt, 4in (102mm) fore and aft of belt.
Armament:	4—9.2in BL, 10—6in BL, 4—6pdr QF, 6—18in TT above water.
Complement:	555

Cruiser counterparts of the Collingwood class battleships, *Imperieuse* was as French-inspired as her name, notably in having a marked tumblehome and in the cruiciform disposition of her main guns. During construction bunker capacity was greatly increased, which, with other alterations, made these ships badly overweight. Concern for their stability led to them being sheathed with 10 inches of teak (instead of four inches), increasing beam by one foot. With belts low in the water and unresponsive under a worse than useless brig rig which only aggravated weight and stability problems, poor *Imperieuse* was the butt of much satirical comment during trials. On her captain's recommendation, masts and rig were removed and the midship derrick replaced by a pole mast with a military top. She was a much better ship for losing her heavy tophamper, and the same modifications were incorporated into *Warspite*, still building.

This ugly pair never quite lived down their initial failure, but serving turns as flagship on the Pacific station, they found their niche in the late Victorian Navy. Satisfactory if slow steamers, able to bring three 9.2in guns to bear in any direction, Russia even flattered them with an imitation in *Admiral Makarof*.

Imperieuse, **1886, as completed. On her (unsuccessful) trials with sailing rig which led to Warspite's completion without (see next page).**

IMPERIEUSE

Built at Portsmouth Dockyard. Laid down 10.8.1881. Launched 18.12.1883. Completed 9.1886. Reserve and refit—masts removed 1886-87. Commissioned for 1887 Review. Reserve 1887-88. Flagship, China 1889-94. Refit 1894-96. Flagship, Pacific 1896-99. Refit and Reserve, Chatham 1899-1905 (commissioned for 1903 Manoeuvres). Depot ship for TBDs at Portland as *Sapphire II* 1905-12. Sold 1913, Ward, Morecambe.

WARSPITE

Built at Chatham Dockyard. Laid down 25.10.1881. Launched 29.1.1884. Completed 6.1888. Reserve 1888-90 (commissioned for Manoeuvres 1888 and '89). Flagship, Pacific 1890-93. Port guard ship, Queenstown 1893-96. Reserve and refit 1896-99. Flagship, Pacific 1899-1902. Chatham Reserve 1902-04. Sold 1905, Ward, Preston.

Warspite, 1897, as completed, showing the completely different appearance without sailing rig.

THE TORPEDO CRUISER

The torpedo was the most fearsome weapon on the naval scene in the late nineteenth century. But until the advent of the submarine the torpedo vessel faced a near-suicidal task, having to endure withering fire before she approached the enemy close enough to loose off her torpedoes. It was therefore essential for the torpedo attacker to present the smallest possible target for the shortest possible time.

The early torpedo boats were indeed small and fast, but too small and frail to be regarded as true ocean-going ships.

The Royal Navy's cycle of torpedo cruisers represents an attempt to evolve a sea-going torpedo carrier. While they were at least proper little ships able to go anywhere in any weather, they all lacked the speed to be effective torpedo craft. Indeed the Archers and Barracoutas, though rated as torpedo cruisers, were primarily gun vessels intended for trade protection and imperial policing.

Fearless, 1887.

SCOUT CLASS (2 ships)

Fearless, Scout

Displacement (tons):	1,580 load.
Dimensions (feet):	229pp, 225oa x 34¼ x 14½
(metres):	67.1pp, 68.6oa, 10.4 x 4.4
Machinery:	2 shaft 2 cyl. HDAC. 4 boilers. 2,000/3,200 HP = 16/17 knots.
Fuel:	Coal 450 tons.
Protection:	Deck over machinery ⅜in (10mm).
Armament:	4—5in BLR (replaced by 4—4.7in QF during 1890s), 8—3pdr QF, 3—14in TT (1 above water, 2 below).
Complement:	147

Britain's first torpedo cruisers. Too slow for their intended role and poor seaboats. Protection was limited to ⅜in plating over the machinery spaces, complemented by wing coal bunkers and good internal subdivision. Rearmed in the 1890s with 4.7in QF guns in place of the 5in BLRs.

FEARLESS

Built by NCA Co. Barrow. Laid down 22.9.1884. Launched 20.3.1886. Completed 7.1887. Mediterranean 1888-1900. Refit, Sheerness 1901. China 1901-04. Sold at Portsmouth 1905. Battle Honour: South Africa 1899-1900.

SCOUT

Built by Thomson, Clydebank. Laid down 8.1.1884. Launched 30.7.1885. Completed 1887. Mediterranean 1887-1903 (Gambia 1901). Sold 1904. Battle Honour: South Africa 1900-01.

Scout, 1887, at Portsmouth with sails fitted.

ARCHER CLASS (8 ships), *Northbrook Programme 1884*

Archer, Brisk, Cossack, Mohawk, Porpoise, Racoon, Serpent, Tartar.

Displacement (tons):	1,770 load.
Dimensions (feet):	225pp, 240oa x 36 x 16
(metres):	68.6pp, 73.2oa, 11 x 4.9
Machinery:	2 shaft 2 cyl. HDAC. 4 boilers. 2,500/3,500 HP = 15/16½ knots. *(Racoon & Serpent* 4,500 HP forced draught = 17½ knots.)
Fuel:	Coal 475 tons.
Protection:	Deck over machinery ⅜in (10mm).
Armament:	6—6in, BLR, 8—3pdr, 3—14in TT above water.
Complement:	176

Developed from the Scouts with the same limited scheme of protection, but aggressively over-gunned, and sheathed and coppered for tropical service. Too slow for torpedo work, they were re-rated third class cruisers soon after completion. Though better seaboats than the Scouts they rolled abnormally at times and were very wet in heavy weather. Not particularly good steamers, their cramped machinery was at least reliable, which explains the class' extensive service and their albeit qualified success.

ARCHER

Built by Thomson, Clydebank. Laid down 2.3.1885. Launched 23.12.1885. Completed 11.1888. Cape 1888-91. China 1891-99. Chatham 1900. Australia 1900-04. Sold 1905, Forrester, Swansea.

BRISK

Built by Thomson, Clydebank. Laid down 2.3.1885. Launched 8.4.1886. Completed 20.3.1888. Cape 1888-89. East Indies 1889-98 (Witu 1890). Chatham 1898. China 1898-1902. Malta Reserve 1902-04. Sold 1906, Ward, Preston.

Battle Honour: East Africa.

COSSACK

Built by Thomson, Clydebank. Laid down 2.3.1885. Launched 3.6.1886. Completed 11.1888. East Indies 1889-1903 (Witu 1890). Chatham 1904. Sold 1905, Garnham.

Archer **as built with 3 masts.**

MOHAWK

Built by Thomson, Clydebank. Laid down 2.3.1885. Launched 6.2.1886. Completed 12.1890. Cape 1890-92. N. America & W.I. 1892-97. Chatham 1897. Australia 1897-1901. Chatham 1902. Mediterranean 1903-04. Sold 1905, Garnham.

PORPOISE

Built by Thomson, Clydebank. Laid down 2.3.1885. Launched 7.5.1886. Completed 12.2.1888. Chinca 1888-97. Australia 1897-1901. Refit, Sheerness 1902-03. East Indies 1903-04. Sold at Bombay, 1905.

RACOON

Built at Devonport Dockyard. Laid down 1.2.1886. Launched 6.5.1887. Completed 1888. Devonport Reserve 1889-91. Cape 1891-97 (M'wele 1895-96). Refit 1897. East Indies 1898-1901 (detached to Cape 1900-01). Sheerness Reserve 1901-refit abandoned. Sold 1905, Cohen.

Battle Honour: South Africa 1900-01.

SERPENT

Built at Devonport Dockyard. Laid down 9.11.1885. Launched 10.3.1887. Completed 3.1888. Devonport Reserve 1888-90 (Annual Manoeuvres 1888 & 89). Commissioned for Cape 1890 but wrecked on passage off Northern Spain, 10.11.1890.

TARTAR

Built by Thomson, Clydebank. Laid down 2.3.1885. Launched 28.10.1886. Completed 1888. Sheerness Reserve 1888-91. N. America & W.I. 1891-97. Refit, Chatham 1898. Cape 1898-1900. Reserve 1900-02. Refit, Haulbowline 1902-03. South Atlantic 1903-04. Sold 1906, Forrester, Swansea.

Battle Honour: South Africa 1899-1900.

Brisk, 1898, showing reduction to 2 masts.

BARRACOUTA CLASS (4 ships), *1887 Programme*

Barracouta, Barrosa, Blanche, Blonde

Displacement (tons):	1,580 load.
Dimensions (feet):	220pp, 233oa, x 35 x 16
(metres):	67.1pp, 71oa, 10.7 x 4.9
Machinery:	2 shaft 3 cyl. TE. 4 double ended cylindrical boilers. 1,750/3,000 HP = 15/16½ knots.
Fuel:	Coal 160 tons.
Protection:	Full length deck 2in-1in (51mm-25mm).
Armament:	6—4.7in QF, 4—3pdr, 2—14in TT above water.
Complement:	160

Designed by William White, and a considerable advance on previous torpedo cruisers. Their vertical steam engines, mounted side by side, took up only half the hull length that horizontal engines would, laid one after the other. This better use of space enabled the Barracoutas to have an effective full length protective deck—the first cruisers of their size to do so, and essential with the advent of the quick firing gun. Steadier ships than their predecessors but poor seaboats, wet in heavy weather, particularly amidships.

Never intended for fleet work, the Barracoutas were sheathed and coppered for service on foreign stations where docking facilities were sparse. After a few years they began to suffer from boiler trouble: *Blonde* and *Blanche* were refitted with Laird boilers in 1900-02.

Barracouta, **1897.**

BARRACOUTA

Built at Sheerness Dockyard. Laid down 1888. Launched 16.5.1889. Completed 1890. At Sheerness 1890-93. S.E. Coast of America 1893-96. Sheerness 1897. Cape 1897-1903. Chatham and Sheerness 1904-05. Sold 1905, McLellan.

Battle Honour: South Africa 1900-01.

BARROSA

Built at Portsmouth Dockyard. Laid down 5.1888. Launched 16.4.1889. Completed 1890. At Portsmouth 1890-94. Channel (temp.) 1894. Cape 1894-1901 (Brass River 1895, M'wele 1895-96). Refit, Haulbowline 1902-03. Cape 1903-05. Sold 1905.

Battle Honours: Benin 1897, South Africa 1899-1900.

Barrosa, **1891, note twin funnels side by side.**

BLANCHE

Built at Pembroke Dockyard. Laid down 5.1888. Launched 6.9.1889. Completed 1890. East Indies 1890-91. Cape 1891-94 (Witu 1893, Juba River 1894). Devonport 1894-96. Mediterranean 1896-97. Devonport 1898-1900—including reboilering. Cape 1900-03. South Atlantic 1903-04. Devonport, laid up 1904-05. Sold 1905, Ward, Preston.

Battle Honour: South Africa 1901.

BLONDE

Built at Pembroke Dockyard. Laid down 5.1888. Launched 22.10.1889. Completed 1890. At Devonport 1890-92. Cape 1892-99 (M'wele 1895-96, Sierra Leone 1898-99). Devonport 1899-1905, including reboilering 1901-02. Sold 1905.

Battle Honour: East Africa 1895.

BARHAM CLASS (2 ships), *1887 Programme*

Barham, Bellona

Displacement (tons):	1,830 load.
Dimensions (feet):	280pp, 293oa x 35 x 13¼
(metres):	85.3pp, 89.3oa, 10.7 x 4
Machinery:	2 shaft 3 cyl. TE. 6 locomotive boilers. 3,600/6,000 HP = 16/19 knots.
Fuel:	Coal 140 tons.
Protection:	Full length deck 2in-1in (51mm-25mm).
Armament:	6—4.7in QF, 4—3pdr, 2—14in TT above water.
Complement:	170

A final fling at the torpedo cruiser concept, the Barhams were really Barracoutas greatly lengthened to double boiler and machinery spaces. Intended for fleet work, they were not sheathed. Sadly, the design speed presupposed an unrealistic degree of forced draught, and after lengthy trials a speed of only 16 knots had to be accepted. Reboiling in 1898-99 raised speed to 18 knots.

Too slow for their intended role, they were employed as dispatch vessels in the Home and Mediterranean fleets.

Bellona, 1904, engine room between boiler rooms giving widely spaced funnels.

BARHAM

Built at Portsmouth Dockyard. Laid down 22.10.1888. Launched 11.9.1889. Completed 1890. Portsmouth (trials) 1890-93. Mediterranean 1893-96. Portsmouth Reserve 1896-98. Reboilered 1898-99. Mediterranean 1899-1902. Portsmouth Reserve 1902-04. Fishery Protection Squadron 1905-06. Attached Mediterranean B.S. 1907-12 (Somaliland 1908-10). Sold 1914, Ward, Preston.

BELLONA

Built by Hawthorn, Hebburn. Laid down 1889. Launched 29.8.1890. Completed 1891. Portsmouth (trials) 1891-92. Channel Squadron 1892-97. Reboilered, Portsmouth 1898-99. Fisheries 1899-1905 (Mediterranean, temp. 1900). Sold. 1906.

BRITISH CRUISER DEPLOYMENT, MARCH 1891

Mediterranean and Red Sea:
  Amphion, Australia, Fearless, Phaeton, Scout, Undaunted.

Channel Squadron:
  Aurora, Immortalite.

North America and West Indies:
  *Canada, *Comus, *Emerald, *Pylades, *Tourmaline.

South East Coast of America:
  *Cleopatra.

Pacific:
  *Champion, *Garnet, Melpomone, Warspite.

Cape of Good Hope and West Coast of Africa:
  Magicienne, Mohawk.

East Indies:
  Blanche, *Boadicea, Brisk, *Conquest (temp.), Cossack, Marathon.

China:
  Archer, *Caroline, *Hyacinth, Imperieuse, Leander, Mercury, Porpoise, Severn.

Australia:
  *Cordelia, *Curacoa, Orlando, *Rapid, *Royalist.

Training Squadron:
  *Active, *Calypso, *Ruby, *Volage.

Ordered Home:
  *Turquoise.

---

*Old corvettes, re-rated as cruisers. Note: Ships in refit or reserve not included.

1892-1919: EXPANSION

1st Class Cruisers: Edgar, Crescent, Powerful and Diadem classes.

2nd Class Cruisers: Apollo, Astraea, Eclipse, Arrogant, Highflyer and Challenger classes.

3rd Class Cruisers: Pelorus class.

The building of cruisers had been neglected by successive Boards of Admiralty ever since the advent of the steamship, because it was believed that merchant ships could be easily converted to act as scouts and assist in commerce protection. At last it was recognised that such conversions would be insufficient, and the Naval Defence Act and the Spencer Programme both placed heavy emphasis on the building of cruisers:

Naval Defence Act 1889. Cost £21.5m over five years.
- 8 battleships (7 Royal Sovereigns, 1 Hood)
- 2 second class battleships (Centurions)
- 9 first class cruisers (7 Edgars, 2 Crescents)
- 8 second class cruisers (Astraeas)
- 21 second class cruisers (Apollos)
- 4 third class cruisers (Pallas)
- 18 torpedo gunboats

Spencer Programme 1893. Cost £31m over five years.
- 7 battleships (Majestics)
- 2 first class cruisers (Powerfuls)
- 6 first class cruisers (Diadems)
- 12 second class cruisers (Eclipses—9 built)
- 6 ram cruisers (Arrogants—4 built)
- 4 third class cruisers (Pelorus)
- 7 torpedo gunboats
- 2 sloops
- 82 torpedo boat destroyers
- 30 torpedo boats
- 1 torpedo depot ship

The Spencer Programme made its mark on history—in that Death Duty was introduced to help pay for it.

Most of the ships in this section were provided under either the Naval Defence Act or the Spencer Programme. By the late 1890s, modern cruisers had almost completely supplanted the old sailing screw-corvettes. One of the problems of this era of expansion was that the Navy could not man all its new ships and many, particularly the Apollos, were held for years in home ports, commissioning only for annual manoeuvres.

In 1890 all cruisers and cruising vessels had been re-classified according to a broad assessment of size, armament and speed. As a general rule, first class cruisers had 9.2in guns, second class cruisers had 6in guns, and third class cruisers were those with no 6in guns. Ships of this last category, which embraced the torpedo cruisers and old screw-corvettes, were not expected to work with the fleet. Little distinction was made between armoured and first class protected cruisers, as the narrow belts of the former conferred no appreciable advantage: the 1890s mark the heyday of the protected cruiser. But the tables turned dramatically in the new century, as light armour plate suddenly made vertical armour in cruisers a worthwhile proposition, and in a short time the large protected cruiser was obsolete.

By 1905 the first class protected cruisers were being brought home and reduced to nucleus crews. As for the second class cruisers, many Apollos were removed from the effective list in 1905; seven became minelayers and nine others were scrapped before 1914. The Astraeas, Eclipses and Highflyers were mostly retained in service for a few more years, partly for lack of replacement, as conventional cruiser building had ceased, and also because they were economical ships, well suited to foreign stations.

All surviving late-Victorian cruisers would have been scrapped soon after 1914 had war not intervened. As it was, most ships still capable of seagoing service were recommissioned in August 1914 to serve a few months in home waters, after which some paid off for subsidiary duties, while others dispersed to join foreign stations where they were little affected by the remainder of the war. Four old Edgars played an active part in the Dardanelles campaign; *Vindictive* and five Apollos met a valiant end as blockships at Zeebrugge and Ostend.

The last Victorian cruiser in commission *Highflyer*, paid off as flagship of the East Indies station at Bombay in 1921.

Hawke, **1893, in early livery.**

EDGAR CLASS (7 ships), *Naval Defence Act 1889*

Edgar, Endymion, Gibraltar, Grafton, Hawke, St George, Theseus

Displacement (tons):	7,350 load (7,700 *Gibraltar* and *St George*, sheathed).
Dimensions (feet):	360pp, 387½oa x 60 (60¾ sheathed) x 23¾ (24 sheathed)
(metres):	109.7pp, 118.1oa x 18.3 (18.5) x 7.2 (7.3)
Machinery:	2 shaft 3 cyl. TE, 4 double ended cylindrical boilers. 10,000/12,000 HP = 18½/20 knots.
Fuel:	Coal 1,250 tons.
Protection:	Full length deck 5in-3in (127mm-76mm).
Armament:	2—9.2in, 10—6in QF, 12—6pdr, 5—3pdr 4—18in TT (submerged).
Complement:	544

Smaller, more economical versions of the Blakes, but with the same armament and protection. By accepting a reduction in power for a speed of 20 knots, and smaller bunkerage for a range of 10,000nm, it was found possible to save 1,800 tons from the Blake's displacement. In fact the whole class exceeded design speed on trials and were regarded as quite the equals of the Blakes—themselves only good for 20 knots. *Gibraltar* and *St George* were sheathed and coppered.

The Edgars gave every satisfaction in service. Their machinery proved exceptionally reliable, and for this reason they saw an unusual amount of sea service for ships of their size.

St George became a Depot Ship in 1910. The rest of the class joined the Northern Patrol in August 1914, but the rigours of operating off the Shetlands and Norway proved a bit much for the old ships, and they were relieved at the end of the year by converted liners. *Gibraltar* then became a Depot Ship whilst *Edgar, Endymion, Grafton* and *Theseus* were refitted with a uniform 6in armament, net sweeping gallows and huge anti-torpedo bulges for service in the Dardanelles. Their 9.2in guns went to the M15 class monitors then being built. From the Dardanelles the four bulged ships went on to serve in the Mediterranean to the end of the war. *Hawke*, the only war loss, was torpedoed in the North Sea in September 1914.

EDGAR

Built at Devonport Dockyard. Laid down 3.6.1889. Launched 24.11.1890. Completed 2.3.1893. Mediterranean 1893-94. China 1894-97. Transport Service 1898-1900. Devonport 1901-02. Guardship, Holyhead 1903-04. Chatham 1905. Boys TS, N. America & W.I. 1905-06. Nucleus crew, Nore 1907. Trooping 1907-08. Portsmouth, 4th Divn 1909-11. 3rd Fleet 1912. Training Squadron, Queenstown 1913-14. 10 CS Northern Patrol 1914. Rebuilt (bulges) 1915. Dardanelles 1915-16. Aegean and Bulgarian Coast 1917. Gibraltar 1918. Queenstown, paid off 1919. Sold 1921, Ward, Morecambe.

Battle Honour: Dardanelles 1915-16.

St George **Flagship of the Cape Squadron circa 1895.**

ENDYMION

Built by Earle, Hull. Laid down 21.11.1889. Launched 22.7.1891. Completed 26.5.1894. Channel 1894-95. Particular Service 1896-97. Held at Chatham 1897-99. China 1899-1902. Refit, Harland & Wolff 1902-03. Channel 1904. Tender to *Wildfire* as Gunnery Training Ship, Sheerness 1905-12. 3rd Fleet, Portsmouth 1912-13. Flagship, Training Squadron, Queenstown 1913-14. 10 CS Northern Patrol 1914. Rebuilt (bulges) 1915. Dardanelles 1915-16. Mediterranean 1916-18. Aegean 1918. Nore, paid off 1919. Sold 1920, Evans, Cardiff.

Battle Honours: China 1900, Dardanelles 1915-16.

Endymion **showing anti-torpedo bulges and gallows.**

GIBRALTAR

Built by Beardmore, Dalmuir. Laid down 2.12.1889. Launched 27.4.1892. Completed 1.11.1894. Particular Service 1894-95. 'Flying Squadron' 1896. Mediterranean 1896-99. Portsmouth 1899-1901. Flagship, Cape 1901-04. N. America & W.I. 1904-06. Devonport, Nucleus Crew and 4th Divn 1906-13 (trooping to Australia 1908; escorted new destroyers *Parramatta* and *Yarra* to Australia 1910-11). Anti-submarine School, Portland 1914. 10 CS Northern Patrol, 1914. Disarmed early 1915. Depot Ship for Northern Patrol, Shetlands 1915-18. Destroyer Depot Ship, Anti-submarine school, Portland 1919-22. Sold 1923, Cashmore, Newport.

GRAFTON

Built by Thames Iron Works. Laid down 1.1.1890. Launched 30.1.1892. Completed 18.10.1894. Particular Service 1894-95. Flagship, China 1895-99. Chatham 1899-1901. Pacific 1902-04. Tender to *Excellent* as Gunnery Training Ship, Portsmouth 1905-13. Training Squadron, Queenstown 1913-14. 10 CS Northern Patrol 1914. Rebuilt (bulges) 1915. Dardanelles 1915-16. Mediterranean 1916-17. Red Sea 1917-18. Aegean 1918. Depot for British ships supporting White Russians, Black Sea 1919. Nore, paid off 1919-20. Sold 1920, Castle, Plymouth.

Battle Honour: Dardanelles 1915-16.

Grafton **fitted out for the Dardanelles Expedition.**

HAWKE

Built at Chatham Dockyard. Laid down 17.6.1889. Launched 11.3.1891. Completed 16.5.1893. Mediterranean 1893-99. Chatham Reserve 1899-1902. Special Service 1902. Home 1903-04 (Special Service 1903). Reserve and training 1904. 4 CS N. America & W.I. 1904-06. Tender to Torpedo School, Sheerness 1906-07. Nore, nucleus crew 1907. 3rd Fleet, Portsmouth and Nore 1908-13 (trooping 1910; collision with SS *Olympic* 1911—repaired with straight bow). Training Squadron, Queenstown 1913-14. 10 CS Northern Patrol 1914. Lost 15.10.1914, torpedoed by U9 in North Sea. 524 lost.

ST GEORGE

Built by Earle, Hull. Laid down 23.4.1890. Launched 23.6.1892. Completed 25.10.1894. Flagship, Cape & W. Africa 1894-98—flew flag of Admiral Sir Harry Rawson at bombardment of Zanzibar 28.8.1896. Portsmouth 1898-99. Cruiser Squadron 1899-1902—escorted Royal Yacht *Ophir* on Empire cruise 1901. Chatham 1902-04. South Atlantic 1904. Boys TS, N. America & W.I. 1904-06. Devonport, nucleus crew 1906-09. Converted to Destroyer Depot Ship, Chatham 1909-10. Depot ship, 3DF Nore 1910-12, 9 DF Firth of Forth 1913-14, 7 DF Humber 1914-15. Mediterranean 1915-17. Converted to Submarine Depot Ship 1917; Aegean 1918-19. Sold 1920, Castle, Plymouth.

Battle Honour: Benin 1897.

Theseus **in Plymouth Sound.**

THESEUS

Built by Thames Iron Works. Laid down 16.7.1890. Launched 8.9.1892. Completed 14.1.1896. 'Flying Squadron' 1896. Mediterranean 1896-98 (detached to Cape 1897). Refit 1898. Mediterranean 1899-1902. Chatham Reserve 1902-05. Tender to *Cambridge* and *Vivid* as Gunnery Training Ship, Devonport 1905-11. 3rd Fleet Devonport, attached to 9 CS but paid off 1912. Training Squadron, Queenstown 1913-14. 10 CS Northern Patrol 1914. Rebuilt (bulges) 1915. Dardanelles 1915-16. Mediterranean 1916-18. Depot ship for trawlers, Aegean 1918. Black Sea 1918-19. Devonport, paid off 1919. Sold 1921, Stanlee. Resold to Slough Trading Co. and broken up in Germany.

Battle Honours: Benin 1897, Dardanelles 1915-16.

CRESCENT CLASS (2 ships), *Naval Defence Act 1889*

Crescent, Royal Arthur

Displacement (tons):	7,700 load.
Dimensions (feet):	360pp, 387½oa x 60¾ x 34
(metres):	109.7pp, 118.1oa x 18.5 x 7.3
Machinery:	2 shaft 3 cyl. TE, 4 double ended cylindrical boilers. 10,000/12,000 HP = 18/20 knots.
Fuel:	Coal 1,250 tons.
Protection:	Full length deck 5in-3in (127mm-76mm).
Armament:	1—9.2in, 12—6in QF, 12—6pdr, 4—18in TT (submerged).
Complement:	544

Identical to the Edgars except for a higher forecastle and a pair of sided 6in guns instead of the forward 9.2in mounting. Both ships were sheathed and coppered. Like the Edgars they saw extensive service and both belonged to the Northern Patrol in 1914, *Crescent* as flagship.

Crescent **with raised forecastle and sided 6 inch guns in lieu of the 9.2 inch gun in the** *Edgars*.

CRESCENT

Built at Portsmouth Dockyard. Laid down 13.10.1890. Launched 30.3.1892. Completed 22.2.1894. Special service as relief on China and Australia Stations 1894-95. Flagship, N. America & W.I. 1895-97. Portsmouth Reserve 1897-99 (commanded by HRH The Duke of York—the future King George V—in 1898 Manoeuvres). Flagship, N. America & W.I. 1899-1902. Portsmouth Reserve 1902-03. Refit, Thames Iron Works 1903-04. Flagship, Cape 1904-07. 3rd Fleet, Portsmouth 1907-13. Training Squadron, Queenstown 1913-14. Flagship, 10 CS Northern Patrol 1914. Guardship, Hoy 1915, Portsmouth 1915-17. Submarine Depot Ship, Scapa Flow 1917-18, Firth of Forth 1919. Sold 1920 to Cohen and broken up in Germany.

ROYAL ARTHUR (ex *Centaur*)

Built at Portsmouth Dockyard. Laid down 20.1.1890. Launched 26.2.1891. Completed 2.3.1893. Flagship, Pacific 1893-96. Refit, Portsmouth 1896-97. Particular service 1897. Flagship, Australia 1897-1904. Refit 1904-05. Flagship, 4 CS, N. America & W.I. 1905-06. Portsmouth, nucleus crew and 4th Divn 1906-13 (trooping 1908). Training Squadron, Queenstown 1913-14. 10 CS Northern Patrol 1914. Guardship, Scapa Flow 1915. Later Depot Ship for Submarines: 12 S/M Flot. 1918, 1 S/M Flot., Rosyth 1919-20. Paid off 1920. Sold 1921 to Cohen and broken up in Germany.

Opposite: *Royal Arthur*

POWERFUL CLASS (2 ships), *Spencer Programme 1893*

Powerful, Terrible

Displacement (tons):	14,200 load.
Dimensions (feet):	500pp, 538oa x 71 x 27
(metres):	152.4pp, 164oa, 21.6 x 8.2
Machinery:	2 shaft 4 cyl. TE, 48 Belleville boilers. 25,000 HP = 22 knots.
Fuel:	Coal 3,000 tons.
Protection:	Full length deck 6in-2in (152mm-51mm).
Armament:	2—9.2in, 12 (later 16)—6in, 16—12pdr, 12—3pdr, 4—18in TT below water.
Complement:	894

Britain's answer to Russia's *Rurik* and *Rossiya*. Armed and protected on the same scale as the Edgars, a vast increase in size was dictated by the requirement for an enormous range and a speed of 22 knots. A hundred feet longer than contemporary battleships, the Powerfuls on completion ranked among the world's largest warships. At £850,000 each they cost twice as much as the Edgars.

The adoption of watertube boilers was a bold step; they saved a great deal of weight, and without them the Powerfuls would not have made their design speed. Inexperienced handling of the boilers sometimes made for difficulties and high coal consumption, but on the whole the ships were excellent steamers, capable of maintaining high speeds for long periods. Built a deck higher than previous cruisers, their lofty freeboard made them splendid seaboats.

Ironically, *Rurik* turned out to be a paper tiger—slow, poorly protected, and with armament badly arranged. The Powerfuls, though successful in their own terms, were much better than they needed to be. Freakish ships meeting no real need, they came to be regarded as expensive white elephants. Both were removed from the effective list before 1914.

Powerful and *Terrible* achieved a measure of fame in the Boer War when they landed the naval brigades at the Cape which assisted in the Relief of Ladysmith.

Powerful, **1897, landed naval brigades in S. Africa.**

POWERFUL

Built by NCA Co. Barrow. Laid down 1894. Launched 24.7.1895. Completed 8.6.1897. Trials and alterations 1897-98. China 1898-1902 (detached to Cape 1899-1901). Refit 1902-03. Portsmouth Reserve 1903-05. Flagship, Australia 1905-11. 3rd Fleet (attached 7 CS) 1912. Subsidiary list 1913 as training hulk, Devonport. Renamed *Impregnable*, 1919. Sold 1929, Hughes Bolckow, Blyth.

Battle Honour: South Africa 1899-1901.

TERRIBLE

Built by Thomson, Clydebank. Laid down 1894. Launched 27.5.1895. Completed 24.3.1898. Took part in Manoeuvres before completion, 1897. Special service 1898-99. China 1899-1902 (detached to Cape 1899-1900). Refit, Clydebank 1902-04. In commission in Reserve, Portsmouth 1905. Escorted *Renown* on Prince and Princess of Wales' cruise to India 1905-06. Trooping to China 1906. Portsmouth nucleus crew and 4th Divn 1907-12. Pembroke Reserve 1913-14. Disarmed and used for trooping to the Dardanelles 1915-16. Accommodation ship, Portsmouth as part of *Fisgard*, 1916-31. Sold 1932, Cashmore, Newport.

Battle Honours: South Africa 1899-1900, China 1900.

DIADEM CLASS (8 ships)

Andromeda, Diadem, Europa, Niobe (1895 Estimates).
Amphitrite, Argonaut, Ariadne, Spartiate (1896 Estimates).

Displacement (tons):	11,000 load.
Dimensions (feet):	435pp, 462½oa x 69 x 25½
(metres):	132.6pp, 141oa x 21 x 7.8
Machinery:	2 shaft 4 cyl. TE, 30 Belleville boilers, 16,500 HP = 20¼ knots (1st batch). 18,000 HP = 20¾ knots (*Ariadne, Spartiate, Amphitrite, Argonaut).*
Fuel:	Coal 1,900 tons.
Protection:	Full length deck 4in-2½in (102mm-64mm).
Armament:	16—6in, 14—12pdr, 3—3pdr, 3—18in TT (2 submerged, 1 above water).

Smaller, more economical versions of the Powerfuls which they generally resembled. Size was cut down by accepting a lower speed, a thinner protective deck, and a uniform 6in armament. The second batch of four ships had more powerful machinery for an extra ½ knot. *Spartiate's* completion was seriously delayed by late delivery of machinery from the contractors. On the whole the class proved good steamers though problems arose in some after a couple of years, notably in *Niobe*.

Though their design was basically sound and served as a basis for future development, the Diadems were fiercely criticised for their slowness and lack of heavy guns. Obsolescence rapidly overtook them with the armoured cruiser's revival. Large, expensive to man, and obsolete at birth, the Diadems rank unhappily among the most useless ships ever built for the Royal Navy, destined to pass most of their time in reserve.

Niobe transferred to Canada in 1910, and four of the class had been reduced to subsidiary duties by 1914. Though *Amphitrite, Argonaut, Europa* and *Niobe* took an active part in the first months of the war, only *Ariadne* and *Amphitrite,* as minelayers, saw any sea service after 1915. *Europa* became flagship at Mudros, more or less a permament feature there.

ANDROMEDA

Built at Pembroke Dockyard. Laid down 2.12.1895. Launched 30.4.1897. Completed 5.9.1899. Mediterranean 1899-1902. Refit 1903-04. China 1904-06. Chatham, nucleus crew 1906. Devonport, nucleus crew & 4th Divn 1907-11. Attached 9 CS 3rd Fleet 1912. Boys TS, Devonport 1913-29. Renamed *Impregnable II,* 1919. Became part of Torpedo School, 1931 and renamed *Defiance.* Broken up, Belgium, 1956.

Diadem, **1898.**

DIADEM

Built by Fairfield, Govan. Laid down 23.1.1896. Launched 21.10.1896. Completed 19.7.1898. Channel 1898-1902. Refit, Fairfield 1902-03. Particular service 1904. Chatham, in commission in Reserve 1905. China 1905-07. Portsmouth, nucleus crew 1907-09, 4th Divn etc., 1909-13 (refit 1909; attached 7 CS 3rd Fleet 1912, but paid off). Stokers' Training Ship, Portsmouth 1914-18 (but closed from 10.1915 to 1.1918). Sold 1921, Ward, Morecambe.

EUROPA

Built by Thomson, Clydebank. Laid down 10.1.1896. Launched 20.3.1897. Completed 23.11.1899. Trooping to Australia 1899-1900. Portsmouth Reserve 1900-04. Devonport, in commission in Reserve etc. & 4th Divn 1904-11 (special service 1908). Attached 9 CS 3rd Fleet 1912-14. Flagship, 9 CS Mid Atlantic 1914-15. Flagship at Mudros 1915-19. Sold at Malta to G. Bletto, 1920. Was to have become an emigrant carrier, but sank in a gale off Corsica in January 1921. Later raised and broken up.

Europa at **Mudros where she served most of WW1 as Flagship.**

NIOBE

Built by Vickers, Barrow. Laid down 16.12.1895. Launched 20.2.1897. Completed 6.12.1898.
Channel 1898-1902 (detached to Cape 1899-1900; escorted Royal Yacht *Ophir* to India 1901).
Refit, Barrow 1903-04. Devonport, nucleus crew, 3rd Fleet etc., 1905-10. Sold to Canada 1910.
Based at Halifax, Nova Scotia 1910-11. Ran aground on Cape Sable, 29.7.1911; towed off by
HMS *Cornwall* and repaired at Halifax until late 1912. Pacific 1914. 4 CS N. America & W.I.
1914-15 (Atlantic patrols). Paid off 10.1915. Depot Ship at Halifax 1915-20. Badly damaged
by the ammunition explosion in Halifax Narrows 6.12.1917, but continued in service without
funnels, ventilators or masts. Sold 1922 and broken up in Philadelphia.

Battle Honour: South Africa 1899-1900.

Diadem class (2nd group)

Amphitrite **as a minelayer, c1917.**

AMPHITRITE

Built by Vickers, Barrow. Laid down 8.12.1896. Launched 5.1.1898. Completed 17.9.1901. Special service 1901-02. China 1902-05. Nucleus crew, Chatham 1905-07, Devonport 1908-09 (trooping 1908). Tender to *Vivid* as Stokers' TS, Devonport 1910-14 (attached 9 CS 3rd Fleet 1912-14). 9 CS Mid Atlantic 1914-15. Harbour service, Portsmouth 1915-16. Converted to Minelayer, Devonport 1916-17. Nore Command 1917-19, replacing *Ariadne* on Dover Barrage. Paid off 6.1919. Portsmouth Reserve 1919-20. Sold 1920, Ward, Milford Haven.

ARGONAUT

Built by Fairfield, Govan. Laid down 23.11.1896. Launched 24.1.1898. Completed 19.4.1900. China 1900-04. Chatham, in commission in Reserve 1904-05, nucleus crew 1906-09. Portsmouth 4th Divn 1909-11, attached 7 CS 3rd Fleet 1912-14. 9 CS Mid Atlantic 1914-15. At Portsmouth, Hospital Ship 1915-17, Accommodation Ship for stokers 1918. Sold 1920, Ward, Milford Haven.

ARIADNE

Built by Thomson, Clydebank. Laid down 29.10.1896. Launched 22.4.1898. Completed 5.6.1902. Flagship, N. America & W.I. 1902-05. Portsmouth, in commission in Reserve, nucleus crew etc., 1905-09. 4th Divn 1909-11, attached 7 CS 3rd Fleet 1912-13. Stokers' Training Ship, Portsmouth 1913-15, Devonport 1915-16. Converted to Minelayer at Devonport 1916-17. Nore Command 1917—laid 708 mines in the Dover Barrage and Heligoland Bight. Lost 26.7.1917—torpedoed by UC65 off Beachy Head.

SPARTIATE

Built at Pembroke Dockyard. Laid down 10.5.1897. Launched 27.10.1898. Completed 17.3.1903. Reserve at Portsmouth 1903-04, Chatham 1905. Portsmouth, nucleus crew 1906-09 (trooping 1907). 4 Divn, Portsmouth 1909-11. Attached 7 CS 3rd Fleet 1912-13. Stokers' TS, Portsmouth from 1913. Renamed *Fisgard* 1915. Sold 1932, Ward, Pembroke Dock.

APOLLO CLASS (21 ships), *Naval Defence Act 1889*

*Aeolus, Andromache, Apollo, *Brilliant, *Indefatigable (later *Melpomone), *Intrepid, *Iphigenia, Latona, Melampus, Naiad, *Pique, *Rainbow, *Retribution, Sappho, Scylla, *Sirius, *Spartan, Sybille, Terpsichore, Thetis, Tribune.
*Sheathed.

Displacement (tons):	3,400 load, 3,600 sheathed vessels
Dimensions (feet):	300pp, 314oa x 43 (sheathed 43¾) x 17½ (sheathed 18½)
(metres):	91.4pp, 95.7oa x 31.1 (13.3) x 5.3 (5.6)
Machinery:	2 shaft 3 cyl. TE. 3 double ended and 2 single ended boilers. 7,000/9,000 IHP = 18½/20 knots (19¾ sheathed)
Fuel:	Coal, 535 tons.
Protection:	Full length deck 2in-1¼in (51mm-32mm). Engine hatch (glacis) 5in (127mm)
Armament:	2—6in QF, 6—4.7in QF, 8—6pdr QF, 1—3pdr QF, 4—MGs, 4—14in TT above water.
Complement:	273

Numerically the Apollos were the largest class of cruisers ever built for the Royal Navy. Derived from the Medeas, but more generously hulled and quite modestly armed for their size—indeed they were fiercely criticised for lack of end-on fire. Poor seaboats, being very wet on account of low freeboard amidships, they were good steamers, though some lost speed after a few years.

Ten ships were sheathed and coppered for tropical service, and some of these saw extensive employment from completion. Many of the class however, spent their prime in reserve, commissioning only for Annual Manoeuvres each spring until, at the turn of the century, they began to be brought forward to replace older cruisers in the active fleet. Obsolete by 1905, a few continued to perform training duties on the North America station almost up to 1914 before being discarded. Eleven survived long enough to serve in the First World War, seven of them as minelayers based at Sheerness and Dover in 1914-15. After 1915 most of them were reduced to secondary duties, being quite worn out. Five were expended as blockships in the Zeebrugge and Ostend raids in 1918.

AEOLUS

Built at Devonport Dockyard. Laid down 10.3.1890. Launched 13.11.1891. Completed 6.1.1894. Mediterranean 1894-95. Detached to China 1895-97. Devonport Reserve 1897-1902. Flagship and Port Guardship, Queenstown 1902-03. Seagoing Drill Ship for RNR, Queenstown 1903-05. Devonport, nucleus crew 1905-11 (refit, Haulbowline 1909; sailed to St Helena 1910). N. America & W.I. 1911-12. Attached Training Squadron 1912-13. Paid off 1913. Sold 1914, Ward, Preston.

ANDROMACHE

Built at Chatham Dockyard. Laid down 4.1889. Launched 14.8.1890. Completed 1892. Held at Chatham 1893-1901. RNR Drill Ship, North Shields 1901-04, and Harwich 1904-05. Laid up, Chatham and Blackwater 1905-07. Converted to Minelayer, Chatham 1907-09. Nucleus crew, Nore 1909-11. ML Squadron, 1912-14. ML Squadron, Dover 1914-15. Depot Ship, Mediterranean 1915. Accommodation Ship, Gibraltar 1916-19. Devonport, paid off 1919. Sold 1920, Castle, Plymouth.

APOLLO

Built at Chatham Dockyard. Laid down 4.1889. Launched 10.2.1891. Completed 1892. Held at Chatham 1892-1901. RNR Drill Ship, Southampton 1901-04. Laid up, Portsmouth 1905-08. Converted to Minelayer, Chatham 1908-09. Nucleus crew, Nore 1909-10, Devonport 1910-11. ML Squadron, 2nd Fleet 1912-14. ML Squadron, Dover 1914-15, Sheerness 1915. Nore Command 1915-17. Depot Ship, Devonport 1917-20 (4 DF 1918, destroyers in C & M 1919). Sold 1920, Castle, Plymouth.

BRILLIANT

Built at Sheerness Dockyard. Laid down 1890. Launched 24.6.1891. Completed 1893. Held at Chatham 1893-1901. Cruiser Squadron 1901-03. South Atlantic 1903-04. RNR Drill Ship, Southampton 1904-05. Attached 4 CS N. America & W.I. 1906-11. 3rd Fleet, paid off 1911-14. North Sea patrols 1914. Depot Ship, Tyne 1914-15, Lerwick 1915-18. Expended as blockship, Ostend 23.4.1918.

Battle Honours: Belgian Coast 1914, Zeebrugge 1918, Ostend 1918.

INDEFATIGABLE

Built by London & Glasgow, Govan. Laid down 1890. Launched 12.3.1891. Completed 1892. Held at Portsmouth 1892-96. N. America & W.I. 1896-1904. Portsmouth 1904-05. Attached 4 CS N. America & W.I. 1906-11—renamed *Melpomone*, 1.1910 to free her old name for a new battlecruiser. Attached Training Squadron 1912-13. Sold 1913, Ward, Preston.

HUSBANDS

Brilliant **expended as a blockship at Ostend.**

INTREPID

Built by London & Glasgow, Govan. Laid down 1890. Launched 20.6.1891. Completed 1892. Held at Portsmouth 1892-96. N. America & W.I. 1896-99. Portsmouth 1899-1902. Mediterranean 1902-04. Harbour service, Portsmouth 1904-09. Converted to Minelayer, Chatham 1909-10. Nucleus crew, Nore 1911. ML Squadron 2nd Fleet 1912-14. ML Squadron, Dover 1914-15. Depot Ship, N. Russia 1915-16, White Sea 1917. Prepared as blockship 1918 and expended at Zeebrugge, 23.4.1918.

Battle Honour: Zeebrugge 1918.

Iphigenia, **1906, fitted as a minelayer with mines showing amidships.**

IMPERIAL WAR MUSEUM

IPHIGENIA

Built by London & Glasgow, Govan. Laid down 1890. Launched 19.11.1891. Completed 1892. Held at Portsmouth 1892-97. China 1897-1900. Portsmouth 1900-03 (Special service 1901-02). China 1903-06. Special service 1906. Converted to Minelayer, Chatham 1906-07. Nucleus crew, Portsmouth 1907-08, Nore 1909-12. ML Squadron, 2nd Fleet 1912-14. ML Squadron, Dover 1914-15. North Russia 1915-16. White Sea 1917. Prepared as blockship 1918 and expended at Zeebrugge, 23.4.1918.

Battle Honour: Zeebrugge 1918.

LATONA

Built by NCA Co. Barrow. Laid down 1889. Launched 22.5.1890. Completed 1892. Held at Portsmouth 1892-1902 (Special service—voyage to Bermuda 1900). Submarine Depot Ship, Home 1902-03. Particular service 1904. Newfoundland Fishery Squadron 1905-06. Converted to Minelayer, Portsmouth 1906-08. Nucleus crew, Portsmouth 1908-12. ML Squadron, 2nd Fleet 1912-14. ML Squadron, Dover 1914-15. Mediterranean 1915-18. Overflow ship, Malta 1919-20. Sold at Malta 1920.

MELAMPUS

Built by NCA Co. Barrow. Laid down 1889. Launched 2.8.1890. Completed 1892. Held at Portsmouth 1892-93. Coast Guard Ship, Kingstown 1893-1905 (commanded by HRH The Duke of York—the future King George V—in 1893 Manoeuvres). Harbour service, Portsmouth 1905-10. Sold 1910, Cohen, Felixstowe.

Latona, **1896, commissioned only for special service/manoeuvres until 1902.**

NAIAD

Built by NCA Co. Barrow. Laid down 1889. Launched 29.11.1890. Completed 1892. Held at Portsmouth 1892-1901. Mediterranean and Red Sea 1901-04 (detached to Cape 1901-02). Laid up, Chatham 1905-07. Converted to Minelayer, Chatham 1907-10. Nucleus crew, Portsmouth 1911. ML Squadron, 2nd Fleet 1912-14. ML Squadron, Dover 1914-15. Depot Ship, Tyne 1917. Sold 1922, King, Troon.

PIQUE

Built by Palmers, Jarrow. Laid dwon 1889. Launched 13.12.1890. Completed 1892. Held at Devonport 1892-95. China 1895-98. Devonport 1898-1900. China 1900-03. Laid up, Sheerness and Blackwater 1904-11. Sold 1911, F. E. Rudge.

RAINBOW

Built by Palmers, Jarrow. Laid down 1890. Launched 25.3.1891. Completed 1892. Held at Devonport 1892-95. China 1895-98. At Malta 1898-99. Devonport 1899-1901. Cruiser Squadron 1901-03. Harbour service 1904-10. To newly formed Royal Canadian Navy 1910. Training Cruiser on Pacific Coast 1910-14. Pacific patrols, based on Esquimalt, British Columbia 1914-15. Depot ship 1915-20. Discarded 1920 and sold as a freighter.

RETRIBUTION

Built by Palmers, Jarrow. Laid down 1890. Launched 6.8.1891. Completed 1892. Held at Devonport 1892-95. Flagship, SE Coast of America 1895-98. Devonport 1898-1902. N. America & W.I. 1902-04. Laid up, Firth of Forth 1904. Sold 1911, F. E. Rudge.

SAPPHO

Built by Samuda, Poplar. Laid down 1890. Launched 9.5.1891. Completed 1892. Held at Chatham 1892-1901 (trooping 1895-96). Cape 1901-02. Chatham 1902-03. RNR Drill Ship, Firth of Forth 1903-05, detached for Newfoundland Fisheries 1906. Nucleus crew, Chatham 1906-07. N. America & W.I. 1907-10. 4th Divn, Portsmouth 1911. Tender to Flagship, IBS Home/Grand Fleet 1912-15. Laid up for subsidiary duties with Grand Fleet 1915-18. Prepared as blockship, but broke down on way to Ostend, 5.1918. Sold 1921, Castle, Plymouth.

Battle Honour: South Africa 1901.

SCYLLA

Built by Samuda, Poplar. Laid down 1890. Launched 17.10.1891. Completed 1892. Held at Chatham 1892-96. Mediterranean 1896-99. Chatham 1900-04. RNR Drill Ship, Harwich 1904-05. Newfoundland Fisheries 1905-06. Nucleus crew, Chatham 1907. 4 CS N. America & W.I. 1907-11. Attached 11 CS 3rd Fleet, paid off 1912. Sold 1914.

SIRIUS

Built by Armstrong, Elswick. Laid down 9.1889. Launched 27.10.1890. Completed 1891. Flagship, SE Coast of America 1892-95. Devonport 1895-97. Particular Service 1897-98. Devonport 1898-1903. China 1903-05. Nucleus crew, Devonport 1906-11 (Special service 1908). Attached 4 CS N. America & W.I. 1912-13. Reserve 1913-14. Nore 1914-15. W. Africa 1915-18. Prepared as blockship at Chatham, 1918, and expended at Ostend 23.4.1918.

Battle Honours: Belgian Coast 1914, Zeebrugge 1918.

SPARTAN

Built by Armstrong, Elswick. Laid down 12.1889. Launched 25.2.1891. Completed 1892. Held at Devonport 1892-93. Mediterranean 1894-95. China (temp.) 1895-97. Devonport Reserve 1897-1903. RNR Drill Ship, Holyhead 1903-05. Harbour service 1906. Tender to *Defiance* at Devonport from 1907. Renamed *Defiance II*, 1921. Sold 1931.

SYBILLE

Built by Stephenson, Newcastle. Laid down 1889. Launched 27.12.1890. Completed 1892. Held at Devonport 1892-95. Mediterranean 1895-98. Portsmouth 1898-1900. Cape 1900-01. Wrecked in Lambert's Bay, South Africa 16.1.1901, the day after landing a Naval Brigade. One man drowned.

Battle Honour: South Africa 1901.

TERPSICHORE

Built by Thomson, Clydebank. Laid down 1889. Launched 30.10.1890. Completed 1892. Held at Chatham 1892-1901. Cape 1901-06 (Gambia 1901). Portsmouth, nucleus crew 1906-07. Laid up 1907-13. Disposal list 1913. Sold 1914, Ward.

Sirius, 1892, prior to becoming Flagship on the SE coast of America station.

THETIS

Built by Thomson, Clydebank. Laid down 1889. Launched 13.12.1890. Completed 1892. Held at Chatham 1892-98. Mediterranean 1898-1901 (detached to Cape 1899-1901). Chatham 1902. China 1902-05. Nucleus crew, Nore 1906. Converted to Minelayer, Portsmouth 1906-07. Nucleus crew, Nore 1907-09 and Portsmouth 1909-11. ML Squadron, 2nd Fleet 1912-14. ML Squadron, Dover 1914-15. Depot ship 1916-17. Prepared as blockship 1918 and expended at Zeebrugge, 23.4.1918.

Battle Honours: South Africa 1899-1901, Zeebrugge 1918.

TRIBUNE

Built by Thomson, Clydebank. Laid down 1889. Launched 24.2.1891. Completed 1892. Held at Chatham 1892-99. N. America & W.I. 1899-1904. Laid up 1905. Sold 1911, Cashmore, Newport.

Intrepid (**nearest camera**) and *Iphigenia* **at Zeebrugge 24 Oct 1918.**

ASTRAEA CLASS (8 ships), *Naval Defence Act 1889.*

Astraea, Bonaventure, Cambrian, Charybdis, Flora, Forte, Fox, Hermione

Displacement (tons):	4,360 load.
Dimensions (feet):	320pp, 339½oa x 49½ x 19
(metres):	97.5pp, 103.5oa x 15.1 x 5.8
Machinery:	2 shaft 3 cyl. TE. 8 cylindrical boilers. 7,500/9,500 HP = 18/19½ knots.
Fuel:	Coal 1,000 tons.
Protection:	Full length deck 2in (51mm). Engine hatch (glacis) 5in (127mm).
Armament:	2—6in QF, 8—4.7in QF, 10—6pdr, 1—3pdr 4—18in TT above water.
Complement:	318

Expanded Apollos, with much improved seakeeping. At last the low midship freeboard which had so blighted the performance of earlier small cruisers was abandoned in favour of a full length weather deck, with no separate forecastle or poop. Little better armed than the smaller Apollos, the Astraeas were considered under-gunned for their size.

The class saw extensive service throughout the world. Though obsolete by 1905, they were so useful and economical that they continued to serve on foreign stations for several more years. *Forte* was sold in 1914, and four others had by then been reduced to secondary duties. Three served as cruisers in the First World War, *Astraea* and *Fox* remaining active through to 1919.

ASTRAEA

Built at Devonport Dockyard. Laid down 14.8.1890. Launched 17.3.1893. Completed 5.11.1895. Mediterranean 1895-98. Refit, Chatham 1898-99. Mediterranean 1899-1900. China (temp.) 1900-02. Refit, Chatham 1902-04. Mediterranean 1904. China 1904-11. 3rd Fleet, Nore 1911-13. Cape 1913-19—bombarded Dar-es-Salaam 8.8.1914. Nore, paid off 1919. Sold 1920, Castle. Broken up in Germany.

Battle Honours: East Africa 1914, Cameroons 1915.

BONAVENTURE

Built at Devonport Dockyard. Laid down 9.12.1890. Launched 2.12.1892. Completed 5.7.1894. Flagship, East Indies 1894-97. Refit 1897-98. China 1898-1901 (grounded on east coast of Korea 5.7.1899; repaired at Hong Kong). Refit, Devonport 1901-03. Pacific 1903-04. China 1904-06. Converted to Submarine Depot Ship, Haulbowline 1906-07. Home 1907-12—escorted submarines C36, C37 and C38, bound for China Station, as far as Malta 1911. Submarine Depot Ship at Harwich 1912-14, Humber 1914, 6 S/M Tyne 1914-16, 2 S/M Tyne 1916-18. For disposal at Chatham 1919. Sold 1920, Forth S'breaking Co. Bo'ness.

Battle Honour: China 1900.

CAMBRIAN

Built at Pembroke Dockyard. Laid down 1890. Launched 30.1.1893. Completed 1894. Mediterranean 1894-97—commanded by Lord Louis Battenberg 1895-96. Refit, Devonport 1898. Cruiser Training Squadron 1899-1900. Flagship, SE Coast of America 1901-03. South Atlantic 1903-04. Refit, Haulbowline 1905. Australia 1906-13 (Flagship 1913). Paid off 1914. Became Stokers' TS at Devonport and renamed *Harlech*, 1916. Renamed *Vivid*, 1921. Sold 1923.

CHARYBDIS

Built at Sheerness Dockyard. Laid down 1891. Launched 15.6.1893. Completed 10.1894. Held at Chatham 1894-95. 'Flying Squadron' 1896. Channel 1896-98. Devonport Reserve 1898-1900. N. America & W.I. 1900- 5. Chatham refit and in commission in Reserve 1905-07. Trooping 1907-08. 3rd Fleet at Nore 1908-10, and Devonport 1911-14. Flagship, 12 CS Western Channel 1914-15. Badly damaged in collision 9.1.1915 and laid up at Bermuda 1915-18. Leased as a cargo carrier 1918-20. Sold at Bermuda, 1922, and broken up in Holland, 1923.

IMPERIAL WAR MUSEUM

Forte

FLORA

Built at Pembroke Dockyard. Laid down 1891. Launched 21.11.1893. Completed 1895. Held at Devonport 1895-96. Trooping to Australia 1896-97. Flagship, SE Coast of America 1898-1901. Devonport 1901-02. Pacific 1902-04. Devonport 1904-05. China 1905-13. Sale list, 1914. Became a workshop at Devonport and renamed *Indus II*, 1915. Sold 1922.

FORTE

Built at Chatham Dockyard. Laid down 21.9.1891. Launched 9.12.1893. Completed 5.11.1895. Mediterranean 1895-98 (detached to Cape 1897). Refit, Chatham 1898-99. Cape 1899-1907. Nucleus crew, Portsmouth 1907-09. Cape 1909-13. Laid up, Kethole Reach (Medway Estuary) 1913. Sold 1914, Tydeman, Holland.

Battle Honours: Benin 1897, South Africa 1899-1900.

HUSBANDS

Fox

FOX

Built at Portsmouth Dockyard. Laid down 1891. Launched 15.6.1893. Completed 14.4.1896. Cape 1896-99 (Sierra Leone 1898-99) Portsmouth 1899-1901. East Indies 1901-06. Nucleus crew, Portsmouth 1906-07. Haulbowline 1907-08. East Indies 1908-14. Captured two German merchantmen off Colombo, 8.1914. East Africa and Egypt 1915-17. Red Sea 1917-18. Archangel 1919. Sold 1920, Cardiff Marine Stores.

Hermione **leaving Portsmouth.**

HERMIONE

Built at Devonport Dockyard. Laid down 17.12.1891. Launched 7.11.1893. Completed 14.1.1896. 'Flying Squadron' 1896. Channel 1896-98. China 1898-1901. Refit, Malta 1901-02. Mediterranean 1902-04. Nucleus crew, Portsmouth 1904-07. Cape 1907-09 (grounded off Zanzibar, 14.2.1914; repairs at Cape Town). Attached 10 CS 3rd Fleet, Portsmouth 1909-13—airship trials, Barrow 1910-12. 4 CS N. America & W.I. 1913-14. Depot ship for patrol vessels, Southampton from 1914. Burnt out 1916, but remained in service. Sold to Multilocular S'breaking Co. 1921, but resold to Marine Society in 1922 and became TS *Warspite* on the Thames. Broken up 1940, T. W. Ward, Gravesend.

Battle Honour: China 1900.

ECLIPSE CLASS (9 ships), *Spencer Programme 1893*

Diana, Dido, Eclipse, Isis, Juno, Minerva, Talbot, Venus

Doris

Displacement (tons):	5,600 load.
Dimensions (feet):	350pp, 373oa x 53½ x 20½
(metres):	106.7pp, 113.7oa x 16.3 x 6.2
Machinery:	2 shaft 3 cyl. TE. 8 cylindrical boilers. 9,600 HP = 19½ knots.
Fuel:	Coal 1,075 tons.
Protection:	Full length deck 3in-1½in (76mm-38mm). Engine hatch (glacis) 6in (152mm).
Armament:	5—6in, 6—4.7in, 8—12pdr, 6-3pdr (later, except *Eclipse*: 11-6in, 9—12pdr), 3—18in TT (2 submerged, 1 above water).
Complement:	450

Expanded Astraeas, with the additional 1,000 tons displacement applied to further improvements in seakeeping. More heavily armed than the Astraeas, the Eclipses were as fiercely attacked for not using their increased size to greater advantage. Their critics were heeded when in 1902-04 all except *Eclipse* were rearmed with a uniform battery of 11-6in guns. Otherwise successful and economical ships, they saw extensive service through to the end of the First World War.

Dido became a Destroyer Depot Ship in 1913. The remainder served in Home waters during the first few months of the war before dispersing to foreign stations in 1915.

DIANA

Built by Fairfield Govan. Laid down 13.8.1894. Launched 5.12.1895. Completed 5.1897. Held at Chatham 1897-99. Trooping to Australia 1900. Mediterranean 1900-04. Rearmed 1904. Attached Mediterranean BS 1905-13 (detached to East Indies 1909). 3rd Fleet, Devonport 1913-14. 12 CS Western Channel 1914-15. Refit 1915. China 1915-17. East Indies 1917-19. Paid off, Queenstown 6.1919. Sold 1920, Castle, Plymouth.

Diana **Rearmed with eleven 6 inch guns.**

DIDO

Built by London & Glasgow, Govan. Laid down 30.8.1894. *Launched 20.3.1896. Completed 10.5.1898. Mediterranean 1898-1901 (detached to China 1900). Chatham 1902. Coast Guard, Hull 1903-04. Attached Channel BS 1904-07. Nucleus crew, Nore 1907-09. Attached Home BS 1909-10. Refit, Chatham 1911. Attached 3 BS, 3rd Fleet, Nore 1911-12. Submarine Depot Ship, 6 S/M Flotilla 1912-14, 3 S/M Flotilla 1914. Destroyer Depot Ship, Harwich, 3 DF. 1914-15, 9DF 1915-17, 10 DF 1918-19. Depot Ship, Reserve Destroyers, Portsmouth 1919-26. Sold 1926, May & Butcher, Maldon.

*Note: Launched 17.3.1896, but ground subsided under slipway and ship not floated for three days.

Battle Honour: China 1900.

DORIS

Built by NCA Co. Barrow. Laid down 29.8.1894. Launched 3.3.1896. Completed 18.11.1897. Flagship, Cape 1897-1901. Devonport 1901-02. Channel Squadron 1902-04. Attached Atlantic BS 1905. Nucleus crew, Devonport 1906-08. Attached Atlantic BS 1909-11. 3rd Fleet 1912-14 (attached 8 BS 1912, 7 BS 1913). 11 CS West of Ireland Coast Patrol 1914—captured a German merchantman, 5.8.1914. East Indies and Egypt 1914-15—sank a Turkish merchantman 12.1914. Dardanelles 1915-16. Mediterranean 1916-17. East Indies 1917-18. Sold at Bombay, 1919.

Battle Honours: South Africa 1899-1901, Dardanelles 1915-16.

ECLIPSE

Built at Portsmouth Dockyard. Laid down 11.12.1893. Launched 19.7.1894. Completed 23.3.1897. Flagship, East Indies 1897-1900. Refit, Chatham 1900-01. China 1901-04. Devonport Reserve 1904-05. Attached 4 CS N. America & W.I. as Cadets' Training Ship, based at Bermuda 1905-06. Portsmouth Reserve 1906-07. Attached to Royal Naval College, Osborne 1907-12. 3rd Fleet, at Portsmouth 1912-13, Devonport 1913-14—escorted new Australian submarines AE 1 and AE 2 to Singapore, 1914. 12 CS Western Channel 1914-15—captured a German merchantman 10.8.1914, another 10.9.1914. Accommodation ship for submarine flotillas 1915-18. Laid up, Devonport 1918-19. Sold 1921, Cohen.

ISIS

Built by London & Glasgow, Govan. Laid down 30.1.1895. Launched 27.6.1896. Completed 10.5.1898. Mediterranean 1898-1901 (detached to China 1900). Chatham 1901-02. Tender to *Britannia* as Cadets' TS 1902-07, attached to 4 CS N. America & W.I. 1905-07. Nucleus crew, Devonport 1907-09. Attached Home BS 1909-10. 3rd Fleet, Devonport 1911-14 (attached 7 BS 1912). 11 CS West of Ireland Coast Patrol 1914-15—captured a German merchantman 10.8.1914. N. America & W.I. 1915-18. At Invergordon 1919. Sold 1920, Granton Shipbreaking.

Battle Honour: China 1900.

JUNO

Built by NCA Co. Barrow. Laid down 22.6.1894. Launched 16.11.1895. Completed 16.6.1897. Held at Devonport 1897-99. Cruiser Squadron 1899-1902—escorted Royal Yacht *Ophir* on Empire cruise 1901. Portsmouth 1902-03. Home 1904. Attached Mediterranean BS 1905-09. Attached Home BS (2nd Divn) 1910. 3rd Fleet, Nore 1911-14 (4th Fleet 1912, attached 7 BS 1912-13). 11 CS West of Ireland Coast Patrol 1914-15. Red Sea and Persian Gulf 1915-17. East Indies 1917-19. Nore, paid off 1920. Sold 1920, Earle. Resold and broken up in Denmark.

IMPERIAL WAR MUSEUM

Minerva, **1897**.

MINERVA

Built at Chatham Dockyard. Laid down 4.12.1893. Launched 23.9.1895. Completed 4.2.1897. Particular Service 1897. Chatham Reserve 1897-99. Cruiser Training Squadron (boiler trials) 1899-1903. Devonport 1903-04. Attached Mediterranean BS 1904-12 (refit 1908). 3rd Fleet Devonport, attached 11 CS 1912. Temporary Depot Ship, 6 DF 1912-13. 3rd Fleet, Portsmouth 1913-14. 11 CS West of Ireland Coast Patrol 1914—captured an Austrian merchantman off Finisterre, 9.1914. East Indies and Egypt 1914-15. Dardanelles 1915—sank Turkish TB *Demirhissar* off Chios 17.4.1915. Egyptian waters 1915-16. East Africa 1916-18. Cape 1918. Sold 1920, Auten.

Battle Honours: Suez Canal 1915, Dardanelles 1915.

TALBOT

Built at Devonport Dockyard. Laid down 5.3.1894. Launched 25.4.1895. Completed 15.9.1896. N. America & W.I. 1896-99. Devonport 1899-1901. China 1901-04. Refit, Chatham 1904-05. Nore Reserve 1905-06. Nucleus crew, Devonport 1906-07 (trooping 1907). Attached Channel BS 1907-09. Attached BS, 2nd Division 1909-10. Stationed at Haulbowline 1911-12. Attached 8 BS 3rd Fleet 1912. Ran aground in Suez Canal whilst trooping 9.1912. Temporary Depot Ship, 7 DF Home 1913. 3rd Fleet, Devonport 1913-14. 12 CS Western Channel 1914-15—captured a German merchantman off the Lizard, 9.1914. Dardanelles 1915-16. East Africa 1916-18. Cape 1918-19. Laid up, Haulbowline 1919. Sold 1921, Multilocular Shipbreaking, Stranraer.

Battle Honour: Dardanelles 1915-16.

HUSBANDS

Venus

VENUS

Built by Fairfield, Govan. Laid down 28.6.1894. Launched 5.9.1895. Completed 9.11.1897. Mediterranean 1897-1901. Rearmed, Chatham 1901-02. Coast Guard Ship, Southampton Water 1903-04. Attached Mediterranean BS 1905-07. Attached Atlantic BS 1907-11. Temporary Depot Ship, 7 DF Home 1911, 1 DF Home 1912. 3rd Fleet at Pembroke 1913-14, Portsmouth 1914. 11 CS West of Ireland Coast Patrol 1914-15—captured two German merchantmen 10.1914. Red Sea and Persian Gulf 1915-16. China 1916-17. East Indies 1917-19. Sold 1921, Cohen. Broken up in Germany.

ARROGANT CLASS (4 ships), *1895 Programme*

Arrogant, Furious, Gladiator, Vindictive

Displacement (tons):	5,750 load.
Dimensions (feet):	320pp, 342oa x 57½ x 20
(metres):	97.5pp, 104.2oa x 17.5 x 6.1
Machinery:	2 shaft 4 cyl. TE. 18 Belleville boilers. 10,000 IHP (forced) = 19 knots.
Fuel:	Coal, 1,175 tons.
Protection:	Full length deck 3in-1½in (76mm-38mm). Engine hatch (glacis) 4in (102mm). Sides forward 2in (51mm).
Armament:	4—6in, 6—4.7in (later 10—6in), 8—12pdr, 3—3pdr 3—18in TT (2 submerged).
Complement:	480

Curious 'ram' variants of the Eclipses, with a shorter, fuller hull form for manoeuvrability and a large, well supported ram bow. Installed power was increased, and water tube boilers necessitated three funnels.

Like the Eclipses, the Arrogants were rearmed in 1902-05 with a uniform battery of 6in guns and reboilered at the same time: their early employment in the Channel and Mediterranean Fleets demanded much faster steaming which evidently wore them out.

Gladiator was lost in a collision in 1908; *Arrogant* became a Submarine Depot Ship in 1911 (to replace *Mercury*); and *Furious* was reduced to harbour service in 1912. *Vindictive* alone served as a cruiser in the First World War, and became famous for her valiant role in the Zeebrugge raid, 23rd April 1918.

ARROGANT

Built at Devonport Dockyard. Laid down 10.6.1895. Launched 26.5.1896. Completed 27.1.1898. Channel Squadron 1898-1901 (crew transferred to *Doris*). Rearmed, Devonport 1902-03. Mediterranean 1903-05. Attached Atlantic BS 1905-09. Trooping to Malta 1909. 3rd Fleet, Devonport 1910. Converted to Submarine Depot Ship, Devonport 1910-11. Submarine Depot Ship at Portsmouth 1911-14 (relieved *Mercury*), and Dover 1914-18 (4 S/M Flotilla 1914-15, 5 S/M Flotilla 1915-18). Base Flagship of Vice Admiral Sir Roger Keyes, Dover Patrol 1915-18. For disposal 1919. Later accommodation ship for Submarine School, Portsmouth. Sold 1923, Hughes Bolckow, and broken up at Blyth.

Arrogant **Keyes flagship in WW1.**

FURIOUS

Built at Devonport Dockyard. Laid down 10.6.1895. Launched 3.12.1896. Completed 1.7.1898. Channel Squadron 1898-1902. Rearmed, Chatham 1903. Mediterranean 1903-05. Seagoing tender to *Vernon*, Torpedo School, Portsmouth 1905-12—wireless experiements in Mediterranean 1911. Harbour service, Portsmouth 1912. Laid up, Motherbank 1913-15. Renamed *Forte*, 6.1915 and attached to *Vernon* as a hulk. Sold 1923, G. Cohen, Swansea.

GLADIATOR

Built at Portsmouth Dockyard. Laid down 1.1896. Launched 18.12.1896. Completed 4.1899. Reserve 1899-1900. Mediterranean 1901-03. Rearmed, Portsmouth 1903-04. Nucleus crew, Portsmouth 1904-08 (trooping 1907). Sank in collision with American liner *St Paul* in the Solent with the loss of 27 lives, 25.4.1908. Raised 10.1908, but was beyond economical repair. Sold 1909.

VINDICTIVE

Built at Chatham Dockyard. Laid down 27.1.1896. Launched 9.12.1897. Completed 4.7.1900. Mediterranean 1900-04. Rearmed, Chatham 1904. Chatham, in commission in Reserve, 3rd Fleet etc. 1904-12. Seagoing tender to *Vernon*, Torpedo School, Portsmouth 1912-14. 9 CS Mid Atlantic 1914-15—captured German merchantman *Schlesien* on 7.8.1914, and *Slawentzitz* on 8.9.1914. SE Coast of S. America 1915-16. White Sea 1916-17. Fitted out as assault ship, 1918 for Zeebrugge Raid, 23.4.1918. Expended as blockship at Ostend 10.5.1918. Raised 1920 and broken up.

Battle Honours: Zeebrugge 1918, Ostend 1918.

Gladiator described by Kipling as having "an air of bristling, hog-backed ferocity".

Vindictive in Dover harbour after the Zeebrugge raid.

HIGHFLYER CLASS (3 ships), *1896 Programme*
CHALLENGER CLASS (2 ships), *1900 Programme*

Hermes, Highflyer, Hyacinth
Challenger, Encounter

Highflyers:

Displacement (tons):	5,600 load.
Dimensions (feet):	350pp, 372oa x 54 x 22
(metres):	106.7pp, 113.4oa x 16.5 x 6.7
Machinery:	2 shaft 4 cyl. TE. 18 Belleville boilers (*Hermes* reboilered with Babcocks 1902-03). 10,000 HP = 20 knots.
Fuel:	Coal 1,100 tons.
Protection:	Full length deck 3in-2in (76mm-51mm). Engine hatch (glacis) 5in (127mm).
Armament:	11—6in, 9—12pdr, 6—3pdr, 2—18in TT submerged.
Complement:	450

Challengers as above except:

Displacement (tons):	5,915 load.
Dimensions (feet):	355pp, 376oa x 56 x 21¼
(metres):	108.2pp, 114.6oa x 17.1 x 6.5
Machinery:	2 shaft 4 cyl. TE. 18 Babcock (*Encounter*, Durr) boilers. 12,500 SHP = 21 knots.

The Highflyers were repeat Eclipses, but incorporating the more powerful machinery and water tube boilers of the Arrogants, and armed from the outset with 11—6in guns.

In April-May 1913 *Hermes* underwent a makeshift conversion into a depot ship for the Naval Wing of the Royal Flying Corps, with a launching platform forward and stowage for three seaplanes aft, beginning the association of the name *Hermes* with naval aviation. After trials and manoeuvres the ship paid off in December 1913, and was hurriedly re-equipped as a cruiser on the outbreak of war in August 1914.

Highflyer was the last cruiser of the Victorian era in active commission, paying off as Flagship of the East Indies Station at Bombay early in 1921.

The Challengers were repeat Highflyers, slightly enlarged to accommodate still more powerful machinery. They replaced the Katoombas on the Australian station, and represent the ultimate stage in a line of development that began with the Apollos.

Hermes later used for early aircraft trials 1913.

HERMES

Built by Fairfield, Govan. Laid down 30.4.1897. Launched 7.4.1898. Completed 5.10.1899. Flagship, N. America & W.I. 1899-1901. Refitted with Babcock boilers, Harland & Wolff, Belfast 1901-03. Channel 1903-04. Portsmouth 1905. Flagship, East Indies 1906-07. Flagship, Cape 1907-13. 3rd Fleet, Nore 1913. Converted to Aircraft Depot Ship, Chatham, 1913. Trials 1913. 3rd Fleet, Nore 1914. Reconverted for cruiser duties 8.1914. Nore Command 1914. Lost 31.10.1914, torpedoed by U27 in Straits of Dover. 44 lost.

Highflyer, **1899, carried out trials of Belleville boilers.**

HIGHFLYER

Built by Fairfield. Govan. Laid down 7.6.1897. Launched 4.6.1898. Completed 7.12.1899. Cruiser Training Squadron (temp.) 1899-1900. Flagship, East Indies 1900-04. Cadets' TS attached N. America & W.I. 1904-06. Nucleus crew, Devonport 1906. East Indies 1906-08. Nucleus crew, Devonport 1908-10. 3rd Fleet, Nore 1910-11. Flagship, East Indies 1911-13. 3rd Fleet, Chatham 1913. TS for Special Entry Cadets 1913-14. 9 CS Mid Atlantic—disabled German AMC *Kaiser Wilhelm der Grosse,* 27.8.1914. 5 CS Mid Atlantic based on Cape Verde 1914-16. West Africa 1916-17. Flagship, N. America & W.I. 1917. East Indies 1918-21 (Flagship 1919-21). Sold at Bombay, 1921.

HYACINTH

Built by London & Glasgow, Govan. Laid down 27.1.1897. Launched 27.10.1898. Completed 3.9.1900. Cruiser Training Squadron (boiler trials) 1900-03. East Indies 1903-06. Nucleus crew, Devonport 1906. Flagship, East Indies 1907-11. Refit, Chatham 1911-12. 3rd Fleet, Nore (attached 5 BS) 1912. Flagship, Cape 1913-19—intercepted German merchantman *Rubens,* 18.5.1915, and sank SS *Tabora* at Dar-es-Salaam, 26.3.1916. Portsmouth, paid off 1919. Sold 1923, Cohen, Swansea.

Challenger **in heavy weather in the Great War.**

CHALLENGER

Built at Chatham Dockyard. Laid down 1.12.1900. Launched 27.5.1902. Completed 3.5.1904. Australia 1904-12. 3rd Fleet, Devonport 1912-14. 9 CS Mid Atlantic based on Portland 1914—captured German steamer *Ulla Boog* in Bristol Channel, 9.1914. Detached to West Africa for Cameroons campaign 1914-15. East Africa 1915-19—roundup of *Konigsberg* 1915, and with *Pioneer* bombarded Dar-es-Salaam, 13.6.1915. Paid off, Portsmouth 1919. Sold 1920, Ward, Preston.

Battle Honours: Cameroons 1914.

ENCOUNTER

Built at Devonport Dockyard. Laid down 28.1.1901. Launched 18.6.1902. Completed 21.11.1905. Australia 1905-14—transferred to RAN 1912. Pacific 1914-15—captured German sailing vessel *Elfriede*, 25.4.1915. China 1915-16. Pacific 1916-18. Permanently transferred to Australia 1919. Receiving ship, Sydney 1919-23. Submarine Depot Ship, renamed *Penguin*, 1923-29. Paid off 1929. Scuttled off Sydney Heads 14.9.1932.

81

PELORUS CLASS (11 ships), *Spencer Programme 1893 and subsequent Estimates*

Pactolus, Pandora, Pegasus, Pelorus, Perseus, Pioneer, Pomone, Prometheus, Proserpine, Psyche, Pyramus

Displacement (tons):	2,135 load.
Dimensions (feet):	300pp, 313½oa x 36½ x 16
(metres):	91.4pp, 95.6oa x 11.1 x 4.9
Machinery:	2 shaft 3 cyl. TE. 16 Thornycorft (*Pomone & Pactolus,* Blechynden; *Pelorus,* Normand; *Pegasus & Pyramus,* Reed) boilers. 5,000/7,000 HP = 18½/20 knots.
Fuel:	Coal 500 tons.
Protection:	Full length deck 2in-1½in (51mm-38mm).
Armament:	8—4in, 8—3pdr, 2—14in TT above water.
Complement:	224

Logical successors to the Pearls, whose general arrangement they followed, but with a longer, thinner hull for greater speed. Guns were disposed as in the Pearls, but of 4in rather than 4.7in calibre to compensate for the narrower beam. Unlike contemporary second-class cruisers, the Peloruses retained a traditional raised forecastle and poop with low freeboard in between, they were consequently very wet, and also rolled heavily.

The class was chosen for comparative trials of a variety of water-tube boilers, and all suffered from a certain amount of boiler trouble—so much in the case of *Pactolus* and *Pomone* that they were withdrawn from service after only a few years. In all ships, best speed soon fell to 15-16 knots.

PACTOLUS

Built by Armstrong, Elswick. Laid down 5.1896. Launched 21.12.1896. Completed 9.1898. Channel 1899-1903. Laid up, Chatham and River Stour 1904-12. Converted to Submarine Depot Ship, 1912. 9 S/M Flotilla, Ardrossan 1914-18. Sold 1921, Multilocular Shipbreaker Co., Stranrear.

PANDORA

Built at Portsmouth Dockyard. Laid down 1896. Launched 17.1.1900. Completed 1901. Mediterranean 1901-04. Nucleus crew, Portsmouth 1904-07. Special service 1908. Cape 1908-12. Sold 1913, Ward, Morecambe.

Pandora

PEGASUS

Built by Palmers, Jarrow. Laid down 5.1896. Launched 4.3.1897. Completed 1898. SE Coast of America 1899-1900. Mediterranean 1901-04. Australia 1905-12 (China, temp. 1912). Cape 1913-14. Sunk by *Konigsberg* off Zanzibar, 20.9.1914. 31 lost.

Perseus **in a gale**

PELORUS

Built at Sheerness Dockyard. Laid down 5.1896. Launched 15.12.1896. Completed 1897. Channel 1897-1901 (detached to Cape 1899-1900). Crew transferred to *Prometheus*, 1901. Reserve 1901-05 (refit, Clydebank 1903). Cape 1905-09. 3rd Fleet, Devonport and Portsmouth 1909-12 (trooping 1911). East Indies 1912-14. Patrols in Bristol Channel 1914. Patrols from Gibraltar 1915-16. Depot ship at Suda Bay 1916-18. Nore, paid off 1919. Sold 1920, Ward, Grays.

Battle Honour: South Africa 1899-1900.

PERSEUS

Built by Earle, Hull. Laid down 5.1896. Launched 15.7.1897. Completed 1901. East Indies 1901-13 (relieved by *Dartmouth*). Sold 1914, Poulson.

PIONEER

Built at Chatham Dockyard. Laid down 16.12.1896. Launched 28.6.1899. Completed 1900. Mediterranean 1900-04. Nucleus crew, Chatham 1905. Drill Ship, Australia 1905-12. Transferred to RAN 12.1912. Paid off 1912-13. Training Ship, Sydney 1914-15. East Africa 1915-16—with *Challenger* bombarded Dar-es-Salaam 13.6.1915. Laid up at Sydney 8.1916. Sold as a hulk, 1924. Scuttled off Sydney Heads 2.1931.

POMONE

Built at Sheerness Dockyard. Laid down 21.12.1896. Launched 25.11.1897. Completed 5.1899. East Indies 1899-1904. Laid up, Chatham and Blackwater 1904-10. Harbour service as Training Ship, Dartmouth 1910-20. Sold 1922, J. H. Lee, Dover.

PROMETHEUS

Built by Earle, Hull. Laid down 1897. Launched 20.10.1898. Completed 1901. Channel 1901-04. Australia 1904-12 (China, Temp. 1912). Sold 1914.

PROSERPINE

Built at Sheerness Dockyard. Laid down 3.1896. Launched 3.12.1896. Completed 1898. N. America & W.I. 1898-1901. Chatham 1902-03. East Indies 1904-12. CS Mediterranean 1913. 3rd Fleet, Sheerness 1913-14. 7 CS Channel 1914. Mediterranean, East Indies, and Egypt 1914-18. Red Sea 1918. Sold at Alexandria 1919 and broken up, Genoa.

Battle Honour: Suez Canal 1915.

PSYCHE

Built at Devonport Dockyard. Laid down 16.11.1897. Launched 19.7.1898. Completed 1900. N. America & W.I. 1900-02. Refit, Hawthorn Leslie 1902-03. Australia 1903-13. New Zealand 1913-15. China 1915. Loaned to RAN 1915. Training Ship for Seamen and Stokers, Sydney 1915-20. Sold 1922 and broken up, Melbourne.

PYRAMUS

Built by Palmers, Jarrow. Laid down 5.1896. Launched 15.5.1897. Completed 1900. Mediterranean 1900-04. Nucleus crew, Chatham 1904-06. Australia 1906-13. New Zealand 1914. Persian Gulf and East Indies 1915. Depot ship at Mudros 1915-18. Devonport, paid off 1919-20. Sold 1920 and broken up in Holland.

BRITISH CRUISER DEPLOYMENT, JUNE 1900

Mediterranean and Red Sea:
Andromeda, Astraea, Barham, Dido, Fearless (det. to Cape), *Isis, Scout, Theseus, Thetis* (det. to Cape), *Venus.*

Channel:
Arrogant, Diadem, Furious, Niobe, (det. to Cape), *Pactolus, Pelorus* (det. to Cape).

North America and West Indies:
Charybdis, Crescent, Hermes, Indefatigable, Pearl, Proserpine, Psyche, Tribune.

South East Coast of America:
Flora, Pegasus.

Pacific:
Arethusa, Leander, Phaeton, Warspite.

Cape of Good Hope and West Coast of Africa:
Barracouta, Barrosa, Doris, Forte, Magicienne, Philomel.

East Indies:
Eclipse (to be relieved by *Highflyer), Marathon, Melpomone* (ordered home), *Pomone, Racoon* (det. to Cape).

China:
Aurora, Bonaventure, Endymion, Hermione, Orlando, Pique, Terrible, Undaunted (tbr *Argonaut).*

Australia:
Katoomba, Mohawk, Porpoise, Royal Arthur, Tauranga, Wallaroo.

Training Squadron:
Cambrian, Juno, Minerva, St George.

Particular Service:
**Calliope,* **Curacoa,* *Diana, Edgar, Europa* (trooping to Australia), **Northampton.*

On Passage Home:
Iphigenia.

---

*Old corvettes except *Northampton,* an old armoured cruiser.
Note: Ships in refit or reserve not included.

1901-19 PART I: THE ARMOURED CRUISER

Cressy, Drake, Monmouth, Devonshire, Duke of Edinburgh, Warrior and Minotaur classes

Three factors prompted Britain's return to the armoured cruiser. First, it was to counter the French *Jeanne d'Arc* and the German *Furst Bismarck*. Second, the new Krupp steel armour was much lighter than the old compound armour for the same strength. Finally, there was the influence of the Italian cruisers *Carlo Alberto* and *Garribaldi*, which were intended to operate in conjunction with the battle fleet and fight in the line as a fast wing. This was the fatally flawed concept, adopted in the Cressys and all subsequent British armoured cruisers (except the Counties), which led ultimately to the battle cruiser. Armoured cruisers meanwhile were expected to carry out the standard cruiser functions in the fleet and on the trade routes.

Except for their belts, the Cressys did not differ radically from the Diadems, and their appearance was very similar. They were also rather slow, only being good for 21 knots. When France and Russia built a number of fast cruisers intended primarily for commerce raiding, Britain raised her speed requirement for armoured cruisers to 23 knots, which the Drakes achieved by increased size and power, and the Counties by reduced armament and protection.

In effect, the Counties were second-class Drakes. Too lightly armed and protected to fight in a fast wing, they were built specifically to counter foreign commerce raiders. With the third-class Gems, they brought to a close the remarkable White era of cruiser design.

In marked contrast to the Counties, Watts' armoured cruisers—the Duke of Edinburgh, Warrior and Minotaur classes—were intended primarily to provide the fleet with a fast wing. Vastly superior to the Drakes and Cressys, they really stood in a class of their own.

Meanwhile, the strategic outlook was changing. For much of the nineteenth century Britain had struggled to maintain the 'Two Power standard', whereby the Royal Navy had to equal the combined strength of the French and Russian navies. But with the passing of the 1898 Navy Law in Germany, the Royal Navy began to face another possible challenger. The sealing of an 'Entente Cordial' with France in 1903 and the rout of the Russian navy at Tsushima in 1905 left Britain with just one serious rival at sea: Germany. In the arms race that ensued the armoured cruiser was abandoned, logically enough, in favour of the battlecruiser.

By 1914 the Cressys were old and the other armoured cruisers past their prime. Only Watts' ships were still regarded as front-line units. As a group they suffered particularly bitter misfortunes: *Aboukir, Cressy* and *Hogue* were lost in a single night; *Good Hope* and *Monmouth* both blew up at Coronel with the loss of all hands; *Argyll* was wrecked and *Natal* destroyed by an internal explosion; *Hampshire's* loss with Lord Kitchener on board sent shock waves around the Empire. Worst of all was the loss of *Black Prince, Warrior* and *Defence* at Jutland.

CRESSY CLASS (6 ships), *1897 Programme*

Aboukir, Bacchante, Cressy, Euryalus, Hogue, Sutlej

Displacement (tons):	12,000 load.
Dimensions (feet):	440pp, 472oa x 69½ x 26
(metres):	134.1pp, 143.9oa x 21.2 x 7.9
Machinery:	2 shaft 4 cyl. TE. 30 Belleville boilers.
	21,000 HP = 21 knots.
Fuel:	Coal 1,600 tons.
Protection:	Long belt, 230ft (70m) from bow 2in-6in (51mm-152mm)
	Full length deck 3in-1in (76mm-25mm)
Armament:	2—9.2in, 12—6in, 12—12pdr, 3—3pdr
	2—18in TT submerged.
Complement:	760

Belted Diadems, heavier, faster, and reverting to the mixed 9.2in and 6in armament of the Powerfuls, the Cressys made a great impression when they first appeared. A fuller hull form gave them better stability than the Diadems, but finer lines forward and the weight of the 9.2in guns increased pitching. The Cressys were the first cruisers intended for foreign service not to be sheathed and coppered, reflecting the improvement in docking facilities around the world. *Euryalus'* completion was delayed for two years by a series of accidents.

At the beginning of the war, the whole class less *Sutlej* formed the 7th Cruiser Squadron, patrolling the southern North sea. Early in the morning of 22nd September 1914, *Aboukir*, *Cressy* and *Hogue* were steaming in company when *Aboukir* was struck by a torpedo and began to sink. Thinking that her sister had been mined, *Hogue* went in to pick up survivors, only to be torpedoed herself. The German submarine *U9* then surfaced, revealing herself as the attacker, and was fired on. Perhaps not comprehending that she would also be attacked, *Cressy* stopped among the survivors from her sisters, and like them, was torpedoed and sunk by *U9*. 1,449 lives were lost that day in one of the most infamous acts of war at sea. A whole term of Dartmouth naval cadets were embarked in the three ships, and many of them perished.

The other three ships of the class survived the war, *Bacchante* remaining in commission until 1919.

ABOUKIR

Built by Fairfield, Govan. Laid down 9.11.1898. Launched 16.5.1900. Completed 3.4.1902. Mediterranean 1902-05. Nucleus crew, Nore 1906, Devonport 1906-07. 3 CS Mediterranean 1907-09. 6 CS Mediterranean 1909-12. 3rd Fleet 1912-14 (attached 4 CS 1912, 6 CS 1913, 7 CS 1914). 7 CS North Sea 1914. With *Cressy* and *Hogue*, torpedoed and sunk by *U9* in North Sea, 22.9.1914.

BACCHANTE

Built by John Brown, Clydebank. Laid down 15.2.1899. Launched 21.2.1901. Completed 25.11.1902. Flagship, Cruiser Division, Mediterranean 1902-04. Nucleus crew, Portsmouth 1905-06. 3 CS Mediterranean 1906-08. 6 CS Mediterranean 1909-12. 3rd Fleet, Nore 1912-14 (attached 6 CS 1912). Flagship, 7 CS North Sea 1914. 12 CS Atlantic Convoys 1914-15. Mediterranean 1915-16. Flagship, 9 CS West Africa based on Sierra Leone 1917-19. Paid off 4.1919. Sold 1920, Castle, Plymouth.

Battle Honours: Heligoland 1914, Dardanelles 1915-16.

CRESSY

Built by Fairfield, Govan. Laid down 12.10.1898. Launched 4.12.1899. Completed 28.5.1901. China 1901-04. Nucleus crew, Portsmouth 1904-07. Boys' TS attached 4 CS N. America & W.I. 1907-09. 3rd Fleet, Nore 1909-14 (attached 6 CS 1912). 7 CS North Sea 1914. With *Aboukir* and *Hogue*, torpedoed and sunk by *U9* in North Sea, 22.9.1914.

Battle Honour: Heligoland 1914.

EURYALUS

Built by Vickers, Barrow. Laid down 18.7.1899. Launched 20.5.1901. Completed 5.1.1904. Flagship, Australia 1904-05. Nucleus crew, Portsmouth 1905-06. Boys' TS, attached 4 CS N. America & W.I. 1906-09. 3rd Fleet, Portsmouth 1909-10, Devonport 1911-13, Nore 1913-14. 7 CS North Sea 1914. 12 CS Atlantic Convoys 1914-15. Mediterranean 1915-16. Flagship, East Indies 1916-17. Under conversion to Minelayer at Hong Kong from 11.1917. Refit abandoned 1918. Sold 1920, Castle, Plymouth. Resold and broken up in Germany.

Battle Honours: Heligoland 1914, Dardanelles 1915.

HOGUE

Built by Vickers, Barrow. Laid down 14.7.1898. Launched 13.8.1900. Completed 19.11.1902. Channel 1902-04. Refit 1904. China 1904-06. Boys' TS, attached 4 CS N. America & W.I. 1906-08 (relieved *St George*). Nucleus crew, Devonport 1908-09. 3rd Fleet, Nore 1909-11. Refit, Chatham 1912-13. 3rd Fleet, Nore 1913-14. 7 CS North Sea 1914. With *Aboukir* and *Cressy*, torpedoed and sunk by *U9*, 22.9.1914.

Battle Honour: Heligoland 1914.

SUTLEJ

Built by John Brown, Clydebank. Laid down 15.8.1898. Launched 18.11.1899. Completed 6.5.1902. Channel 1902-04. Refit 1904. China 1904-06. Boys' TS, attached 4 CS N. America & W.I. 1906-09. 3rd Fleet, Devonport 1909-14 (Flagship 1909-12, attached 6 CS 1912-13, 7 CS 1913, 6 CS 1913-14). 9 CS Mid Atlantic 1914. 11 CS West Coast of Ireland 1914-15. Repairs at Devonport 1916. 9 CS West Africa 1916-17. Overflow ship at Rosyth 1917-18. Sold 1921, Ward, Preston.

Cressy, 1910, lost with Abouki and Hogue.

DRAKE CLASS (4 ships), *1898 Programme*

Drake, Good Hope, King Alfred, Leviathan

Displacement (tons):	14,150 load.
Dimensions (feet):	500pp, 533½oa x 71⅓ x 26
(metres):	152.4pp, 162.6oa x 21.7 x 7.9
Machinery:	2 shaft 4 cyl. TE. 43 Belleville boilers. 30,000 HP = 23 knots.
Fuel:	Coal 2,500 tons.
Protection:	Long belt, 400ft (122m) from bow 3in-6in (76mm-152mm). Full length deck 3in-1in (76-25mm).
Armament:	2—9.2in, 16—6in, 14—12pdr, 3—3pdr, 2—18in TT submerged.
Complement:	900

Enlarged Cressys, with the increase in size devoted mainly to the more powerful machinery necessary for a speed of 23 knots. Hailed by the First Lord, Lord Goschen, as 'mighty cruisers', they were as big as the Powerfuls and much better protected. Among the fastest ships in the world on completion, they often exceeded their trial speed in service. Good seaboats and exceptional steamers, they were capable for many years of long periods of fast steaming.

Armament was similar to that of the Cressys, but the 9.2in guns were of an improved type, 45 calibre instead of 40. Deck fittings were kept to a minimum to reduce the risk of fire, giving the Drakes a neat, uncluttered appearance. Usually employed as cruiser squadron flagships, as befitted their size and prestige.

DRAKE

Built at Pembroke Dockyard. Laid down 24.4.1899. Launched 5.3.1901. Completed 13.1.1903. Cruiser Squadron, Channel 1903-04. Flagship, 2 CS Atlantic 1905-08. Flagship, 1 CS Channel 1908-10. 5 CS Atlantic 1910-11. Flagship, Australia 1911-13. 2nd Fleet (attached 6 CS) 1913-14. 6 CS Grand Fleet 1914-15. Refit late 1915. N. America & W.I. (Atlantic convoys) 1916-17. Torpedoed and sunk by *U79* off Rathlin Island, N. of Ireland, 2.10.1917.

GOOD HOPE (ex Africa)

Built by Fairfield, Govan. Laid down 11.9.1899. Launched 21.2.1901. Completed 8.11.1902. Cruiser Squadron, Channel 1903-04. Flagship 1 CS Channel 1905-07. Flagship 2 CS Atlantic 1907-09 (visited South Africa 1908). Refit, Portsmouth 1910. 5 CS Atlantic 1911, Mediterranean 1912. 2nd Fleet (attached 6 CS) 1913-14. 6 CS Grand Fleet 1914—sent to South Atlantic as flagship of Rear Admiral Sir Christopher Cradock. Blew up at battle of Coronel with loss of all hands, 1.11.1914.

Good Hope, 1907, lost as Admiral Cradock's flagship at Coronel.

Drake, **1917, at Sheerness with lower 6 inch casemates removed.**

KING ALFRED

Built by Vickers, Barrow. Laid down 11.8.1899. Launched 28.10.1901. Completed 22.12.1903. Particular Service 1904. Nucleus crew, Chatham 1905. Flagship, C in C China 1906-10. 3rd Divn, Devonport 1911. 2nd Fleet (attached 5 CS 1912, 6 CS 1913-14). 6 CS Grand Fleet 1914. 9 CS Mid Atlantic 1915-17. N. America & W.I. (Atlantic convoys) 1917-19. Sold 1920, F. Rijdijk, Holland.

LEVIATHAN

Built by John Brown, Clydebank. Laid down 30.11.1899. Launched 3.7.1901. Completed 16.6.1903. Cruiser Squadron, Channel 1903-04. 3 CS Mediterranean 1905-06. Refit, Chatham 1907. 5 CS Home 1908-09. 4 CS N. America & W.I. 1909-12. Flagship, Training Squadron 1912. 3rd Fleet (attached 6 CS) 1913-14. 6 CS Grand Fleet 1914-15 (temp. 5 CS Dec. 1914—Jan. 1915). Flagship, N. America & W.I. 1915-19 (Atlantic convoys 1918). Sold 1920, Hughes Bolckow, Blyth.

MONMOUTH CLASS (10 ships)

Essex, Kent (1898 Programme, Supplementary Estimates)
Bedford, Monmouth (1899 Programme)
Berwick, Cornwall, Cumberland, Donegal, Lancaster, Suffolk (1900 Programme)

Displacement (tons):	9,800 load.
Dimensions (feet):	440pp, 463½oa x 66 x 25
(metres):	134.1pp, 141.3oa x 20.1 x 7.6
Machinery:	2 shaft 4 cyl. TE. 31 Belleville boilers. 22,000 HP = 23 knots.
Fuel:	Coal 1,600 tons.
Protection:	Long belt, 330ft (101m) from bow 2in/4in/—(51mm/102mm/—). Full length deck 2in (51mm).
Armament:	14—6in (2 x 2, 10 x 1), 10—12pdr, 3—3pdr, 2—18in TT submerged.
Complement:	675-720

Second-class Drakes, intended for trade protection rather than fleet work. As fast as the Drakes, but scaled down in size, armament and protection.

Originally the armament was to have included a single 7.5in gun fore and aft, but novel electrically operated twin 6in turrets were adopted instead. Unfortunately these turrets were too cramped for efficient operation and prone to electrical problems.

In general good seaboats, the Monmouths' very fine lines fore and aft, combined with the weight of the twin turrets, caused heavy pitching in bad weather. Excellent steamers, they kept their speed for many years. The *Kent*, which had difficulty making her contract speed when new, attained 25 knots during the battle of the Falklands in December 1914-very low on fuel and burning wardroom furniture to gain the last knot. She again excelled herself in the chase for the *Dresden* in the following March: hurtling through a choppy sea in a strong southerly wind, spray flying about her forecastle and flames leaping from her funnels thirty feet into the air, while her crew sat on the quarterdeck to make the propellers 'bite', she must have been a memorable sight. But that day at least, the *Dresden* got away.

ESSEX

Built at Pembroke Dockyard. Laid down 1.1.1900. Launched 29.8.1901. Completed 22.3.1904. 2 CS Atlantic 1904-06. Nucleus crew, Devonport 1906. Nucleus crew, Portsmouth, and Home Fleet 1907-09. 4 CS N. America & W.I. 1909-12. Training Squadron 1912. Refit 1913. 4 CS N. America & W.I. 1914-16—captured a German merchantman 10.8.1914, another 7.9.1914 and another 5.1916. Became Destroyer Depot Ship 1916. Devonport, paid off 1919-20. Sold 1921 to Slough Trading Co. Broken up in Germany.

Berwick, **1905, note searchlight only on foremast.**

KENT

Built at Portsmouth Dockyard. Laid down 12.2.1900. Launched 6.3.1901. Completed 1.10.1903. 1 CS Channel 1903-05. China 1906-13. Refit 1913-14. SE Coast of America 1914-15—sank German light cruiser SMS *Nurnberg* at Falklands 8.12.1914. With *Glasgow* sank SMS *Dresden* at Mas a Fuera, Chile, 14.3.1915. Pacific 1915-16. Cape 1916-18. China 1918. Vladivostock 1.1919. Paid off for disposal 1919. Sold at Hong Kong, 1920.

Battle Honour: Falklands 1914.

BEDFORD

Built by Fairfield, Govan. Laid down 19.2.1900. Launched 31.8.1901. Completed 11.11.1903. 1 CS Channel 1903-06. Nucleus crew, Nore 1906-07. China 1907-10. Wrecked at Quelport Island in China Sea, 21.8.1910. Wreck sold 10.1910.

MONMOUTH

Built by London & Glasgow, Govan. Laid down 29.8.1899. Launched 13.11.1901. Completed 2.12.1903. 1 CS Channel 1903-06. China 1906-13. 3rd Fleet 1913-14. 5 CS Mid Atlantic 1914, and sent to S. Atlantic. Sunk at battle of Coronel with loss of all hands, 1.11.1914.

BERWICK

Built by Beardmore, Dalmuir. Laid down 19.4.1901. Launched 20.9.1902. Completed 9.12.1903. 1 CS Channel 1903-04. 2 CS Atlantic 1904-07. Portsmouth Divn, Home Fleet 1908—rammed and sank destroyer HMS *Tiger* during night exercises off Isle of Wight, 2.4.1908. Refit 1908-09. 4 CS N. America & W.I. 1909-19 (Training Squadron 1912). Captured German merchantman *Spreewald* in S. Atlantic 10.9.1914. Atlantic convoys during war. 8 LCS N. America & W.I. 1919. Devonport, paid off 1919. Sold 1920, Castle. Broken up in Germany.

CORNWALL

Built at Pembroke Dockyard. Laid down 11.3.1901. Launched 29.10.1902. Completed 1.12.1904. 2 CS Atlantic 1904-06. Refit, Devonport 1907. Cadets' TS attached N. America & W.I. 1908-14. 5 CS Mid Atlantic 1914—captured German merchantman *Syra*, 6.8.1914. South America 1914-15—with *Glasgow* sank SMS *Leipzig* at the Falklands, 8.12.1914. Blockade of *Konigsberg*, E. Africa 1915. Dardanelles 1915. China 1915-17. N. America & W.I. (Atlantic convoys) 1917-19. Cadets' TS 1919. Devonport, paid off 1919. Sold 1920, Ward, Briton Ferry.

Battle Honours: Falklands 1914, Dardanelles 1915

CUMBERLAND

Built by London & Glasgow, Govan. Laid down 19.2.1901. Launched 16.12.1902. Completed 1.12.1904. 2 CS Atlantic 1904-06. Nucleus crew, Devonport 1907. Cadets' TS, attached N. America & W.I. 1907-14. 5 CS Mid Atlantic 1914—sent to West Africa 1914-15. 6 CS Grand Fleet 1915. N. America & W.I. (including Atlantic convoys) 1915-19. Cadets' TS 1919-21. Sold 1921, Ward, Briton Ferry.

Battle Honour: Cameroons 1914.

Monmouth **later lost at Coronel, 1914.**

AUTHORS COLLECTION

DONEGAL

Built by Fairfield, Govan. Laid down 14.2.1901. Launched 4.9.1902. Completed 5.11.1903. 1 CS Channel 1903-05. Commissioned for China Station, 1906, but ran aground on passage out. Repairs, Chatham 1906. Nucleus crew, Devonport and Home Fleet 1907-09. 4 CS N. America & W.I. 1909-12. Training Squadron 1912. 3rd Fleet (attached 5 CS) 1913-14. Refitting 8.1914. 5 CS Mid Atlantic (based on Sierra Leone) 1914. 6 CS Grand Fleet 1915. 7 CS Grand Fleet Nov 1915-16—escorting convoys to White Sea (Archangel). 2 CS Grand Fleet from March 1916. 9 CS Mid Atlantic Sep. 1916-17. 4 CS N. America & W.I. 1917-18. Paid off 5.1918. Devonport Reserve 1918-19. Sold 1920, Castle. Resold to Granton Shipbreaking Co.

LANCASTER

Built by Armstrong, Elswick. Laid down 4.3.1901. Launched 22.3.1902. Completed 5.4.1904. 3 CS Mediterranean 1904-09. 6 CS Mediterranean 1909-12. 5 CS, 2nd Fleet 1912-13. 4 CS N. America & W.I. 1913-15. 7 CS Grand Fleet 1915. Refit 1915-16. Pacific 1916-19. Partially dismantled at Birkenhead 1919. Sold 1920, Ward, Preston.

SUFFOLK

Built at Portsmouth Dockyard. Laid down 25.3.1901. Launched 15.1.1903. Completed 21.5.1904. 3 CS Mediterranean 1904-09. 6 CS Mediterranean 1909-12. 4 CS N. America & W.I. 1913-16 (Flagship 1914). Captured a German merchantman, 8.8.1914. Refit 1917. Flagship, China 1917-18. Vladivostock 1918-19. Devonport, paid off 1919-20. Sold 1920, Castle. Resold and broken up in Germany.

DEVONSHIRE CLASS (6 ships), *1901 Programme*

Antrim, Argyll, Carnarvon, Devonshire, Hampshire, Roxburgh

Displacement (tons):	10,850 load.
Dimensions (feet):	450pp, 473½oa x 68 x 24
(metres):	137.2pp, 144.3oa x 20.7 x 7.3
Machinery:	2 shaft 4 cyl. TE. 6 cylindrical boilers + 15-17 watertube: *Antrim, Hampshire,* 17 Yarrow; *Argyll* 16 Babcock; *Roxburgh* 17 Durr; *Devonshire* 15 *Carnarvon* 17 Niclausse. 21,000 HP = 22¼ knots.
Fuel:	Coal, 1,950 tons.
Protection:	Long belt, 325ft (99m) from bow 2in/6in/— (51mm/152mm/—). Full length deck 2in (51mm).
Armament:	4—7.5in, 6—6in, 2—12pdr, 18—3pdr, 4—18in TT submerged.
Complement:	655-700

In one of his last designs before retiring as DNC, Sir William White wanted to correct shortcomings he had always seen in the Monmouths. The increase in displacement in the Devonshires was limited to 1,000 tons, and with the same installed power as the Monmouths, a drop in speed of ¾ knot was accepted. Four 7.5in guns were carried, two instead of the Monmouth's twin 6in turrets fore and aft, and another pair in wing turrets on the upper deck, just abaft and below the forecastle.

Better ships all round than the Monmouths, all managed to exceed 23 knots on trials. In the long term, however, their odd mixture of cylindrical and water tube boilers let them down, and the Devonshires became indifferent steamers.

ANTRIM

Built by John Brown, Clydebank. Laid down 27.8.1902. Launched 8.10.1903. Completed 23.6.1905. 1 CS Channel 1905-06. 1 CS Atlantic 1906-07. 2 CS Atlantic 1907-09. 3rd Fleet, Nore 1909-11. 5 CS 2nd Fleet 1912. 3 CS 2nd Fleet 1913-14. Flagship, 3 CS Grand Fleet 1914-16. Captured a German merchantman 6.8.1914. Present at Heligoland 28.8.1914. At Archangel, 6.1916. N. America & W.I. 1916-18 (paid off Dec. 1917—Aug. 1918). Nore Reserve 1919. Asdic Trials Ship 1920-21. Cadets' TS 1922. Sold 1922, Hughes Bolckow, Derwenthaugh.

ARGYLL

Built by Scotts, Greenock. Laid down 1.9.1902. Launched 3.3.1904. Completed 12.1905. 1 CS Atlantic 1906-07. 1 CS Channel 1907-09. 5 CS Atlantic 1909-12—detached to escort King George V to India 1911-12. 3 CS 2nd Fleet 1913-15. 3 CS Grand Fleet 1914-15—captured a German merchantman 6.8.1914. Heligoland 1914. Wrecked on Bell Rock, east coast of Scotland, 28.10.1915.

CARNARVON

Built by Beardmore, Dalmuir. Laid down 1.10.1902. Launched 7.10.1903. Completed 29.5. 1905. 3 CS Mediterranean 1905-07. 2 CS Atlantic 1907-09. 3rd Fleet, Devonport 1909-11. 5 CS 2nd Fleet 1912-14. Flagship, 5 CS Mid Atlantic 1914; captured a German merchantman 24.8.1914. South Atlantic 1914-15—struck shoal off Abrolhos Rocks, Brazil 2.1915 and repaired at Rio de Janeiro. N. America & W.I. 1915-18 (Atlantic convoys 1917). Cadets' TS 1919-21. Sold 1921, Slough Trading Co. and broken up in Germany.

Battle Honour: Falklands 1914.

DEVONSHIRE

Built at Chatham Dockyard. Laid down 25.3.1902. Launched 30.4.1904. Completed 24.3.1905. 1 CS Channel 1905-06. 1 CS Atlantic 1906-07. 2 CS Atlantic 1907-09. 3rd Fleet, Devonport 1909-11. 3 CS 2nd Fleet 1913-14. 3 CS Grand Fleet 1914-16—captured a German merchantman 6.8.1914. At Heligoland and Dogger Bank actions. Nore 1916. 7 CS Grand Fleet 1916. N. America & W.I. 1916-19. Devonport, paid off 1919-20. Sold 1921, Ward. Broken up at Preston and Barrow.

HAMPSHIRE

Built by Armstrong, Elswick. Laid down 1.9.1902. Launched 24.9.1903. Completed 15.7.1905. 1 CS Channel 1905-06. 1 CS Atlantic 1906-07. 1 CS Channel 1907-08. Refit, Portsmouth 1909. 3rd Fleet, Portsmouth 1909-11. 6 CS Mediterranean 1911-12. China 1912-14. Captured a German merchantman, 11.8.1914, and took part in hunt for SMS *Emden*. 6 CS Grand Fleet, Dec. 1914. 7 CS Grand Fleet, Jan. 1915-16 (Northern Patrols). Sunk by mine off the Orkneys with Lord Kitchener aboard, 5.6.1916. 650 lost.

Battle Honour: Jutland 1916.

ROXBURGH

Built by London & Glasgow, Govan. Laid down 13.6.1902. Launched 19.1.1904. Completed 5.9.1905. 1 CS Channel 1905-06. 1 CS Atlantic 1906-07. 1 CS Channel 1907-09. 3rd Fleet, Portsmouth 1909-11. 5 CS 2nd Fleet 1912. 3 CS 2nd Fleet 1913-14. 3 CS Grand Fleet 1914-15. Captured a German merchantman 6.8.1914. Bows seriously damaged by torpedo from *U39*, 20.6.1915; repairs to 4.1916. 3 CS Grand Fleet 1916. N. America & W.I. 1916-19 (N. America Patrols 1917). Rammed and sank German *U89* off N. Ireland 12.2.1918. Wireless Training Ship 1919-20. Sold 1921, Slough Trading Co. and broken up in Germany.

Carnarvon

DUKE OF EDINBURGH CLASS (2 ships), *1902 Programme*

Black Prince, Duke of Edinburgh

Displacement (tons):	13,550 load.
Dimensions (feet):	480pp, 505½oa x 73½ x 26
Dimensions (metres):	146.3pp, 154.1oa x 22.4 x 7.9
Machinery:	2 shaft 4 cyl. TE. 20 Babcock, 6 cylindrical boilers. 23,500 SHP = 23½ knots.
Fuel:	Coal 2,150 tons.
Protection:	Full length belt 4in/6in/3in (102mm/152mm/76mm). Decks (full length): main 1in-¾in (25mm-19mm); lower 1½in-¾in (38mm-19mm). Upper deck 1in (25mm) amidships.
Armament:	6—9.2in, 10—6in, 22—3pdr, 3—18in TT submerged.
Complement:	700-850

Homologues of the King Edward VII class battleships, the Dukes, as they were known, represented a significant advance on previous designs. Better armed and protected than the Drakes, with more extensive belts and their horizontal armour spread over three decks, great things were expected of these first cruisers of the Watts era. Unfortunately they were marred by serious design errors; the 6in secondary armament was considered too light for the armoured cruisers new fleet role, and the 3pdrs were hopelessly inadequate for their intended use against torpedo boat destroyers. Also, incredibly, they repeated the mistake made in the Drakes of mounting their 6in battery in casemates so near the water that the guns were awash in any but the calmest sea. The ignominious defeat of the *Black Prince* by the supposedly inferior *Leviathan* in mock battle manouevres in 1906 set the seal on the class' failure. The sad reputation of the Dukes was in stark contrast to the outstanding success of their half-sisters, the Warriors.

In 1917 *Duke of Edinburgh* was taken in hand to have all her secondary armament mounted at main deck level.

BLACK PRINCE

Built by Thames Iron Works. Laid down 3.6.1903. Launched 8.11.1904. Completed 17.3.1906. 2 CS Atlantic 1906-08. 1 CS Channel 1908-09. 5 CS Atlantic 1909-12. 1 CS Mediterranean 1912-14—captured a German merchantman in Red Sea 8.1914. 1 CS Grand Fleet, Dec. 1914-16. Lost by gunfire at Jutland, 1.6.1916. 857 lost.

Battle Honour: Jutland 1916.

Duke of Edinburgh. **The only ship of her squadron to survive Jutland.**

DUKE OF EDINBURGH

Built at Pembroke Dockyard. Laid down 11.2.1903. Launched 14.6.1904. Completed 20.1.1906. 2 CS Atlantic 1906-08. 1 CS Channel 1908-09. 5 CS Atlantic 1909-13. 1 CS Mediterranean 1913-14—captured a German merchantman in Red Sea 8.1914. Persian Gulf 11.1914. 1 CS Grand Fleet, Dec. 1914-16. 2 CS Grand Fleet, June 1916-17. Refit 1917. Atlantic convoys 1917-18. N. America & W.I. 1918. Immingham, paid off, 1919. Sold 1920, Hughes Bolckow.

Battle Honour: Jutland 1916.

WARRIOR CLASS (4 ships), *1903 Programme*

Achilles, Cochrane, Natal, Warrior

Displacement (tons):	13,550 load.
Dimensions (feet):	480pp, .505½oa x 73½ x 25
(metres):	146.3pp, 154.1oa x 22.4 x 7.6
Machinery:	2 shaft 4 cyl. TE. 19 Yarrow, 6 cylindrical boilers. 23,000 SHP =23 knots.
Fuel:	Coal 2,050 tons.
Protection:	Full length belt 4in/6in/3in (102mm/152mm/76mm). Decks (full length): main lin-¾in (25mm-19mm); lower 2in-¾in (51mm-19mm). Upper deck 1in (25mm) amidships.
Armament:	6—9.2in, 4—7.5in, 26—3pdr, 3—18in TT submerged.
Complement:	700-850

Originally to have been repeats of the Dukes, but modified in the light of experience with the earlier ships. Casemates were abandoned and the secondary armament, increased to 7.5in, was mounted entirely at main deck level. With a higher centre of gravity than the Dukes they were steadier ships and excellent gun platforms. The Warriors enjoyed an enormously high reputation and Service opinion of them was well summarised by Jane's Fighting Ships 1914: 'Are held by all who have served in them to be the best cruisers ever turned out.'

ACHILLES

Built by Armstrong, Elswick. Laid down 22.2.1904. Launched 17.6.1905. Completed 22.4.1907. 5 CS Home 1907-09. 2 CS Home 1909-14. 2 CS Grand Fleet 1914-18—sank German raider *Leopard* north of Shetlands, 16.3.1917. Refit, Feb-Nov 1918. Reserve as Stokers' TS, Chatham 1918-19. Sold 1920, Ward, Briton Ferry.

COCHRANE

Built by Fairfield, Govan. Laid down 24.3.1904. Launched 20.5.1905. Completed 18.2.1907. 5 CS Home 1907-08. 2 CS Home 1909-14. 2 CS Grand Fleet 1914-17. N. America & W.I. 1917. 2 CS Grand Fleet 1918—detached to White Sea (Murmansk) and trapped in ice, N. Russia, 1918. Wrecked in Mersey estuary 14.11.1918.

Battle Honour: Jutland 1916.

Natal, **1907**.

NATAL

Built by Vickers, Barrow. Laid down 6.1.1904. Launched 30.9.1905. Completed 5.3.1907. 5 CS Home 1907-09. 2 CS Home 1909-14. 2 CS Grand Fleet 1914-15. Blown up by internal explosion, Cromarty Firth, 30.12.1915 with the loss of 404 lives.

WARRIOR

Built at Pembroke Dockyard. Laid down 5.11.1903. Launched 25.11.1905. Completed 12.12.1906. 5 CS Home 1907-09. 2 CS Home 1909-13. 1 CS Mediterranean 1913-14. Sent to Adriatic, 8.1914 to try to prevent the breakout of battlecruiser SMS *Goeben*; thence to Suez Canal, Gibraltar and Sierra Leone, 2CS Grand Fleet Dec 1914-16. Badly damaged by gunfire early in the battle of Jutland; taken in tow by HMS *Engadine*. but foundered 1.6.1916. 71 lost.

Battle Honour: Jutland 1916.

MINOTAUR CLASS (3 ships), *1904 Programme*

Defence, Minotaur, Shannon

Displacement (tons):	14,600 load.
Dimensions (feet):	490pp, 519oa x 74½ *(Shannon* 75½) x 26
(metres):	149.4pp, 158.2oa x 22.7 x (23) x 7.9
Machinery:	2 shaft 4 cyl. TE. 24 Yarrow *(Minotaur* Babcock) boilers. 27,000 SHP = 23 knots.
Fuel:	Coal 2,060 tons.
Protection:	Full length belt 4in/6in/3in (102mm/152mm/76mm). Decks (full length): main 1in-¾in (25mm-19mm); lower 2in-¾in (51mm-19mm). Upper deck 1in (25mm) amidships.
Armament:	4-9.2in (2 x 2), 10—7.5in, 16—12pdr, 5—18in TT submerged.
Complement:	755-850

Homologues of the Lord Nelson class battleships, these aggressively armed ships mounted their 9.2in guns in twin turrets fore and aft. This superior disposition of the main battery, without wing turrets, gave the Minotaurs as heavy a broadside with four guns as the Warriors had with six. Less successful than the Warriors and regarded as overgunned, it was felt that the rise in displacement would have been better devoted to improvements in protection. *Shannon* had a modified hull form, one foot wider than her sisters.

Before the war, *Defence* and *Minotaur* were sent to the China Station to counter the presence in the Far East of the German armoured cruisers *Scharnhorst* and *Gneisenau*. The two opposing pairs were very evenly matched, except that the Minotaurs had ten guns in their secondary armament against the Germans' nine. In a gesture of friendly rivalry the ships' officers agreed in Hong Kong that if they ever met in battle the Minotaurs would each withhold fire from one 7.5 gun to make a fair fight of it.

DEFENCE

Built at Pembroke Dockyard. Laid down 22.2.1905. Launched 27.4.1907. Completed 9.2.1909. 5 CS Home 1909. 1 CS Home 1909-11. China 1912-13. Flagship, 1 CS Mediterranean 1913-14. Took part in hunt for *Goeben* and *Breslau*, 8.1914. Sent to South Atlantic to reinforce Cradock's squadron, but diverted to Cape of Good Hope, 11.1914. Flagship, 1 CS Grand Fleet, Jan 1915-16. Sunk by gunfire of German battleship *Friedrich Der Grosse* at Jutland, 31.5.1916. 893 lost.

Battle Honour: Jutland 1916.

Shannon **in wartime camouflage.**

MINOTAUR

Built at Devonport Dockyard. Laid down 2.1.1905. Launched 6.6.1906. Completed 1.4.1908. 5 CS Home 1908-09. 1 CS Home 1909-10. Flagship, China 1910-14—captured and sank German merchantman *Elsbeth*, 6.8.14; bombarded German W/T station on Yap in the Pacific. Escorted Australian troop convoys, Nov. 1914. Flagship, Cape, Dec. 1914. Refit 1915-16. Flagship, 2 CS Grand Fleet 1916-19. Reserve 1919-20. Sold 1920, Ward, Milford Haven.

Battle Honour: Jutland 1916.

SHANNON

Built at Chatham Dockyard. Laid down 2.1.1905. Launched 20.9.1906. Completed 10.3.1908. 5 CS Home 1908-09. 2 CS Home 1909-12. Flagship, 3 CS Home 1912-13, 2 CS Home 1913-14. 2 CS Grand Fleet 1914-19—Murmansk, 11.1916; Atlantic convoys 1917-18. Sheerness, paid off 1919, becoming accommodation ship to HMS *Actaeon* torpedo school until 1922. Sold 1922, McLellan, Bo'ness.

Battle Honour: Jutland 1916.

1901-19 PART II:
TOWARDS THE LIGHT CRUISER

Topaze (Gem), Adventure, Forward, Pathfinder, Sentinel, Boadicea, Blonde and Active classes

These small cruisers were all faster than hitherto, necessary for the Gems to keep up with the fleet, and for the scouts to work with destroyer flotillas. Whereas the Gems were fairly orthodox third class protected cruisers, the scouts pioneered the destroyer leader concept and lacked the range, protection, and firepower of proper cruisers. Both lines of development later converged in the light cruiser.

The first batch of eight commerically designed scouts had reciprocating engines and full length protection. Seven Admiralty-designed ships followed them, turbine powered but virtually unarmoured. The Admiralty design, expanded and given a heavier armament and extensive side armour, became the basis for the Arethusa class light cruisers, which successfully merged the small cruiser and scout categories.

Early in the war, several of the Grand Fleet destroyer flotillas were led by Arethusa or 'C' class light cruisers, but from 1915 they began to be replaced by the Marksman and subsequent classes of destroyer leaders, which were enlarged versions of contemporary destroyers. Later, the destroyer leader became almost indistinguishable from the ships of her flotilla, the only difference being the Leader's extra accommodation for the Captain (D) and his staff.

TOPAZE (GEM) CLASS (4 ships)

Amethyst, Topaze (1902 Programme), *Diamond, Sapphire* (1903 Programme)

Displacement (tons):	3,000 load.
Dimensions (feet): **(metres):**	360pp, 373¾oa x 40 x 14½ 109.7pp, 113.9oa x 12.2 x 4.4
Machinery:	2 shaft 4 cyl. TE except *Amethyst*, turbines. Normand Laird boilers except *Diamond*, Yarrow and *Amethyst*, Yarrow (curved). 9,800 HP = 21¾knots, except *Amethyst*, 12,000 HP = 22½ knots.
Fuel:	Coal 300 tons normal, 500 max.
Protection:	Full length deck 2in (51mm).
Armament:	12—4in, 8—3pdr, 2—18in TT above water.
Complement:	296

The Gems link the late Victorian family of cruisers with the Towns and Arethusas of the 1914-18 war. Unlike previous third class cruisers, they were intended to operate with the fleet and so were larger, faster and better armed than their predecessors. Compared with *Pelorus*, machinery was more powerful, length/beam ratio was further increased, and seakeeping greatly improved. *Amethyst* was the first cruiser powered by steam turbines.

Four additional ships provided under the 1904 Estimates were never ordered.

AMETHYST

Built by Armstrong, Elswick. Laid down 7.1.1903. Launched 5.11.1903. Completed 17.3.1905. Attached Atlantic BS 1905-07. Nucleus crew, Portsmouth 1907-09. Atlantic (SE Coast of America and West Coast of Africa) 1909-11. 8 DF Home (Patrol Flotilla) 1912-14. Commodore (T) 3 DF Harwich 1914. Attached 1 LCS Grand Fleet 1914. Mediterranean 1915. South America 1916-19. Queenstown, paid off 1919. Sold 1920, Towers, Milford Haven.

Battle Honours: Heligoland 1914, Dardanelles 1915.

TOPAZE

Built by Cammell Laird, Birkenhead. Laid down 14.8.1902. Launched 23.7.1903. Completed 11.1904. Attached Channel BS 1904-07. Home (full crew) 1907-09. SO Ship 4 DF, Portsmouth 1909-12. Attached 6 BS (2nd Fleet) 1913. Attached 5 BS Channel 1914-15. Mediterranean 1915-17. Red Sea 1917-18. Portsmouth, paid off 1919. Sold 1921, Cohen, and broken up in Germany.

Amethyst. **First cruiser fitted with turbine engines.**

DIAMOND

Built by Cammell Laird, Birkenhead. Laid down 24.3.1903. Launched 6.1.1904. Completed 1.1905. 4 CS N. America & W.I. 1905-07. Attached 5 BS Atlantic 1907. Attached Channel BS 1907-09. SO Ship, 3 DF Nore 1909-12. 5 DF Nore 1912-13. Attached 5 BS Channel (2nd Fleet) 1913-15. Attached 5 BS Grand Fleet 1915-18. Mediterranean 1918 (used as 'CMB carrier', with six 40ft Coastal Motor Boats carried in davits). Nore, paid off 1919. Sold 1921, Ward, Grays.

SAPPHIRE

Built by Palmers, Jarrow. Laid down 30.3.1903. Launched 17.3.1904. Completed 7.2.1905. Flagship, Rear Admiral (D), Portland 1905-07. Captain (D), Channel 1907-09. SO Ship, 5 DF Devonport 1909-12. 7 DF Home (Patrol Flotilla) 1912. Attached 5 BS Channel (2nd Fleet) 1912-13. Attached 4 BS. Grand Fleet 1914-15. Mediterranean 1915-16. East Indies 1916-19. Nore, paid off 1919-20. Sold 1920, Ward, Grays.

Battle Honours: Belgian Coast 1914, Dardanelles 1915.

ADVENTURE CLASS (2 ships)

Adventure, Attentive

Displacement (tons):	2,640 load.
Dimensions (feet):	374pp, 395oa x 38¼ x 12¼
(metres):	114pp, 120.4oa x 11.7 x 3.7
Machinery:	2 shaft 3 cyl. TE. 12 Yarrow boilers. 16,000 IHP = 25 knots.
Fuel:	Coal 450 tons.
Protection:	Full length deck 2in-¾in (51mm-19mm)
Armament:	10—12pdr, 8—3pdr (later 9—4in, 1—3in AA), 2—18in TT above water.
Complement:	268

FORWARD CLASS (2 ships)

Foresight, Forward

Displacement (tons):	2,860 load.
Dimensions (feet):	365pp, 379oa x 39¼ x 14¼
(metres):	111.3pp, 115.5oa x 12 x 4.3
Machinery:	2 shaft 3 cyl. TE. 12 Thornycroft boilers. 16,500 IHP = 25 knots.
Fuel:	Coal 500 tons.
Protection:	Belt abreast boiler and machinery spaces 2in (51mm). Deck fore and aft of belt ⅝ (16mm).
Armament:	As in *Adventure*
Complement:	268

PATHFINDER CLASS (2 ships)

Pathfinder, Patrol

Displacement (tons):	2,900 load.
Dimensions (feet):	370pp, 379oa x 38½ x 13
(metres):	112.8pp, 115.5oa x 11.8 x 4
Machinery:	2 shaft 4 cyl. TE. 12 Laird-Normand boilers. 16,500 IHP = 25 knots.
Fuel:	Coal 600 tons.
Protection:	Belt abreast engine room only, 2in (51mm). Full length deck 1½in-⅝in (39mm—16mm).
Armament:	As in *Adventure*
Complement:	268

SENTINEL CLASS (2 ships)

Sentinel, Skirmisher.

Displacement (tons):	2,880 load.
Dimensions (feet):	360pp, 381oa x 40 x 14
(metres):	109.7pp, 116.1oa x 12.2 x 4.3
Machinery:	2 shaft 4 cyl. TE. 12 Vickers-Express boilers. 17,000 IHP = 25 knots.
Fuel:	Coal 410 tons.
Protection:	Full length deck 1½in-⅝in (39mm-16mm).
Armament:	As in *Adventure*.
Complement:	268

Adventure, Forward, Pathfinder and Sentinel classes.

With the large River class, the torpedo boat destroyer at last came of age as a proper sea-going ship.

The need arose for a new type of cruiser to work in company with the destroyers. Their function was to act as scouts, lead torpedo attacks, and to back up their flotillas when attacked by other destroyers. Four destroyer builders were each asked to design and build a pair of Scouts to the Admiralty's broad specifications. These were: a speed of 25 knots; an armament of 10—12pdr, 8—3pdr and 2 TT; a 1½in protective deck or equivalent side armour; and shallow draught for working in inshore waters.

The four designs varied considerably, especially as regards protection, but all had the same armament and speed. Soon after completion all ships received an additional pair of 12 pdrs, and all were re-armed in 1911-12 with 9—4in guns. By 1914 they had become too slow for destroyer work, and were employed during the war more or less as ordinary third class cruisers.

HUSBANDS

Adventure. **Note curved bow and 4 funnels.**

ADVENTURE (ex Eddystone)

Built by Armstrong, Elswick. Laid down 7.1.1904. Launched 8.9.1904. Completed 10.1905. Nucleus crew, Nore 1905-07. Leader, 1 DF Home 1907-10. Attached 2 DF Home 1910-13. 3LCS (temp.) for 1913 Manoeuvres. Attached 6 DF Portsmouth 1913-14, Dover 1914-15. 6 LCS Humber (temp.) 1915. Flagship, Queenstown 1915-17. Convoys to Gibraltar 1918. Mediterranean 1918-19. Laid up, Immingham 1919-20. Sold 1920, Ward, Morecambe.

ATTENTIVE

Built by Armstrong, Elswick. Laid down 8.1.1904. Launched 24.11.1904. Completed 10.1905. Nucleus crew, Nore 1905-09—sank destroyer *Gala* and holed *Ribble* in double collision, 27.4.1908. Leader, 3 DF Nore (3rd Fleet) 1909-10. Scout, 2 DF Home 1910-12. 3 LCS (temp.) for 1913 Manoeuvres. Attached 1 DF Home 1913. Leader, 6 DF Portsmouth (Patrol Flotilla) 1914, 6 DF Dover 1914-18. Gibraltar convoys 1918. White Sea 1918. For disposal 1919. Sold 1920, Ward, Preston.

Battle Honours: Belgian Coast 1914-18, Zeebrugge 1918.

Forward. **Note poop deck aft,** *Pathfinder* **was similar but without a poop.**

FORWARD (ex *Nore*)

Built by Fairfield, Govan. Laid down 22.10.1903. Launched 27.8.1904. Completed 22.8.1905. Nucleus crew, Portsmouth 1905-07. Channel 1907-09. Leader, 2 DF Home 1909. Attached 4 DF Portsmouth (3rd Fleet) 1909-10. Scout, 3 DF Nore (3rd Fleet) 1910-14—3 LCS (temp.) for 1913 Manoeuvres. 9 DF Shetland Patrol 1914. Leader, 7 DF Humber 1914-15. 6 LCS (temp.) in Humber 1915. Mediterranean 1915-18. Nore, paid off 1919. Sold 1921, Foyer, Sunderland.

FORESIGHT

Built by Fairfield, Govan. Laid down 24.10.1903. Launched 8.10.1904. Completed 8.9.1905. Nucleus crew, Portsmouth 1905-09. Leader, 2 DF Home 1909-10. Attached 3 DF Nore (3rd Fleet) 1910-12. Chatham Reserve 1912-13. Leader, 6 DF Portsmouth (Patrol Flotilla) 1913-14, 6 DF. Dover 1914-15. 6 LCS (temp.) Humber 1915. Mediterranean 1915-19—in Aegean from 7.1916. Paid off, Chatham 6.1919. Sold 1920, Granton Shipbreaking.

Battle Honours: Belgian Coast 1914, Dardanelles 1915-16.

PATHFINDER (ex *Fastnet*)

Built by Cammell Laird, Birkenhead. Laid down 15.8.1903. Launched 16.7.1904. Completed 18.7.1905. Atlantic 1905-06. Channel (special service) 1906-07. Nucleus crew, Nore 1907-08. Scout, 1 DF Home 1909-10 Scout, 4DF Portsmouth (3rd Fleet) 1910-12. Reserve 1912-13. Attached 8 DF Nore 1913-14, 8 DF Forth 1914. Sunk by *U21* in North Sea, 5.9.1914. 259 lost.

PATROL

Built by Cammell Laird, Birkenhead. Laid down 31.10.1903. Launched 13.10.1904. Completed 26.9.1905. Channel (special service) 1905-07. Nucleus crew, Portsmouth 1907-08, Nore 1908. 3 DF Nore 1909-10. (Temp. Leader, 1 DF Home 1909.) Attached 1 DF Home 1910-11. Attached 3 DF Nore (3rd Fleet) 1912. Chatham Reserve 1912. Stationed at Haulbowline 1913-14. Attached 9 DF Nore 1914, 9 DF Forth/Tyne 1914-15. 7 DF Humber 1915-18. Irish Sea 1918. 9 DF Nore 1918-19. Sold 1920, Machinehandel Co. and broken up in Holland.

HUSBANDS

Sentinel. **Note turtleback forecastle cowls.**

SENTINEL (ex *Inchkeith*)

Built by Vickers, Barrow. Laid down 8.6.1903. Launched 19.4.1904. Completed 4.1905. Channel (special service) 1905-07. Nucleus crew, Devonport 1907-09. Attached 5 DF Devonport (3rd Fleet) 1909-12. Refit 1912. 3 LCS (temp.) for 1913 Manoeuvres. Leader, 9 DF Nore 1913. Attached 6 DF Portsmouth/Dover 1913-14. 8 DF Forth 1914-15. 6 LCS Humber (temp.) 1915. Mediterranean 1915-18. Aegean 1918. Black Sea 1918-19. Paid off at Sheerness, 4.1919. Mechanics' T.S. Chatham 1920-22. Sold 1923, Young, Sunderland.

SKIRMISHER

Built by Vickers, Barrow. Laid down 29.7.1903. Launched 7.2.1905. Completed 7.1905. Nucleus crew, Devonport 1906-07. Attached Channel Flotilla 1907-09. 2 DF Home 1909-10. Scout, 4 DF Portsmouth (3rd Fleet) 1910-12. Refit 1912. 3 LCS (temp.) for 1913 Manoeuvres. 7 DF Devonport 1913-14. 7 DF Humber 1914-15. 6 LCS Humber (temp.) 1915. Mediterranean 1916-19. Immingham 1919. Sold 1920, Ward, Preston.

BOADICEA CLASS (2 ships), *1907 Programme*

Bellona, Boadicea

Displacement (tons):	3,300 normal, 3,800 deep load
Dimensions (feet): **(metres):**	385pp, 405oa x 41 x 14 117.3pp, 123.4oa x 12.5 x 4.3
Machinery:	4 shaft Parsons turbines. 12 Yarrow boilers. 18,000 SHP = 25 knots.
Fuel:	Coal 850 tons. Oil 200 tons.
Protection:	Partial plating over machinery 1in (25mm).
Armament:	6—4in, 4—3pdr, 2—18in TT above water (p & s)
Complement:	317

Bigger and heavier than the commercially designed Scouts but more lightly armed and protected, the most notable advance in these ships was the adoption of turbine propulsion—as in all future British cruisers. Deck protection was limited to a partial plating over machinery spaces.

During the war, four additional 4in guns were added in the waist, as in the Blonde and Active classes, and a 3in AA gun was mounted on the quarterdeck. The 3in gun was replaced by a 4in AA mounting in 1918.

Both ships were converted for minelaying in 1917.

BLONDE CLASS (2 ships), *1909 Programme*

Blanche, Blonde

As *Boadiceas*, except:

Displacement (tons):	3,350 normal, 3,850 deep load.
Dimensions: **Machinery:**	Beam 41½ft (12.6m). Speed 24½ knots.
Fuel:	Coal 780 tons. Oil 190 tons.
Protection:	Partial plating over machinery 1½in (38mm).
Armament:	10—4in, 4—3pdr. 2—21in TT above water (p & s).
Complement:	314

Very similar to *Boadicea*, but with 21in TT and four additional 4in waist-mounted guns. Deck armour, increased to 1½in was still only a partial covering over the machinery.

Both ships were converted for minelaying in 1917.

Boadicea, **1909. The first class fitted with turbine machinery.**

BELLONA

Built at Pembroke Dockyard. Laid down 5.6.1908. Launched 20.3.1909. Completed 2.1910. SO Ship 2 DF (H Class) 1910-12. Attached Battle Squadrons, Grand Fleet 1913-19. Converted for minelaying, 6.1917. For disposal 1919. Sold 1921, Ward, Lelant.

Battle Honour: Jutland 1916.

BOADICEA

Built at Pembroke Dockyard. Laid down 1.6.1907. Launched 14.5.1908. Completed 6.1909. SO Ship 1 DF (later 3DF) Home 1909-13. Attached Battle Squadrons, Grand Fleet 1913-19. Converted for minelaying, 1917. Nore Reserve 1919. Harbour service, Dartmouth 1920-26 (replaced *Pomone*). Sold 1926, Alloa, Rosyth.

Battle Honour: Jutland 1916.

BLANCHE

Built at Pembroke Dockyard. Laid down 12.4.1909. Launched 25.11.1909. Completed 11.1910. Scout, 1 DF (later 3DF) Home 1910-13. Attached Battle Squadrons, Grand Fleet 1913-19. Converted for minelaying 3.1917. Paid off, 1919. Sold 1921, Foyer, Sunderland.

Battle Honour: Jutland 1916.

BLONDE

Built at Pembroke Dockyard. Laid down 6.12.1909. Launched 22.7.1910. Completed 5.1911. SO Ship 7 DF (I Class, later 1 DF) 1911-13. Attached Battle Squadron, Grand Fleet 1913-19. Converted for minelaying, 9.1917. Sold 1920, TC Pas, Holland.

ACTIVE CLASS (3 ships), *1910 and 1911 Programmes*

Active, Amphion, Fearless

Displacement (tons):	3,440 normal, 4,000 deep load.
Dimensions (feet):	385pp, 406oa x 41½ x 15½
(metres):	117.3pp, 123.7oa x 12.6 x 4.7
Machinery:	4 shaft Parsons turbines. 12 Yarrow boilers. 18,000 SHP = 25 knots.
Fuel:	Coal 780 tons. Oil 190 tons.
Protection:	Partial plating over machinery 1in (25mm).
Armament:	10—4in, 4—3pdr, 2—21in TT deck, p & s.
Complement:	321-325

Near-repeats of the Blondes, but more modern-looking with their graceful 'plough' bows. They reverted to 1in plating over the machinery, but had thicker shell plating amidships as limited protection against light gunfire.

Amphion became the first British naval loss of the war. The surviving pair received a 3in AA gun, *Active* in 1916, *Fearless* in 1918. Both had two 4in guns taken out in 1918.

ACTIVE

Built at Pembroke Dockyard. Laid down 27.10.1910. Launched 14.3.1911. Completed 12.1911. Ship, 2 DF (H Class) 1912-14. Harwich Force 1914. Attached Battle Squadrons, Grand Fleet 1915-16. Attached 4 DF Portsmouth 1916-17. Queenstown 1917-18. Mediterranean 1918. Reserve 1919. Sold 1920 and broken up in Norway.

Battle Honour: Jutland 1916.

AMPHION

Built at Pembroke Dockyard. Laid down 15.3.1911. Launched 4.12.1911. Completed 3.1913. SO Ship, 3DF (L Class) 1913-14. Harwich Force 1914. First casualty of the war when she ran into a minefield laid by SMS *Koningen Luise*, which she and her flotilla had just sunk, 6.8.1914. 148 lost.

FEARLESS

Built at Pembroke Dockyard. Laid down 15.11.1911. Launched 12.6.1912. Completed 10.1913. SO Ship, 1 DF 1913-17 (Grand Fleet from 1914). 12th Submarine Flotilla (K Class) 1917-19. Reserve 1919-20. Sold 1921, Slough Trading Co. and broke up in Germany.

Battle Honour: Jutland 1916.

Fearless.

NUCLEUS CREWS AND FLEET REORGANIZATION

Until 1904, ships in the Fleet Reserve were manned by small care and maintenance parties. For Annual Manoeuvres they were made up to full complements, drawn ad hoc partly from naval depots and partly from the Royal Naval Reserve. These hastily assembled crews did their best, but being quite unused to their ships, gunnery firing results were poor and breakdowns frequent. In theory the ships of the Fleet Reserve were available for immediate service, but in practice their value as a reserve force was dubious. There was also a Dockyard Reserve, consisting of ships in refit, plus a great number of obsolete ships (a 'miser's hoard of useless junk'), which were laid up unmanned and sometimes partially dismantled.

The nucleus crew system—probably the best reserve manning system ever devised—was one of the most significant of the Fisher reforms, as it gave the Royal Navy a large and effective reserve fleet in Home waters, where forces were being concentrated. Ships were kept 'in commission in reserve' with two-fifths of their normal complements, including all the key personnel in the gunnery and mechanical departments. The nucleus crew took their ship to sea once a quarter for 10-14 days, and thoroughly mastered her idiosyncrasies. Once a year, ships were made up to full complements for Manoeuvres, now much more satisfactory than before. Obsolete ships in the Dockyard Reserve were ruthlessly scrapped, although some old ships continued to be kept, unmanned, in the Material Reserve.

In order to find the manpower for the nucleus crews, many ships were withdrawn from foreign stations and either paid off or reduced to reserve. The Navy's commands were reorganised into five fleets, corresponding to Fisher's belief that 'five strategic keys lock up the world'—namely Singapore, the Cape, Alexandria, Gibraltar, and Dover.

Readily able to concentrate on Singapore were the East Indies, China, and Australia squadrons which form the new Eastern Fleet: the squadrons remained separate commands in peacetime, but they would assemble each year at Singapore for joint exercises at the end of their annual manoeuvres. The Pacific squadron, based at Esquimault, British Columbia, was withdrawn. The Cape squadron took over the South Atlantic and North America stations. The former North America and West Indies squadron became the 4th Cruiser (or Particular Service) Squadron, based at Devonport and employed in training, though it continued to show the flag in the West Indies and in South American waters: in wartime it would join either the Mediterranean or Channel Fleet. Based at Gibraltar, the Atlantic Fleet (formerly the Channel Fleet) could reinforce either the Mediterranean or Channel Fleet; it exercised twice a year with the former and once a year with the latter. The Channel Fleet (formerly the Home Fleet) had its strategic centre at Dover, but cruised between Ireland and Gibraltar. The Channel, Atlantic, and Mediterranean Fleets each had an armoured cruiser squadron attached, and of course, other cruisers were attached to the Battle Squadrons of each Fleet. Nucleus crew ships at the Nore, Portsmouth and Devonport formed the new Home Fleet. Ships were no longer attached to the RNR as drillships, or to the Coastguard, which became a separate service.

The nucleus crew system and the fleet reorganisation was put into effect in December 1904. Care was taken not to antagonize Germany, and the overwhelming advantage these reforms gave to the Royal Navy in home waters was played down. But it could not be concealed that, as Balfour stated in 1906, 'this new Reserve scheme has augmented the fighting power of the British fleet not once or twice, but threefold'.

The logical culmination of the fleet reforms came with the abolition of the Channel Fleet as a separate command in April 1909, creating a unified Home Fleet with four Divisions: the First Division, based at the Nore, consisted of ships in full commission; the Second Division, based at Portland, had full complements including a proportion of trainees; the Third Division based at Portsmouth and Devonport consisted of nucleus crew ships; Fourth Division ships had care and maintenance parties rather than nucleus crews, and could only commission for service on the full mobilization of reserves.

BRITISH CRUISER DEPLOYMENT, FEBRUARY 1910

Home Fleet, First Division (full crews)
  Attached 1 BS: *Dido, Isis.*
  1 CS: *Defence* (with battlecruisers *Indomitable, Inflexible, Invincible).*
  Attached 1 DF: *Adventure, Boadicea, Pathfinder.*

Home Fleet, Second Division (full crews, including some trainees)
  Attached 2 BS: *Juno, Talbot.*
  2 CS: *Achilles, Cochrane, Natal, Shannon, Warrior.*
  Attached 2 DF: *Bellona, Foresight, Skirmisher.*

Home Fleet, Third Division (nucleus crews)
  Nore: *Antrim, Charybdis, Cressy, Hawke* (trooping), *Hogue.* Attached: *Andromache, Apollo.*
  Portsmouth: *Hampshire, Hermione, Roxburgh,* Attached: *Latona, Thetis.*
  Devonport: *Arrogant, Carnarvon, Devonshire, Niobe, Sutlej.*
  Attached to Destroyer Flotillas: *Diamond* (Nore), *Topaze* (Portsmouth).

Home Fleet, Fourth Division (care and maintenance parties)
  Portsmouth: *Ariadne, Diadem, Spartiate, Argonaut, Terrible, Crescent, Edgar,
    Royal Arthur.*
  Devonport: *Europa, Amphitrite, Andromeda, Gibraltar.*

4 CS Home Fleet (N. America and West Indies)
  Berwick, Donegal, Essex, Leviathan. Attached: *Brilliant, Melpomone, Scylla.*
  Special Service (Cadet Training Ships): *Cornwall, Cumberland.*

Atlantic Fleet
  Attached BS: *Doris, Venus.* Attached: *Amethyst.*
  5 CS: *Argyll, Black Prince, Drake, Duke of Edinburgh.*

Mediterranean Fleet
  Attached BS: *Barham, Diana, Medea, Minerva.*
  6 CS: *Aboukir, Bacchante, Lancaster, Suffolk.*

China:
  Astraea, Bedford, Flora, Kent, King Alfred, Monmouth.

Australia:
  *Cambrian, Challenger, Encounter, Pegasus, Pioneer, Powerful, Prometheus,
  Psyche, Pyramus.*

Cape:
  Forte, Hermes, Pandora.

East Indies:
  Fox, Hyacinth, Perseus, Philomel, Proserpine.

1910-30: THE LIGHT CRUISER

Bristol, Weymouth, Chatham, Birkenhead, Arethusa, Caroline, Calliope, Cambrian and Centaur classes.

Since the Gems completed in 1904-05 the Royal Navy had not ordered any true cruisers; the armoured cruisers were virtually second-class battleships, while the scouts were in essence North Sea ships, lacking the protection to work with the fleet and the range to undertake the cruiser's traditional role.

Fisher's plans for the Navy had no place for cruisers; the way ahead lay with battle cruisers and fast destroyers like his beloved brain-child *Swift*. But battlecruisers were far too expensive to replace cruisers ship for ship, and *Swift* proved a disappointment in service.

Meanwhile, the German Navy had pressed ahead with the construction of a large series of third class cruisers, armed with ten excellent 4.1in guns and named after German towns. With an eye firmly on the German ships, the Royal Navy turned back to cruiser construction, appropriately naming its ships after British towns.

In 1911 the old system of cruiser classification was abolished. Instead, ships over 6,000 tons, effectively meaning all armoured and first class protected cruisers, were rated simply 'cruisers', while the smaller protected cruisers, scouts, and the new Towns became 'light cruisers'.

The Bristol design evolved through the Weymouths into the very successful Chatham and Birmingham classes. Their dimensions limited numbers, however, and the Arethusas at around 3,000 tons served as a basis for fresh development through the subsequent Caroline, Cambrian and Centaur classes. The Towns, Arethusas and early 'C' classes bore the brunt of the fighting in the North Sea in the First World War. Completed in 1910-16, all except the rather cramped Bristols and Arethusas saw extensive post war service.

The Chathams and Birminghams were especially valued in the immediate post-war years, being among the few ocean going ships in a predominantly short range cruiser force built for operations in the North Sea. Their coal firing was an advantage on some foreign stations.

The early 'C's, which nearly all carried four 6in guns by the 1920s, were regarded as under armed in comparison with later ships. They were also less economical, with their quadruple screws and direct drive turbines. Nevertheless, most of them were retained to keep up numbers, as new ships arrived too slowly to provide for their timely replacement. Their fates were sealed as they fell foul of the tonnage quotas set by the 1930 London Naval Treaty, which had the effect of limiting the Royal Navy's cruiser strength to around fifty ships.

BRISTOL CLASS (5 ships), *1908 Programme*

Bristol, Glasgow, Gloucester, Liverpool, Newcastle

Displacement (tons):	4,800 normal, 5,300 full load.
Dimensions (feet):	430pp, 453oa x 47 x 15½
(metres):	131.1pp, 138.1oa x 14.3 x 4.7
Machinery:	4 shaft Parsons turbines (*Bristol*: 2 shaft Brown Curtis). 12 Yarrow boilers. 22,000 SHP = 25 knots.
Fuel:	Coal 1,350 tons. Oil 250 tons. Range 5.070nm at 16 knots.
Protection:	Full length deck 2in-¾in (51mm-19mm).
Armament:	2—6in, 10—4in, 4—3pdr, 2—18in TT submerged (beam).
Complement:	480

Cast in the mould of the third class protected cruiser, but owing something as well to the Boadiceas. Originally an all 4in armament was proposed; the 6in guns were added to go one better than contemporary German ships, but the mixed armament was, as usual, a mistake. Freeboard amidships was too low, preventing the waist guns from being worked in a seaway, and the Bristols were also rather cramped, especially after wartime additions. A large metacentric height, intended to preserve stability in the damaged state, gave them a lively roll.

As often happens in warship design, the Bristols were outshone by their successors. They spent most of their war service—not without distinction—on overseas stations, while the newer Towns fought in the more hotly contested waters nearer home. Unlike the later Towns, the Bristols found no place in the post-war fleet and were scrapped soon after hostilities ended.

Liverpool, **1910, first true cruiser since the Gem Class.**

BRISTOL

Built by John Brown, Clydebank. Laid down 23.3.1909. Launched 23.2.1910. Completed 12.1910. Attached 2 BS Home 1910-12. 2 LCS Home 1913. 5 CS Home 1914. 4 CS N. America & W.I. from 8.1914—briefly engaged *Karlsruhe*, 6.8.1914; with AMC *Macedonia* captured German colliers in Falklands battle; took part in hunt for *Dresden*, 12.1914. Mediterranean 1915-16. Adriatic 1916-17. South America 1918-19. Portsmouth Reserve 1919. For disposal 1920. Sold 1921, Ward, Hayle.

Battle Honours: Falklands 1914, Adriatic 1917.

GLASGOW

Built by Fairfield, Govan. Laid down 25.3.1909. Launched 30.9.1909. Completed 9.1910. Attached 2 BS Home 1910-11. SE Coast of America 1911-15—captured German SS *Catherina*, 16.8.1914; at battle of Coronel, 1.11.1914; with *Cornwall* helped sink *Leipzig* at Falklands 8.12.1914; with *Kent*, sank SMS *Dresden* at Mas a Fuera, Chile, 14.3.1915. Mediterranean 1915-16—hunt for raider *Mowe*, Feb. and Sept. 1916. 8 LCS Adriatic 1917-18. At Gibraltar 6.1919. Portsmouth Reserve 1919. For disposal 1920. Stokers' TS, Portsmouth 1921-26. Sold 1927, Ward, Morecambe.

Battle Honour: Falklands 1914.

GLOUCESTER

Built by Beardmore, Dalmuir. Laid down 15.4.1909. Launched 25.10.1909. Completed 10.1910. Attached 1 BS Home 1912-12. 2 LCS/1 LCS Mediterranean 1913-15—chased *Goeben* and *Breslau* 8.1914; search for AMC *Kronprinz Wilhelm*, W. coast of Africa 1914-15. 3 LCS Grand Fleet 1915-16—captured German supply ship *Macedonia*, 2.1915; shelled Galway during Easter uprising, 4.1916. 2 LCS Grand Fleet 1916. 8 LCS Adriatic 1916-19. Devonport 1919. For disposal 1920. Sold 1921, Ward, Briton Ferry.

Battle Honour: Jutland 1916.

LIVERPOOL

Built by Vickers, Barrow. Laid down 17.2.1909. Launched 30.10.1909. Completed 10.1910. Attached 1 BS Home 1910-12. 2 LCS Home 1913-14. 5 CS Grand Fleet 1914. 2 LCS Grand Fleet Jan-Feb 1915. 3 LCS Grand Fleet 1915—search for *Kronprinz Wilhelm* off W. Africa, then boiler repairs at Liverpool, 6.1915. Mediterranean Nov 1915-18. 8 LCS Aegean Nov1918. Black Sea 1918-19. Devonport Reserve 1919. For disposal 1920. Sold 1921, Slough Trading Co. and broken up in Germany.

Battle Honour: Heligoland 1914.

NEWCASTLE

Built by Armstrong, Elswick. Laid down 14.4.1909. Launched 25.11.1909. Completed 9.1910. China 1910-14 (replaced *Bedford*)—Shanghai Rebellion 23.6.1913. Searched off S. America for German AMC *Prinz Eitel Freidrich*, 1914. Pacific 1915-16—captured German prize *Mazatlan*, 1916. Mediterranean (Mudros, East Indies, Adriatic) 1917. SE Coast of America 1918-19. Nore Reserve 1919-20. Sold 1921, Ward, Lelant.

Newcastle, 1918, at Montevideo, note stump mainmast.

WEYMOUTH CLASS (4 ships), *1909 Programme*

Dartmouth, Falmouth, Weymouth, Yarmouth

Displacement (tons):	5,250 normal, 5,800 full load.
Dimensions (feet):	430pp, 453oa x 48½ x 15½
(metres):	131.1pp, 138.1oa x 14.8 x 4.7
Machinery:	4 shaft Parsons compound reaction turbines (*Yarmouth*: 2 shaft Brown Curtis) 12 Yarrow boilers. 22,000 SHP = 25 knots.
Fuel:	Coal 1,290 tons. Oil 260 tons. Range 4,500nm at 16 knots.
Protection:	Full length deck 2in-¾in (51mm-19mm).
Armament:	8—6in, 4—3pdr.2—21in TT submerged (beam).
Complement:	475

Described in the 1909 Estimates as an 'Improved Bristol class', the most significant advance being their uniform armament of 8—6in guns. To overcome the freeboard problems of the earlier ships the forecastle deck was extended some way aft, and the waist guns enclosed in a bulwark.

All ships received a 3in AA gun in 1915, mounted between the second and third funnels. After *Falmouth's* loss the remaining three ships were fitted in 1917 with tripod foremasts and director control for the 6in guns. Aircraft platforms, fitted in *Weymouth* and *Yarmouth* in 1918 and extending over the CT and forward 6in gun, were removed after the war. *Weymouth* and *Dartmouth* shipped an extra 3in AA gun on the quarterdeck.

Robust and well armed, the Weymouths were considered worth retaining after the war, but were less actively employed than the subsequent Chatham and Birmingham classes.

Weymouth.

IMPERIAL WAR MUSEUM

DARTMOUTH

Built by Vickers, Barrow. Laid down 19.2.1910. Launched 14.12.1910. Completed 10.1911. Attached 3 BS Home 1911-13. East Indies 1913-14—captured German tug *Adjutant*, 10.1914. South Atlantic Jan 1915—search for *Karlsruhe*. Dardanelles, Feb—May 1915. 8 LCS Adriatic (based at Brindisi) 1915-19—torpedoed by *UC25*, 15.5.1917. 7 LCS South America 1919-21. Devonport Reserve 1921-24. Refit 1924-26. Trooping 1926-27. Flagship VAC Reserves, Portsmouth 1927-28. Trooping to Mediterranean and China 1928-29. Reserve 1929, temporarily attached to *Defiance*, 1930. Sold 1930, Alloa, Rosyth.

Battle Honour: Dardanelles 1915.

FALMOUTH

Built by Beardmore, Dalmuir. Laid down 21.11.1909. Launched 20.9.1910. Completed 9.1911. Attached 2 BS Home 1911-13. 2 LCS Home 1913-14. 5 CS Mid Atlantic 1914—sank German merchantmen *Fasolt, Ochtum, Borkum* and *Hude,* 8.1914. Flagship, 1 LCS Grand Fleet, Dec 1914—Feb 1915. 3 LCS Grand Fleet 1915-16 (flagship from 6.1916). Torpedoed in North Sea by *U66* and again by *U52*, 19.8.1916, and sank following day off Flamborough Head.

Battle Honours: Heligoland 1914, Jutland 1916.

WEYMOUTH

Built by Armstrong, Elswick. Laid down 19.1.1910. Launched 18.11.1910. Completed 10.1911. Attached 3 BS Home 1911-13. 2 LCS Home 1913. 1 CS Mediterranean 1913-14—detached to East Indies in hunt for *Emden* 1914-15. East Africa (roundup of *Konigsberg* Feb—July 1915. Mediterranean 1915-16. 6 LCS Grand Fleet 1916-17. Mediterranean 1917-18. Commodore, 8 LCS. Adriatic 1918-19—damaged by torpedo from Austrian submarine *U28* off Durazzo, 2.10.1918. Malta refit 1919-20. 7 LCS South America 1920-21. Nore Reserve 1921-27 (refit 1924, Flagship, VA Nore Reserve 1925-27). Sold 1928, Hughes Bolckow, Blyth.

YARMOUTH

Built by London & Glasgow, Govan. Laid down 27.1.1910. Launched 12.4.1911. Completed 4.1912. Attached 4 BS Home 1912-13. China 1913-14. Hunt for *Emden* 1914; captured one of her colliers and sank another, 10.1914. 2 LCS Grand Fleet, Dec 1914-15. 3 LCS Grand Fleet, Feb 1915-18. 2 LCS Grand Fleet 1918-19. Flagship, Cape (temp.) 1919. Refit 1919. 7 LCS South America 1919-20. Nore Reserve 1920-22. Attached Signal School, Portsmouth 1922-24. Refit 1924-25. Trooping 1925-27. Attached Signal School, Portsmouth 1927. Flagship, RA Submarines, Falmouth 1928. Sold 1929, Alloa, Rosyth.

Battle Honour: Jutland 1916.

Yarmouth. **Note aircraft sited above "A" gun.**

CHATHAM CLASS (3 ships), *1910 Programme and R.A.N. (3 ships)*

Chatham, Dublin, Southampton, Brisbane, Melbourne, Sydney

Displacement (tons):	5,400 normal, 6,000 deep load.
Dimensions (feet):	430pp, 458oa x 49 x 16
(metres):	131.1pp, 139.6oa x 14.9 x 4.9
Machinery:	4 shaft Parsons (*Southampton* 2 shaft Brown Curtis) turbines. 12 Yarrow boilers. 25,000 SHP = 25½ knots.
Fuel:	Coal 1,240 tons. Oil 260 tons. Range 4,500 nm at 16 knots.
Protection:	Full length belt 2in (51mm) nickel steel on 1in (25mm) shell plating. Full length deck 1½in—⅜in (38mm-10mm).
Armament:	8—6in, 4—3pdr, 2—21in TT submerged (beam).
Complement:	475

Sea experience with the preceding classes had exposed the weakness of low freeboard amidships. In the Chathams the forecastle deck extended aft for two thirds of the ship's length, and five of the eight 6in guns carried at this height. The protective deck was thinned to ⅜in over most of its length, and the weight thus saved devoted to a 2in waterline belt of nickel steel laid on top of 1in shell plating—an early instance of protection forming an integral part of ship structure. The new Mark XII 45 calibre gun was more accurate than the old Mark XI 50 calibre weapon, despite its lower velocity. A low metacentric height reduced roll and made the Chathams steady gun platforms. They were distinguished from the earlier Towns by their long forecastle deck and clipper or 'plough' bows.

In 1915 all were given a 3in AA gun. In 1917-18 they were fitted with tall searchlight platforms and tripod foremasts. *Dublin, Melbourne, Southampton* and *Sydney* were also given aircraft platforms, removed in 1919.

CHATHAM

Built at Chatham Dockyard. Laid down 3.1.1911. Launched 9.11.1911. Completed 12.1912. 1 LCS Home 1912-13 (detached to Mediterranean 1913). 1 CS Mediterranean 1914). Red Sea and East Indies (including roundup of *Konigsberg*) 1914-15—captured German SS *Prasident* in Lindi River, 19.10.1914. Mediterranean and Dardanelles 1915. Flagship, 3 LCS Grand Fleet 1916-19—mined off Norfolk 26.5.1916; repaired at Chatham. Nore Reserve 1919-20. New Zealand Division 1920-24. Flagship, 4 LCS East Indies 1924-25. Paid off, Devonport 11.1925. Sold 1926, Ward, Pembroke Dock.

Battle Honour: Dardanelles 1915-16.

DUBLIN

Built by Beardmore, Dalmuir. Laid down 4.1911. Launched 30.4.1912. Completed 3.1913. Attached 1 BS Home 1913. 1 CS Mediterranean 1913-15. Dardanelles 1915. Based on Brindisi 1915—damaged by torpedo from Austrian U Boat, 9.6.1915. 2 LCS Grand Fleet 1916-19. Reserve 1919. 3 LCS Mediterranean (temp.) 3.1920. 6 LCS Africa 1920-24. Nore Reserve 1924. Sold 1926, King, Troon.

Battle Honours: Dardanelles 1915, Jutland 1916.

SOUTHAMPTON

Built by John Brown, Clydebank. Laid down 6.4.1911. Launched 16.5.1912. Completed 11.1912. Attached 1 BS Home 1913. 1 LCS Home/Grand Fleet 1913-15. Flagship, 2 LCS Grand Fleet 1915-17. At Jutland sank German TB 530 and cruiser *Fraunlob*: sustained severe damage. 3 LCS Grand Fleet 1917-19. Flagship 7 LCS South America 1919-20. Refit, Cape 1920-21. Flagship, 4 LCS East Indies 1921-24. Material Reserve, Nore 1924. Sold 1926, Ward, Pembroke Dock.

Battle Honours: Heligoland 1914, Dogger Bank 1915, Jutland 1916.

BRISBANE

Built at Cockatoo Dockyard. Laid down 25.1.1913. Launched 30.9.1915. Completed 11.1916. Pacific 1916-17. East Indies 1917. Australia—GB convoys 1918. Aegean Squadron 11.1918. Australia 1919-35. (Training Ship from 1928). Paid off Portsmouth, 9.1935. Sold 1936, Ward, Briton Ferry.

HMAS *Melbourne* flying off platform fitted forward, 1917/8.

MELBOURNE

Built by Cammell Laird, Birkenhead. Laid down 14.4.1911. Launched 30.5.1912. Completed 1.1913. Pacific 1913-14. N. America & W.I. 1914-16. 2 LCS Grand Fleet 1916-19. Australia 1919-28. (Flagship, RAN 1927-28). Paid off, Portsmouth 1928. Sold 1928, Alloa, Rosyth.

SYDNEY

Built by London & Glasgow, Govan. Laid down 11.2.1911. Launched 29.8.1912. Completed 6.1913. Pacific 1913-14. New Guinea expedition 9.1914. Sank SMS *Emden*, 9.11.1914. N. America & W.I. 1914-16. 2 LCS Grand Fleet 1916-19. Australia 1919-28 (refit, Cockatoo 1923). Paid off 5.1928. Broken up, Cockatoo 1929-30.

Battle Honour: *Emden* 1914.

RNZN

Chatham arriving Auckland Jan 1921.

BIRMINGHAM CLASS (3 ships), *1911 Programme and R.A.N.* (1 ship)

Birmingham, Lowestoft, Nottingham, Adelaide

Displacement (tons):	5,440 normal, 6040 deep (*Adelaide* 5,550, 6,160).
Dimensions (feet):	430pp, 457oa x 50 x 16 (*Adelaide* 462¾oa)
(metres):	131.1pp, 139.3oa x 15.2 x 4.9 (141oa)
Machinery:	4 shaft Parsons turbines. 12 Yarrow boilers. 25,000 SHP = 25½ knots.
Fuel:	Coal 1,165 tons. Oil 235 tons. Range 4,140nm at 16 knots.
Protection:	Full length belt 2in (51mm) nickel steel on 1in (25mm) shell plating. Full length deck 1½in-⅜in (38mm-10mm).
Armament:	9—6in, 4—3pdr, 2—21in TT submerged (beam).
Complement:	480

Near repeats of the Chathams, slightly wider, and with a pair of 'sided' 6in guns on the forecastle instead of a single centreline mounting. Greater flare forward improved lift and reduced spray. All were fitted with a 3in AA gun in 1915, but none received aircraft equipment.

Birmingham and *Lowestoft* survived the war and were retained for some years, serving mainly on the Africa station. *Adelaide* was not completed until 1922; during modernisation in 1938-39 she was converted for oil fuel only, losing her forefunnel and two boilers, while armament was altered to 8—6in and 3—4in AA guns.

This most successful class marks the end of the Town cycle of medium sized broadside cruisers. Their dimensions limited numbers, and the smaller Arethusas which followed them provided a basis for fresh development.

BIRMINGHAM

Built by Armstrong, Elswick. Laid down 10.6.1912. Launched 7.5.1913. Completed 2.1914. 1 LCS Home/Grand Fleet 1914-15—sank two German merchantmen, 8.14, and *U15* on 9.8.14. the first U-boat sunk in the war. 2 LCS Grand Fleet 1915-19. 6 LCS Africa 1919-21. Nore Reserve 1921-22. Trooping to East Indies, early 1923. Flagship, 6 LCS Africa 1923-28. SO Reserves, Nore 1929. Sold 1931, Ward, Pembroke Dock.

Battle Honours: Heligoland 1914, Dogger Bank 1915, Jutland 1916.

Lowestoft, 16 Sept 1929, with tripod foremast fitted.

LOWESTOFT

Built at Chatham Dockyard. Laid down 29.7.1912. Launched 23.4.1913. Completed 4.1914. 1 LCS Home/Grand Fleet 1914-15—sank German merchantman *Fernbellin*, 8.14. 2 LCS Grand Fleet 1915-16. Flagship, 8 LCS Mediterranean 1916-17. Refit, Malta 1917. Flagship, 8 LCS Adriatic 1918-19. 6 LCS Africa 1919-24 (Flagship from 1921). Refit 1924-25. 6 LCS Africa 1925-29. Paid off, Devonport 10.1929. Sold 1931, Ward, Milford Haven.

Battle Honours: Heligoland 1914, Dogger Bank 1915.

NOTTINGHAM

Built at Pembroke Dockyard. Laid down 13.6.1912. Launched 18.4.1913. Completed 4.1914. 1 LCS Home/Grand Fleet 1914-15. 2 LCS Grand Fleet 1915-16. Torpedoed and sunk by *U52* in North Sea, 16.8.1916. 38 lost.

Battle Honours: Heligoland 1914, Dogger Bank 1915, Jutland 1916.

ADELAIDE

Built at Cockatoo Dockyard. Laid down 1.1915. Launched 27.7.1918. Completed 8.1922. Australia 1922-28 (Empire Cruise 1924). Sydney Reserve 1928-38. Refit 1938-39. Australia 1939-45. Laid up 1945. Broken up, Australian Iron & Steel, Port Kembla 1949.

IMPERIAL WAR MUSEUM

HMAS *Adelaide* **during WW2, forefunnel removed.**

BIRKENHEAD CLASS (2 ships)

Birkenhead, Chester

Displacement (tons):	5,185 normal, 5,795 deep load. *(Chester* 5,235 normal, 5,845 deep load.)
Dimensions (feet):	430pp, 446 *(Chester* 456)oa x 50 x 16
(metres):	131.1pp, 135.9, (139)oa x 15.2 x 4.9
Machinery:	4 shaft Parsons turbines. 12 Yarrow boilers. 25,000 SHP = 25½ knots *(Chester* 31,000 SHP = 26½ knots).
Fuel:	Coal 1,070 tons, oil 352 tons. *(Chester* 1,161 tons oil only).
Protection:	Full length belt 2in (51mm) nickel steel on 1in (25mm) shell plating. Full length deck 1½in-⅜in (38mm-10mm).
Armament:	10—5.5in, 1—3in AA 2—21in TT submerged (beam).
Complement:	500

Ordered by Greece in early 1914, the contracts were taken over by the British Admiralty early in 1915, after the first ship had been launched. Copies of *Birmingham*, but armed with 10-5.5in 50 calibre guns of a new model made by Coventry Ordnance Works.

After the war their resale to Greece was considered but rejected, and both ships were scrapped.

BIRKENHEAD (ex Antinavarhos Kontouriotis)

Built by Cammell Laird, Birkenhead. Laid down 27.4.1914. Launched 18.1.1915. Completed 5.1915. 3 LCS Grand Fleet 1915-19. Portsmouth Reserve 1919-20. Sold 1921, Cashmore, Newport.

Battle Honour: Jutland 1916.

CHESTER (ex Lambros Katsonis)

Built by Cammell Laird, Birkenhead. Laid down 7.10.1914. Launched 8.12.1915. Completed 5.1916. 3 LCS Grand Fleet 1916-19. Nore Reserve 1919-20. Sold 1921, Rees, Llanelli.

Battle Honour: Jutland 1916.

Chester in which **Boy Cornwell won his VC at Jutland.**

BRITISH CRUISER DEPLOYMENT, AUGUST 1914

Mediterranean
1 CS   *Defence* (Flag), *Black Prince, Duke of Edinburgh, Warrior* and light cruisers *Chatham, Dublin, Gloucester, Weymouth.*

Grand Fleet
1 LCS *Southampton* (Flag), *Birmingham, Lowestoft, Nottingham.*
2 CS   *Shannon* (Flag), *Achilles, Cochrane, Natal.*
3 CS   *Antrim* (Flag), *Argyll, Devonshire, Roxburgh.*

N. America and West Indies
4 CS   *Suffolk* (Flag), *Berwick, Essex, Lancaster* and light cruiser *Bristol,* supported by two French cruisers.

Mid Atlantic
5 CS   *Carnarvon* (Flag), *Cornwall, Cumberland, Monmouth.*

Nominally Grand Fleet, but mostly on detached duties
6 CS   *Drake, King Alfred, Good Hope, Leviathan.*

Southern area of North Sea
7 CS   *Bacchante* (Flag), *Aboukir, Cressy, Euryalus, Hogue.*

Mid Atlantic
9 CS   *Europa* (Flag), *Amphitrite, Argonaut, Challenger, Highflyer, Vindictive.*

Northern Patrol
10 CS *Crescent* (Flag), *Edgar, Endymion, Gibraltar, Grafton, Hawke, Royal Arthur, Theseus.*

West of Ireland Coast Patrol
11 CS *Juno* (Flag), *Doris, Isis, Minerva, Venus.*

Western Channel Patrol
12 CS *Charybdis* (Flag), *Diana, Eclipse, Talbot,* supported by a French cruiser squadron.

Attached to Grand Fleet Battle Squadrons (and Fleet Flagship):
        Bellona, Blanche, Blonde, Boadicea, (and *Sappho*).

Attached to Channel Fleet Battle Squadrons (pre-Dreadnoughts):
        Brilliant, Diamond, Proserpine, Sapphire, Sirius, Topaze.

Minelayer Squadron:
        Andromache, Apollo, Intrepid, Iphigenia, Latona, Naiad, Thetis.

Attached to Destroyer Flotillas:
        1st (Harwich); *Fearless.* 2nd (GF); *Active.* 3rd (Harwich); *Amphion.*
        6th (Dover Patrol); *Adventure, Attentive, Foresight.* 7th (Humber Patrol);
        Skirmisher.
        8th (Tyne Patrol); *Pathfinder, Sentinel.* 9th (Forth Patrol); *Forward, Patrol.*

China:	*Minotaur* (Flag), *Hampshire, Newcastle, Yarmouth.*
East Indies:	*Fox, Dartmouth, Weymouth.*
Cape of Good Hope:	*Hyacinth* (Flag), *Astraea, Pegasus.*
Australian Fleet:	*Encounter, Melbourne, Pioneer, Sydney.*
New Zealand Division:	*Philomel, Psyche, Pyramus.*
Canada:	*Niobe* (joined 4 CS), *Rainbow* (Pacific patrol).
SE Coast of America	*Glasgow.*

THE ARETHUSA'S

With the K and L classes, destroyer speeds reached 29-31 knots—too fast for existing Scouts to work effectively with them. A new class of fast Scouts was called for, and Churchill as First Lord set up a Cruiser Committee in 1911 to consider the alternatives. There were two options: a light armed, unprotected but very fast super-Swift, or a well armed and protected but slower super-Amphion. Fisher characteristically backed the former, attracted by the promised speed of 37 knots, but Churchill backed the 'cruiser admirals', and the super-Amphion became the basis of the Arethusa design. To emphasize that they were the smallest cruisers with side armour, Churchill described them to Parliament as 'light armoured cruisers'.

ARETHUSA CLASS (8 ships), *1912 Programme*

Arethusa, Aurora, Galatea, Inconstant, Penelope, Phaeton, Royalist, Undaunted

Displacement (tons):	3,750 load, 4,400 deep load.
Dimensions (feet):	410pp, 436oa x 39 x 13½
(metres):	125pp, 132.9oa x 11.9 x 4.1
Machinery:	4 shaft Parsons (*Arethusa* & *Undaunted* Brown Curtis) turbines. 8 boilers. 40,000 SHP = 28½ knots.
Fuel:	Oil 875 tons.
Protection:	Full length belt 2in-1½in (51mm-38mm), on 1in (25mm) plating amidships. Partial plating over machinery 1in (25mm).
Armament:	2—6in, 6—4in, 1—3pdr AA. 4—21in TT (deck)
Complement:	276-282

The Arethusas brought two innovations to cruiser design: oil fuel only, and fast-running destroyer machinery. As in the Chathams, the belt was laid over 1in side plating, so making protection contribute to structural strength. The protective deck was abandoned; over the machinery spaces the two outboard strakes of deck plating, each about 15ft wide, were of 1in thickness, but this was as much for strength as protection. Armament was an unhappy compromise between the 10-4in of the Scouts and a proposal for 5—6in guns. Unfortunately the 4in QF Mk IV gun was prone to jamming, and in ranging the guns it was hard to distinguish a 4in shell splash from a 6in one (the standard objection to a mixed armament).

The original 3pdr was replaced in all ships by a single 3in AA mounting in 1915. In 1917 all were re-armed with two 3in AA guns, except *Penelope* and *Undaunted* which received a single 4in AA gun instead. An additional pair of TT was fitted in all ships in 1917. A tripod replaced the pole foremast in 1918, when all except *Undaunted* were fitted for minelaying, and *Galatea, Inconstant, Penelope* and *Phaeton* had the after pair of 4in guns replaced by a single 6in mounting on the centreline.

Briefly in 1915 four ships had been fitted with a sloping runway over the forecastle for launching a French monoplane. In 1917-18 *Galatea, Phaeton, Royalist* and *Undaunted* were given a quarterdeck winch for towing a kite balloon, and all received a flying-off platform over the forward 6in gun in 1918.

Like the Scouts, the Arethusas were essentially North Sea ships, and wartime additions had made these already tight ships very cramped. Having initiated a highly successful cycle of cruiser development, they were quite outclassed by their successors and discarded soon after the war.

Aurora, **July 1917—in dock at Hull.**

ARETHUSA

Built at Chatham Dockyard. Laid down 28.10.1912. Launched 25.10.1913. Completed 11.8.1914. Leader, 3 DF Harwich 1914-15—Heligoland; covered Cuxhaven raid, 25.12.1914; Dogger Bank. 5 LCS Harwich, June 1915-16—covered Borkum raid, 7.1915; took part in chase of minelayer *Meteor*, 8.1915; captured four German trawlers, Sept—Oct 1915. Mined off Felixstowe, 11.2.1916; taken in tow but broke loose and broke her back running aground on Cutler Shoal.

Battle Honours: Heligoland 1914, Dogger Bank 1915.

AURORA

Built at Devonport Dockyard. Laid down 24.10.1912. Launched 30.9.1913. Completed 5.9.1914. Leader, 1 DF Grand Fleet 1914-15. Leader, 10 DF Harwich 1915. 5 LCS Harwich, June 1915-18—took part in sinking of *Meteor*, 8.1915; covered Hoyer seaplane raid, 24.3.1916. Rearmed 1917-18. 7 LCS Grand Fleet 1918-19. Devonport Reserve 1919. Gifted to Royal Canadian Navy, 1920, but paid off 1921 and hulked 1923. Sold 1927, Lasseque, Sorel PQ.

Battle Honour: Dogger Bank 1915.

GALATEA

Built by Beardmore, Dalmuir. Laid down 9.1.1913. Launched 14.5.1914. Completed 12.1914. Leader, 2 DF Harwich 1914-15. Leader, 1 DF Grand Fleet, based at Rosyth Feb 1915-18—with *Phaeton* shot down Zeppelin L7, 4.5.1916. 1 LCS Grand Fleet, Sept 1918-19 (Baltic, end 1918-19; collision with SS *Moto* off Northumberland, 10.12.1918.) 2 LCS Atlantic 1919-20. Portsmouth Reserve 1920. Sold 1921, Multilocular Shipbreaking Co. Stranraer.

Battle Honour: Jutland 1916.

INCONSTANT

Built by Beardmore, Dalmuir. Laid down 3.4.1913. Launched 6.7.1914. Completed 1.1915. 1 LCS Grand Fleet 1915-19—took part in search for *Meteor*, 8.1915. SNO Ship, Baltic early 1919. 2 LCS Harwich 1919. Captain S/M, 1st Submarine Flotilla, Atlantic 1919-22. Sold 1922, Cashmore, Newport.

Battle Honour: Jutland 1916.

PENELOPE

Built by Vickers, Barrow. Laid down 1.2.1913. Launched 25.8.1914. Completed 10.12.1914. Harwich Force 1915-18 (5 LCS from 8.1915)—covered Hoyer raid, 3.1915; captured four German trawlers, 9.1915. Damaged by torpedo from *UB 29* off Norfolk coast, 25.4.1916. 7 LCS Grand Fleet 1918-19. Nore Reserve 1919-21. For disposal 1921. Sold 1924, Stanlee, Dover.

PHAETON

Built by Vickers, Barrow. Laid down 12.3.1913. Launched 21.10.1914. Completed 2.1915. 4 LCS Grand Fleet 1915. Dardanelles, Mar-Sept 1915. 1 LCS Grand Fleet 1915-18—with *Galatea* shot down Zeppelin L 7, 4.5.1916. 7 LCS Grand Fleet 1918-19. 2 LCS Harwich 1919-20. Refit, Devonport 1920-21. Devonport Reserve 1921-22. Sold 1923, King, Troon.

Battle Honour: Jutland 1916.

Inconstant.

ROYALIST

Built by Beardmore, Dalmuir. Laid down 3.6.1913. Launched 14.1.1915. Completed 3.1915. 4 LCS Grand Fleet 1915. Leader, 12 DF Grand Fleet 1915-16. 4 LCS Grand Fleet 1916-17 (Jutland). 1 LCS Grand Fleet 1917-19—Baltic 1919. 2 LCS Harwich 1919-20. Portsmouth Reserve 1920-22. Sold 1922, Cashmore, Newport.

Battle Honour: Jutland 1916.

UNDAUNTED

Built by Fairfield, Govan. Laid down 21.12.1912. Launched 28.4.1914. Completed 29.8.1914. Leader, 3 DF Harwich 1914-15—in action with her flotilla against German destroyers off Flanders coast, 17.10.1914; covered Cuxhaven raid, 25.12.1914. Leader, 9 DF Harwich 1915-17—damaged in collision with destroyer *Landrail*, 4.1915; captured a German trawler, 9.1915; damaged in collision with *Cleopatra*, 24.3.1916—repairs on Tyne. Leader, 10 DF Harwich 1917-18. 4 LCS Grand Fleet 1918-19. Nore Reserve 1919-22 (trooping to Mediterranean 1921). Sold 1923, Cashmore, Newport.

Battle Honours: Dogger Bank 1915, Belgian Coast 1916.

CAROLINE CLASS (6 ships), *1913 Programme*

Caroline, Carysfort, Cleopatra, Comus, Conquest, Cordelia

Displacement (tons):	4,219 load, 4,733 deep.
Dimensions (feet):	420pp, 446oa x 41½ x 14¾
(metres):	128pp, 135.9oa x 12.6 x 4.5
Machinery:	4 shaft Parsons independent reduction (*Carysfort* Brown Curtis) turbines. 8 Yarrow boilers. 40,000 SHP = 28½ knots.
Fuel:	Oil 916 tons. Range 1,075/3,680 miles at 28/18 knots.
Protection:	Full length belt 2in-1½in (51mm-38mm), on 1in (25mm) plating amidships. Partial plating over machinery 1in (25mm).
Armament: as built;	2—6in, 8—4in, 1—13pdr, 4—3pdr, 4—21in TT (deck).
1919;	4—6in, 2—3in AA, 4—21in TT (deck).
Complement:	325

Expanded Arethusas, sharing the same machinery and scheme of protection, but with a heavier armament differently disposed. Both 6in guns were mounted aft, one superfiring over the other, while the forecastle carried a pair of sided 4in guns. The latter proved ineffective, and were replaced in 1916-17 by a single 6in mounting on the centreline. In 1917-18 the remaining 4in guns were taken out to make way for one 6in gun amidships, and thus the Carolines evolved from ten gun mixed calibre to four gun single calibre ships. Retained for some years after the war, they were considered under-armed in comparison to the Centaur and subsequent classes.

CAROLINE

Built by Cammell Laird, Birkenhead. Laid down 28.1.1914. Launched 29.9.1914. Completed 4.12.1914. Leader, 4 DF Grand Fleet 1914-15. 1 LCS Grand Fleet, Jan-Nov 1915. 4 LCS Grand Fleet 1916-19, 4 LCS East Indies 1919-22. Paid off 1922. Became RNVR Drill Ship at Belfast, 1926, and is still (1987) afloat there.

Battle Honour: Jutland 1916.

CARYSFORT

Built at Pembroke Dockyard. Laid down 25.2.1914. Launched 14.11.1914. Completed 8.6.1915. Leader, 4 DF Grand Fleet 1915-16. 5 LCS Harwich, Apr 1916-17. 7 LCS Grand Fleet 1917-19 (Flagship 1918). 2 LCS Harwich 1919 (Baltic 1919-20). 2 LCS Atlantic 1920-23 (Irish Patrols 1922, detached for Turkish crisis 1922-23). Devonport Reserve 1923-31 (trooping 1924 and 1929). Sold 1931, McLellan, Bo'ness.

Caroline **as built with pole foremast—note sided 4 inch guns on forecastle.**

CLEOPATRA

Built at Devonport Dockyard. Laid down 26.2.1914. Launched 14.1.1915. Completed 1.6.1915. 5 LCS Harwich 1915-18—rammed and sank German destroyer G194, 25.3.1916: struck British mine off Dutch coast, 4.8.1916; repairs 1916-17. 7 LCS Grand Fleet 1918-19. 2 LCS Harwich 1919 (Baltic). 1 LCS Atlantic 1919-21. Nore Reserve 1921-22. Refit, Pembroke 1923-24. 3 LCS Mediterranean (temp.) 1924. 1 CS Atlantic 1925-26. Refit 1927. Nore Reserve 1927-31 (SNO 1928-31, trooping to Mediterranean 1928 and China 1929). Sold 1931, Hughes Bolckow, Blyth.

Battle Honour: Belgian Coast 1916.

COMUS

Built by Swan Hunter, Wallsend. Laid down 3.11.1913. Launched 16.12.1914. Completed 21.5.1915. 4 LCS Grand Fleet 1915-19—sank German raider *Greif*, 29.2.1916. 1 LCS Grand Fleet, Mar—Apr 1919. Rosyth Refit 1919. 4 LCS East Indies 1919-22. Refit 1922-23. 3 LCS Mediterranean 1923-24. Nore Reserve 1925. 2 CS Atlantic 1925-30. Devonport Reserve 1930-33 (SNO 1931-33). Sold 1934, Ward, Barrow.

Battle Honour: Jutland 1916.

CONQUEST

Built at Chatham Dockyard. Laid down 3.3.1914. Launched 20.1.1915. Completed 1.6.1915. 5 LCS Harwich 1915-18. Mined 7.18; repairs to 4.19. Nore Reserve 1919-22. Captain S/M, 1st Submarine Flotilla, Atlantic 1922-26. Captain S/M, 1st Submarine Flotilla, Mediterranean 1927-28. Portsmouth Reserve 1928-30. Sold 1930, Metal Industries, Rosyth.

CORDELIA

Built at Pembroke Dockyard. Laid down 21.7.1913. Launched 23.2.1914, Completed 3.1.1915. 1 LCS Grand Fleet 1915-17. 4 LCS Grand Fleet 1917-19. Gunnery TS, Devonport 1919. Nore Reserve 1919. 2 LCS Atlantic 1920-22 (Irish Patrols 1922). Nore Reserve 1923. Sold 1923, Cashmore, Newport.

Battle Honour: Jutland 1916.

Conquest, 1923.

CALLIOPE CLASS (2 ships), *1913 Programme*

Calliope, Champion

Displacement (tons):	4,228 normal, 4,695 deep load.
Dimensions (feet):	420pp, 446oa x 41½ x 14¾ mean.
(metres):	128pp, 135.9oa x 12.6 x 4.5
Machinery:	4 shaft (*Champion* 2 shaft) Parsons geared turbines. 6 Yarrow boilers. 37,500 SHP = 28½ knots (*Champion* 40,000 SHP = 29 knots).
Fuel:	Oil 805-895 tons. Range 1,300/4,000 miles at 28/18 knots.
Protection:	Full length belt 3in-1in (76mm-25mm) on 1 in (25mm) plating amidships. Partial plating over machinery 1in (25mm).
Armament: as built;	2—6in, 8—4in, 1—13pdr, 4—3pdr, 2—21in TT submerged (beam).
1920;	4—6in, 2—3in AA, 2—21in TT submerged (beam).
Complement:	324

In the last two ships of the 1913 Programme opportunity was taken to incorporate larger boilers and experiment with geared turbines. Boilers were reduced in number from eight to six, and funnels from three to two, giving rise to the classic 'C class' profile. *Calliope*'s gearing accepted some reduction in power, while *Champion*, with a two shaft arrangement, was the faster ship. Protection was similar to the Carolines', but the belt was thicker. The torpedo tubes were under water (and unworkable at speed) rather than deck-mounted; gun armament was the same as the Carolines', and evolved by similar stages into a uniform battery of four 6in guns. Two pairs of deck-mounted 21in TT added in 1916 were removed after the war to save topweight.

CALLIOPE

Built at Chatham Dockyard. Laid down 1.1.1914. Launched 17.12.1914. Completed 6.1915. 4 LCS Grand Fleet 1915-19. Badley damaged at Jutland. Reserve 1919. 8 LCS N. America & W.I. 1919-20. Nore Reserve 1920-24. 2 LCS Atlantic 1924-25. Trooping 1925-26. Refit and Nore Reserve 1926-28. 3 CS Mediterranean 1928-29. Portsmouth Reserve 1929. Sold 1931, Ward, Inverkeithing.

Battle Honour: Jutland 1916.

Champion. **Post war with tripod foremast—retained searchlight platform aft.**

CHAMPION

Built by Hawthorn Leslie, Hebburn. Laid down 9.3.1914. Launched 29.5.1915. Completed 20.12.1915. Leader, 13 DF Grand Fleet 1915-18. 2 LCS Harwich 1919. Attached to *Vernon* Torpedo School, Portsmouth 1919-24. Gunnery Training Ship 1925-28. Attached Signal School 1928-33. Sold 1934, Metal Industries, Rosyth.

Battle Honour: Jutland 1916.

CAMBRIAN CLASS (4 ships), *1914 Programme*

Cambrian, Canterbury, Castor, Constance

Displacement (tons):	4,320 normal, 4,799 deep load.
Dimensions (feet):	420pp, 446oa x 41½ x 14¾ mean.
(metres):	128pp, 135.9oa x 12.6 x 4.5
Machinery:	4 shaft Parsons (*Canterbury* Brown Curtis) turbines. 6 Yarrow boilers. 40,000 SHP = 28 knots.
Fuel:	Oil 841 tons. Range 980/3,380 miles at 28/18 knots.
Protection:	Full length belt 2in-1in (51mm-25mm) on 1in (25mm) plating amidships. Partial plating over machinery 1in (25mm),
Armament: as built;	2 *(Cambrian 3)*—6in, 8 *(Cambrian 6)*—4in, 4—3pdr, 1—13pdr AA, 2—21in TT submerged (beam).
1920;	4—6in, 2—3in AA, 2—21in TT submerged (beam).
Complement:	323

Very similar to the Calliopes, but reverting to the standard four shaft direct-drive machinery and thinner belts of the Carolines. *Cambrian* was completed with three 6in guns (one forward, two aft), starting the move towards the all 6in armament. In due course all were rearmed like the preceding classes to end up with four 6in guns. *Canterbury* was given two pairs of deck-mounted 21in TT, removed after the war.

Cambrian **fitted with 6 inch guns before joining the fleet.**

CAMBRIAN

Built at Pembroke Dockyard. Laid down 8.12.1914. Launched 3.3.1916. Completed 5.1916. 4 LCS Grand Fleet 1916-19. 8 LCS N. America & W.I. 1919-22. 2 LCS Atlantic 1922-24 (Turkish crisis 1922-23). Refit 1924-26. 2 CS Atlantic 1926-29. Trooping to China 1929. Nore Reserve 1929-33 (SNO 1931-33). Sold 1934, Metal Industries, Rosyth.

CANTERBURY

Built by John Brown, Clydebank. Laid down 14.10.1914. Launched 21.12.1915. Completed 9.5.1916. Attached 3 BS Grand Fleet 1916. 5 LCS Harwich 1916-18. Aegean and Black Sea 1918-19. 1 LCS Atlantic 1919. Gunnery Training Ship, Portsmouth 1919-22. Portsmouth Reserve 1922-24. 2 CS Atlantic 1924-25. Refit and Nore Reserve 1925-26. 2 CS Atlantic 1926-30. Nore Reserve 1930-33, trooping 1930-31 (to China) and 1932-33. Sold 1934, Metal Industries, Rosyth.

CASTOR

Built by Cammell Laird, Birkenhead. Laid down 28.10.1914. Launched 28.7.1915. Completed 12.11.1915. Leader, 11 DF Grand Fleet 1915-16. Commodore (D) Grand Fleet 1916-19. Commodore (D) Atlantic 1919-20 (Black Sea 1919-20). 2 LCS Atlantic 1920-23 (Irish Patrols 1922). Gunnery Training Ship, Portsmouth 1923-24. Nore Reserve 1924-27 (refit 1925-26). Trooping to China 1927-28. Det., China 1928-30. Devonport Reserve 1930-35. Sold 1935, Metal Industries, Rosyth.

Battle Honour: Jutland 1916.

WRIGHT & LOGAN

Constance, **July 1929, showing post war layout.**

CONSTANCE

Built by Cammell Laird, Birkenhead. Laid down 25.1.1915. Launched 12.9.1915. Completed 26.1.1916. 4 LCS Grand Fleet 1916-19. 8 LCS N. America & W.I. 1919-26. Chatham Refit 1926-27. Flagship, Portsmouth Reserve 1928. 5 CS China 1928-30. Portsmouth Reserve 1930-35 (Flagship VACR 1930-32). Sold 1936, Arnott Young, Dalmuir.

Battle Honour: Jutland 1916.

CENTAUR CLASS (2 ships), *1914 Programme*

Centaur, Concord

Displacement (tons):	4,165 normal, 4,870 deep.
Dimensions (feet):	420pp, 446oa x 42 x 14½
(metres):	128pp, 135.9oa x 12.8 x 4.4
Machinery:	4 shaft Parsons impulse reaction geared turbines. 6 Yarrow boilers. 40,000 SHP = 29 knots.
Fuel:	Oil 824 tons. (Range 980/3,880 miles at 28/18 knots.)
Protection:	Full length belt 2in-1in (51mm-25mm) on 1in (25mm) plating amidships. Partial plating over machinery 1in (25mm).
Armament:	5—6in, 1—13pdr, 2—3in AA 2—21in TT submerged (beam).
Complement:	336

Known as the Armstrong design, using machinery and materials assembled for two cancelled Turkish ships. Similar to the Cambrians, but with a uniform 6in armament and a fifth gun, worked in between the bridge and fore funnel. In spite of an increase in beam to accommodate the extra topweight, the Centaurs rolled considerably, and the concentration of weight forward made them liable to bury their bows in a head sea. Nevertheless, with their heavy uniform armament, the Centaurs were a great advance on the preceding classes.

Centaur had No. 2 gun removed in 1925; *Concord* lost Nos. 2 and 4 guns in 1928 when she became a tender to the Signal School.

CENTAUR

Built by Armstrong, Elswick. Laid down 24.1.1915. Launched 6.1.1916. Completed 8.1916. 5 LCS Harwich 1916-19. Baltic 1918-19. 3 LCS Mediterranean 1919-23 (Flagship 1920). Devonport Reserve 1923-24. Rosyth Refit 1924-25. Commodore (D) Atlantic 1925-32. Portsmouth Reserve 1932. Sold 1934, King, Troon.

CONCORD

Built by Armstrong, Elswick. Laid down 1.2.1915. Launched 1.4.1916. Completed 18.12.1916. 5 LCS Harwich 1916-19. 3 LCS Mediterranean 1919-23. Devonport Refit 1923-24. 3 LCS Mediterranean 1924. Attached Australia, 1925 and China 1925-26. 3 CS Mediterranean 1926-27. Reserve and refit, Portsmouth 1927-28 (trooping to China 1928). Attached Signal School, Portsmouth 1928-33. Dockyard control 1933. Sold 1935, Metal Industries, Rosyth.

Centaur. **Designed to carry uniform armament of 6 inch guns. The first cruiser built with a tripod foremast.**

1917-45: FROM ONE WAR TO ANOTHER

Caledon, Ceres, Capetown, Danae, Emerald and Cavendish classes.

All these ships were built under Emergency War Programmes, though many were not completed until some years after the Armistice. All except the Cavendish class are related to the line of development that began with the Arethusas and Carolines. They were the backbone of the Royal Navy's cruiser strength in the 1920s and well into the '30s, supplemented for many years by the Towns and older 'C' classes.

Replaced only gradually in the active Fleet by the trickle of new cruisers, all except the ill-fated *Cassandra* and *Raleigh* survived until 1939, by which time they were outdated and quite outclassed by newer ships. A number of the 'C's had been converted to anti-aircraft vessels, and others were similarly converted in the course of the war. In spite of their age all these classes saw strenuous war service particularly in the Mediterranean, and took heavy losses. Those that survived were worn out by 1945. Only *Frobisher* saw any post-war service, reverting briefly to her previous role of Cadet Training Ship.

The tonnages in this chapter are based on the 1922 assessment of standard displacement.

Caledon **Suez Bay 1941.**

CALEDON CLASS (4 ships), *Emergency War Programme*

Caledon, Calypso, Caradoc, Cassandra

Displacement (tons):	4,180 standard, 5,150 full load.
Dimensions (feet):	425pp, 450oa x 42¾ x 14¾ mean.
(metres):	129.5pp, 137.2oa x 13 x 4.5
Machinery:	2 shaft Parsons SR geared turbines. 6 Yarrow boilers. 40,000 SHP = 29 knots.
Fuel:	Oil 935 tons. Range 1,290/5,900 at 28½/10 knots.
Protection:	Full length belt 2in-1in (51mm-25mm) on 1in (25mm) plating amidships. Partial plating over machinery 1in (25mm).
Armament:	5—6in, 2—3in AA, 4—3pdr, 8—21in TT (4x2).
Caledon **1943:**	6—4in AA (3x2), 4—40mm AA (2x2), 12—20mm AA (6x2).
Complement:	334-400 (437 as flagships).

Ordered in December 1915. Very similar to *Centaur,* but with two shaft single reduction fully geared turbines, and slightly more beam to improve stability. Experience had shown that submerged torpedo tubes were unworkable at speed, and so the Caledons mounted theirs on deck. Straight, 'cut away' bows distinguished these and subsequent ships from the earlier 'C' groups.

Cassandra was lost in the Russian campaign in December 1918. The others were the oldest British cruisers to survive until 1939, little altered apart from modifications to the bridge and after superstructure, and the removal of a flying-off platform in *Caledon*. During the Second World War, light AA armament was increased and radar fitted. In 1942-43 *Caledon* underwent a full AA vessel conversion, which involved the rebuilding of her forward superstructure on the lines of the Ceres/Capetown classes.

CALEDON

Built by Cammell Laird, Birkenhead. Laid down 17.3.1916. Launched 25.11.1916. Completed 6.3.1917. 6 LCS Grand Fleet 1917. Flagship, 1 LCS Grand Fleet 1917-19 (Baltic 1.1919). 2 LCS Atlantic 1919-26 (Flagship 1919-21). Refit 1926-27. 3 CS Mediterranean 1927-31. Devonport and Nore Reserve 1931-39. 7 CS Home 1939-40. 3 CS Mediterranean 1940. Red Sea 1940-41. East Indies and Eastern Fleet 1942. Anti-aircraft conversion, Sep 1942-Dec 1943. Mediterranean 1944-45. Reserve 1945. Broken up, Dover Industries, Dover 1948.

Battle Honours: Mediterranean 1940, South France 1944, Aegean 1944.

Calypso, **July 1935, lost before AA conversion could be undertaken.**

CALYPSO

Built by Hawthorn Leslie, Hebburn. Laid down 7.2.1916. Launched 24.1.1917. Completed 21.6.1917. 6 LCS Grand Fleet 1917-19 (Baltic end 1918-19). 3 LCS Mediterranean 1919-28. Refit 1928-29. 3 CS Mediterranean 1929-32. Devonport Reserve 1932-39. 7 CS Home 1939-40. Mediterranean 1940. Torpedoed and sunk by Italian submarine *Bagnolini* south of Crete, 12.6.1940. 39 lost.

CARADOC

Built by Scotts, Greenock. Laid down 21.2.1916. Launched 23.12.1916. Completed 15.6.1917. 6 LCS Grand Fleet 1917-19 (Baltic end 1918-19). 3 LCS Mediterranean 1919-27 (China, temp. 1926-27). Refit 1927-28. 8 CS America & W.I. 1928-30. Reserve 1930. 5 CS China 1930-34. Devonport Reserve 1934-39. Channel Force 1939. America & W.I. 1939-42. Eastern Fleet 1942-43. South Atlantic 1943-44. Base ship, Colombo 1944-45. Broken up, Ward, Briton Ferry 1946.

Battle Honour: Atlantic 1940.

CASSANDRA

Built by Vickers, Barrow. Laid down 3.1916. Launched 25.11.1916. Completed 29.6.1917. 6 LCS Grand Fleet 1917-18 (Baltic, end 1918). Sunk by mine in Gulf of Finland, 5.12.1918. 11 lost.

CERES CLASS (5 ships): CAPETOWN CLASS (5 ships),
Emergency War Programme

Cardiff, Ceres, Coventry, Curacoa, Curlew
Cairo, Calcutta, Capetown, Carlisle, Colombo

Displacement (tons):	4,290 normal, 5,280 full load (Capetowns: 4,200 standard, 5,220 full load).
Dimensions (feet):	425pp, 450 (Capetowns 451½)oa x 43½ x 14¼ mean.
(metres):	129.5pp, 137.2oa (137.6)oa x 13.3 x 4.3
Machinery:	2 shaft Brown Curtis (*Curlew, Cairo, Calcutta, Capetown,* Parsons) SR geared turbines. 6 Yarrow boilers. 40,000 SHP = 29 knots.
Fuel:	Oil 935 tons. Range 1,290/5,900 miles at 28½/10 knots.
Protection:	Full length belt 2in-1in (51mm-25mm) on 1in (25mm) plating amidships. Partial plating over machinery 1in (25mm).
Armament: as built; **AA conversions;**	5—6in, 2—3in AA, 2—2pdr, 8—21in TT (4 x 2). 10 (later 8)—4in AA, 8—2pdr AA in *Coventry* and *Curlew*. Others: 8-4in AA (4x2), 4—2pdr AA (1x4), 8—.5in AA (2x4) except *Colombo*, similar to *Caledon*. *Cardiff, Ceres* and *Capetown* unconverted.
Complement:	334-400 (437 as flagships).

The finest light cruisers of their day, the Ceres class ordered in March 1916 were a great advance on the earlier Cs. A most advantageous re-arrangement of the fore part of the ship was made possible by moving boilers and funnels a few feet aft; the bridge was brought well back almost to the forefunnel, and the second 6in gun, instead of being sited between bridge and funnel with restricted arcs of fire, was moved to 'B' position, forward of the bridge and superfiring over 'A' gun. Bow fire was thereby doubled, and with the weight of the bridge further aft, *Ceres* was less prone to bury her bows in a head sea.

Dubbed 'Tyrwhitt's Dreadnoughts' in the Harwich Force because the disposition of their armament resembled that of a 13.5in gun battleship, the Ceres class make an interesting comparison with the Carolines, of the same approximate dimensions.

The Capetowns, ordered in June—July 1917 were identical to the *Ceres* except for their so-called 'trawler bow'—a marked sheer forward which reduced spray and wetness. None of this group were completed before the Armistice. *Capetown* and *Carlisle* had an aircraft hangar forward, later removed.

In 1935, *Coventry* and *Curlew* were re-armed with 10 single 4in guns in prototype conversions to anti-aircraft vessels. Improved conversions were later extended to *Curacoa, Cairo, Calcutta, Carlisle* and *Colombo*, which received four (*Colombo* three) twin 4in AA mountings. *Cardiff, Ceres* and *Capetown* were not converted, and ended their careers largely unaltered.

153

Cardiff, **1929.**

CARDIFF *(ex Caprice)*

Built by Fairfield, Govan. Laid down 22.7.1916. Launched 12.4.1917. Completed 25.6.1917. Flagship, 6 LCS Grand Fleet 1917-19 (Baltic end 1918-19). Led German High Seas Fleet to surrender 11.1918. 3 LCS Mediterranean 1919-29. Devonport Refit 1929-31. 6 CS Africa 1931-33. Nore Reserve 1933-38. 5 CS China 1938-39. 12/11 CS Home 1939. Training Ship, Home 1940-45. Reserve 1945. Broken up, West of Scotland Shipbreaking, Troon 1946.

CERES

Built by John Brown, Clydebank. Laid down 11.7.1916. Launched 24.3.1917. Completed 1.6.1917. 6 LCS Grand Fleet 1917-19 (Baltic end 1918-19). 3 LCS Mediterranean 1919-29. Chatham Refit 1929-31. Reserve 1931-32. 3 CS Mediterranean 1932-33. Nore and Devonport Reserve 1933-39. 11 CS Home 1939. Mediterranean 1940. East Indies 1940-42. Eastern Fleet 1942-43. Reserve as Accommodation Ship 1944-45. Broken up, Hughes Bolckow, Blyth 1946.

Battle Honour: Normandy 1944.

COVENTRY *(ex Corsair)*

Built by Swan Hunter, Wallsend. Laid down 4.8.1916. Launched 6.7.1917. Completed 21.2.1918. 5 LCS Harwich 1918-19. 1 LCS Atlantic 1919-20. Commodore (D) Atlantic 1920-24. Flagship (D) Mediterranean 1924-28. Refit 1928-30. Flagship (D) Mediterranean 1930-34. Anti-aircraft conversion, Portsmouth 1935. Mediterranean 1936. Reserve 1936-39. 3 CS Mediterranean 1939. Humber Force 1939-40. Mediterranean 1940-41—damaged by near miss 17.5.41: repairs at Bombay Oct 41—June 42. Mediterranean 1942. Bombed and sunk by Italian aircraft off Tobruk, 14.9.1942. 63 lost

Battle Honours: Norway 1940, Spartivento 1940, Atlantic 1941, Greece 1941, Crete 1941, Libya 1941, Mediterranean 1941.

Curacoa. **Note wartime pennant number (D allocated to older cruisers at that time).**

CURACOA

Built at Pembroke Dockyard. Laid down 7.1916. Launched 5.5.1917. Completed 18.2.1918. Flagship, 5 LCS Harwich 1918-19. Flagship, 1 LCS Atlantic 1919—mined in Baltic, 5.1919; repairs to late 1919. 2 LCS Atlantic 1919-28 (Turkish crisis 1923). 3 CS Mediterranean 1929-32. Tender to Gunnery and Torpedo School, Portsmouth 1932-39. Anti-aircraft conversion, Chatham 1939-40. Home 1940-42. Accidentally rammed and sunk by liner *Queen Mary* west of Ireland, 2.10.1942. 338 lost.

Battle Honours: Norway 1940, Atlantic 1940, North Sea 1940-42, Arctic 1942.

CURLEW

Built by Armstrong, Walker. Laid down 21.8.1916. Launched 5.7.1917. Completed 14.12.1917. 5 LCS Harwich 1917-19 (Baltic early 1919). 1 LCS Atlantic (temp.) 1919. 5 LCS China 1920-22. 8 LCS America & W.I. 1922-26 (Empire Cruise 1923-24). 5 CS China 1927-28. Refit 1928-29. 3 CS Mediterranean 1929-33. Nore Reserve 1933-35. Anti-aircraft conversion, Chatham 1935-36. Nore Reserve 1937-39. Home 1939-40. Bombed and sunk by German aircraft off Norway, 26.5.1940. 9 lost.

Battle Honours: Norway 1940.

Curlew, 1937. Converted as an AA ship. 2 x 4 inch guns were later removed, in 1940, when multiple pompoms were fitted.

NATIONAL MARITIME MUSEUM

Capetown, 4th Sept 1925, at Vancouver BC showing trawler bow.

NATIONAL MARITIME MUSEUM

WRIGHT & LOGAN

Cairo, **Nov 1934.**

CAIRO

Built by Cammell Laird, Birkenhead. Laid down 28.11.1917. Launched 19.11.1918. Completed 14.10.1919. 5 LCS China 1919-22. 4 LCS East Indies 1922-25. 8 CS America & W.I. 1926-28. Flagship (D) Mediterranean 1928-30. Refit 1930-32. Flagship (D) Home 1932-37. Anti-aircraft conversion, Chatham 1938-39. Home 1939-42 (Channel Force 9.1939, Humber Force 1939-40). Mediterranean 1942. Torpedoed by Italian submarine *Axum* off Bizerta and finally sunk by destroyer HMS *Pathfinder*, 12.8.1942. 24 lost.

Battle Honours: Norway 1940, Atlantic 1940-41, Malta Convoys 1942.

CALCUTTA

Built by Armstrong, Walker. Laid down 18.10.1917. Launched 9.7.1918. Completed 8.1919. 8 LCS N. America & W.I. 1919-27 (Flagship 1925). Reserve 1927-28. Flagship, 6 CS Africa 1928-31. Nore Reserve 1931-38. Anti-aircraft conversion, Chatham 1938-39. Home 1939. Humber Force 1939-40. Mediterranean 1940-41. Bombed and sunk by German and Italian aircraft N.W. of Alexandria, 1.6.1941. 116 lost.

Battle Honours: Norway 1940, Dunkirk 1940, Greece 1941, Crete 1941, Libya 1941, Malta Convoys 1941, Mediterranean 1941.

CAPETOWN

Built by Cammell Laird, Birkenhead. Laid down 23.2.1918. launched 28.6.1919. Completed 10.4.1922. Completed at Pembroke Dockyard. 8 L.C.S. N. America & W.I. 1922-29. Devonport Reserve 1929-34. 5 CS China 1934-37. Devonport Reserve 1937-39. N. Atlantic (Gibraltar) 1939. Mediterranean 1939-40. East Indies 1941-42. Eastern Fleet 1942-43. Home 1944. Reserve as Accommodation Ship 1944-45. Broken up, Ward, Preston 1946.

Battle Honours: Mediterranean 1940, Normandy 1944.

Carlisle, **1919, with hangar fitted under bridge.**

CARLISLE (ex *Cawnpore)*

Built by Fairfield, Govan. Laid down 2.10.1917. Launched 9.7.1918. Completed 16.11.1918. 5 LCS Harwich 1918-19. 5 LCS China 1919-28. Refit 1928-29. 6 CS Africa 1929-37. Devonport Reserve 1937-39. Anti-aircraft conversion, Chatham 1939-40. Home 1940. Red Sea 1940. Mediterranean 1941-43. Bombed by Italian aircraft—constructive total loss 9.10.1943. Base ship at Alexandria 1943-45. Scrapped at Alexandria 1949.

Battle Honours: Norway 1940, Greece 1941, Crete 1941, Libya 1941-42, Sirte 1942, Malta Convoys 1941-42, Sicily 1943, Aegean 1943.

COLOMBO

Built by Fairfield, Govan. Laid down 8.12.1917. Launched 18.12.1918. Completed 18.6.1919. 5 LCS China 1919-20. 4 LCS East Indies 1921-26. 8 CS America & W.I. 1926-29. Chatham Refit 1929-31. 3 CS Mediterranean 1932. 4 CS East Indies 1933-36. Nore and Devonport Reserve 1936-39. N. Atlantic (Gibraltar) 1939. 11 CS Home 1939-40. East Indies 1940-42. Eastern Fleet 1942. Anti-aircraft conversion, Devonport, Aug 42-June 43. Mediterranean 1943-45. Reserve 1945. Broken up, Cashmore, Newport 1948.

Battle Honours: Atlantic 1939-44, Sicily 1943, Aegean 1944, South France 1944, Adriatic 1944.

DANAE CLASS (8 ships), *Emergency War Programmes*

Danae, Dauntless, Dragon (1st group).
Delhi, Dunedin, Durban ((2nd group).
Despatch, Diomede (3rd group).

Displacement (tons):	4,850 standard, 5,800 full load.
Dimensions (feet):	445pp, 472½oa x 46¼ x 14½ mean.
	(1st group 471oa, 3rd group beam 46¾).
(metres):	135.6pp, 144oa x 14.1 x 4.3 (143.6 oa, 14.2)
Machinery:	2 shaft Brown Curtis (*Dauntless, Diomede* Parsons) SR geared turbines.
	6 Yarrow boilers. 40,000 SHP = 29 knots.
Fuel:	Oil 1,050 tons. Range 2,300 miles at 27 knots.
Protection:	Full length belt 2in-1in (51mm-25mm) on 1 in (25mm) plating amidships.
	Partial plating over machinery 1in (25mm).
Armament:	6—6in, 2—4in AA (originally 2—3in AA in all but *Durban, Despatch* and *Diomede*: increased later to 3—4in AA), 2—2pdr AA, 12—21in (4x3) TT.
Complement:	350-450 (469 as flagship).

Erroneous intelligence reports indicated that Germany was building powerful new light cruisers, and the Admiralty responded by ordering the first three 'D' or Danae class ships in September 1916. These were stretched versions of the *Ceres*, lengthened by 20 feet to enable them to ship a sixth 6in gun between the fore funnel and the bridge. Their torpedo armament of four triple 21in tubes was the heaviest of any British cruiser.

The second batch of three ships ordered in July 1917 had trawler bows like the Capetowns, as did the third batch of six ships, slightly wider, ordered in March 1918. Of this last batch four were cancelled in November 1918. *Dragon* and *Dauntless* were completed with a large hangar within the bridge structure, later removed. For a while *Delhi, Despatch, Diomede* and *Durban* carried a revolving flying-off platform just forward of the searchlight position amidships.

A proposal in 1920 to complete *Despatch* as a Royal Yacht came to nothing.

Aesthetically the long, low, assymetrical shape of the 'D's lacked the classic balance and beauty of the 'C' classes. They were satisfactory ships, however, and represent the ultimate development of the original Arethusa concept.

DANAE

Built by Armstrong, Walker. Laid down 1.12.1916. Launched 26.1.1918. Completed 22.6.1918. 5 LCS Harwich 1918-19. 1 LCS Atlantic 1919-24—Empire Cruise 1923-24. 1 CS Mediterranean 1925-29. Refit 1929-30. 8 CS America & W.I. 1930-35. Devonport and Portsmouth Reserve 1935-39. 9 CS Atlantic 1939, China 1939-42. Eastern Fleet 1942-44. Home 1944-45—served as Polish *Conrad* Oct 1944-46. Broken up, Ward, Barrow 1948.

Battle Honour: Normandy 1944.

DAUNTLESS

Built by Palmers, Jarrow. Laid down 3.1.1917. Launched 10.4.1918. Completed 2.12.1918. Detached service, West Indies 1919. 1 LCS Atlantic 1919-24—Empire Cruise 1923-24. 1 CS Mediterranean 1925-27. China 1927. 8 CS America & W.I. 1928—grounded off Halifax, NS 2.7.1928 and badly damaged; repairs 1928-29. Reserve 1929-30. 8 CS America & W.I. 1930-32. 3 CS Mediterranean 1932-35. Portsmouth Reserve 1935-39. 9 CS S. Atlantic 1939, China 1939-42. Eastern Fleet 1942-43. Training Ship, Home 1943-45. Broken up, Ward, Inverkeithing 1946.

Battle Honour: Atlantic 1939.

DRAGON

Built by Scotts, Greenock. Laid down 24.1.1917. Launched 29.12.1917. Completed 16.8.1918. 5 LCS Harwich 1918-19. 1 LCS Atlantic 1919-25—Empire Cruise 1923-24. 1 CS Mediterranean 1925-28 (China, temp. 1927). Refit 1928-30. 8 CS America & W.I. 1930-38. Nore Reserve 1938-39. 7 CS Home 1939-40. Mediterranean, West Indies 1940. S. Atlantic 1940-41. Eastern Fleet 1942. Home 1943-44—manned by Polish Navy (name unchanged) from Jan 1943. Badly damaged by a Marder, 8.7.1944, and expended as a breakwater, Normandy beaches.

Battle Honour: Arctic 1944.

DELHI

Built by Armstrong, Walker. Laid down 29.10.1917. Launched 23.8.1918. Completed 7.6.1919. Flagship 1 LCS Atlantic 1919-24—Empire Cruise 1923-24. 1 CS Mediterranean 1925-28 (China, temp. 1927). Refit 1928-29. 8 CS America & W.I. 1929-32. 3 CS Mediterranean 1932-38. Devonport Reserve 1938-39. 12 CS/11 CS Home 1939-40. Mediterranean 1940. S. Atlantic 1941. Re-armed at New York Navy Yard, May-Dec. 1941 and completed Plymouth, Apr 1942. Home 1942. Mediterranean 1943-45. Damaged at Split 12.2.1945; repairs abandoned. Broken up, Cashmore, Newport 1948.

Battle Honours: Atlantic 1940, North Africa 1942, Sicily 1943, Salerno 1943, Anzio 1944, S. France 1944, Adriatic 1944.

DUNEDIN

Built by Armstrong, Walker. laid down 5.11.1917. Launched 19.11.1918. Completed 10.1919. 1 LCS Atlantic 1919-24. New Zealand Division 1924-37 (refit 1931-32). Portsmouth Reserve 1937-39. 12 CS/11 CS Home 1939-40. America & W.I. 1940. S. Atlantic 1941—captured a German auxiliary, 7.41. Torpedoed and sunk by German U-boat *U124* north of Pernambuco 24.11.1941. 418 lost.

Battle Honour: Atlantic 1941.

Dauntless showing searchlight platform amidships.

Dunedin, Oct 1938—note no topmasts.

Durban **in WW2 camouflage.**

DURBAN

Built by Scotts, Greenock. Laid down 22.6.1918. Launched 29.5.1919. Completed 31.10.1921. Completed at Devonport. 5 LCS China 1921-28. 8 CS America & W.I. 1928-30. Refit 1930-31. 8 CS America & W.I. 1931-34. 3 CS Mediterranean 1934-36. Portsmouth Reserve 1936-39. 9 CS S. Atlantic 1939, China 1939-42. Bombed during evacuation of Singapore, 12.2.42; repairs to Aug 42. Eastern Fleet 1942-43. Home 1944. Expended as a breakwater, Normandy beaches 9.6.1944.

Battle Honour: Normandy 1944.

DESPATCH

Built by Fairfield, Govan. Laid down 8.7.1918. Launched 24.9.1919. Completed 30.6.1922. Completed at Chatham. 5 LCS China 1922-27. 8 CS America & W.I. 1927-31. Reserve 1931-32. Refit 1932-33. 3 CS Mediterranean 1933-37. Portsmouth Reserve 1937-39. 9 CS S. Atlantic 1939. America & W.I. 1939-42. S. Atlantic 1942-43. Refit, Portsmouth Oct 43—May 44. Nore 1944. Reserve as Accommodation Ship 1945. Broke up, West of Scotland S'breaking, Troon 1946.

Battle Honours: Atlantic 1939, Spartivento 1940, Normandy 1944.

DIOMEDE

Built by Vickers, Barrow. Laid down 3.6.1918. Launched 29.4.1919. Completed 7.10.1922. Completed at Portsmouth. 5 LCS China 1922-25. New Zealand Division 1925-36 (refit 1929-30). Mediterranean 1936. Reserve 1936-39. Boys' Training Ship, Devonport 1938-39. 7 CS Home 1939-40. America & W.I. 1940-42. S. Atlantic 1942. Refit and conversion to Training Ship, Rosyth July 42-Sep 43. Training Ship, Home 1943-45. Reserve, Falmouth 1945. Broken up, Arnott Young, Dalmuir 1946.

Cancelled 11.1918: *Daedalus* (Armstrong), *Daring* (Beardmore), *Desperate* (Hawthorn Leslie), *Dryad* (Vickers).

BRITISH CRUISER DEPLOYMENT, NOVEMBER 1918

2 CS Grand Fleet
Minotaur (Flag), *Achilles, Shannon (Cochrane* detached to White Sea).

1 LCS Grand Fleet (Battle Cruiser Force)
Caledon (Flag), *Galatea, Inconstant, Phaeton, Royalist.*

2 LCS Grand Fleet (Battle Cruiser Force)
Birmingham (Flag), *Dublin, Melbourne, Sydney, Yarmouth.*

3 LCS Grand Fleet (Battle Cruiser Force)
Birkenhead (Flag), *Chatham, Chester, Southampton.*

4 LCS Grand Fleet
Calliope (Flag), *Cambrian, Caroline, Comus, Constance, Cordelia.*

5 LCS Harwich Force
Curacoa (Flag), *Canterbury, Centaur, Cleopatra, Concord, Conquest, Coventry, Curlew, Danae, Dragon.*

6 LCS Grand Fleet (Battle Cruiser Force)
Cardiff (Flag), *Calypso, Caradoc, Cassandra, Ceres.*

7 LCS Grand Fleet
Carysfort (Flag), *Aurora, Penelope, Undaunted.*

8 LCS Adriatic
Lowestoft (Flag), *Dartmouth, Glasgow, Gloucester, Weymouth.*

Attached to Grand Fleet Battle Squadrons
Bellona, Blanche, Blonde, Boadicea.

Attached to Flotillas
Castor (Commodore (D), Grand Fleet), *Champion* (13 DF Grand Fleet), *Fearless* (12 S/M Flot).

Aegean Squadron
Endymion, Forward, Liverpool, Sentinel, Skirmisher, Theseus.

N. America and W. Indies Squadron
Antrim, Berwick, Carnarvon, Cornwall, Cumberland, Devonshire, Donegal, Duke of Edinburgh, Highflyer, Isis, King Alfred, Leviathan, Roxburgh.

East Indies
Euryalus, Diana, Doris, Juno, Venus.

Red Sea
Grafton, Fox, Proserpine, Sapphire, Topaze.

Australian Fleet
Brisbane, Encounter, Pioneer, Psyche.

China
Suffolk, Kent.

Pacific
Lancaster.

SE Coast of America
Newcastle, Amethyst, Bristol.

Cape of Good Hope
Hyacinth (Flag), *Talbot.*

E. Coast of Africa
Challenger, Minerva.

W. Coast of Africa
Astraea (and *Bacchante* (Flag), at Sierra Leone).

Gibraltar
Edgar, Active, Adventure, (Attentive detached to White Sea).

Queenstown
Patrol.

1st Mining Squadron
Amphitrite.

Cardiff leading German High Seas Fleet to surrender Nov 1918.

EMERALD CLASS (2 ships), *Emergency War Programme*

Emerald, Enterprise

Displacement (tons):	7,550 standard (*Enterprise* 7,580).
Dimensions (feet):	535pp, 570oa x 54½ x 16¼ mean.
(metres):	163.1pp, 173.7oa x 16.6 x 5.0
Machinery:	4 shaft Brown Curtis SR geared turbines. 8 Yarrow small-tube boilers. 80,000 SHP = 33 knots.
Fuel:	Oil 1,746 tons. Range 1,380/3,850 miles at 32/20 knots.
Protection:	Full length belt 2in-1in (51mm-25mm) on 1in (25mm) plating amidships. Main deck over after engine room and partial plating over boiler rooms and forward engine rooms 1in (25mm). Magazines: 1in (25mm) crowns, ¾in (19mm) sides and ends.
Armament:	7—6in, 3—4in AA, 4—3pdr, 2—2pdr AA, 12 (later 16)—21in TT (4x3, later 4x4), 1 aircraft.
Complement:	572

In this class, ordered in March 1918, the overriding feature was a speed of 32 knots in the deep condition to meet a late 1917 Staff requirement for ships to counter the fast German cruisers then (mistakenly) thought to be under construction. Loosely described as enlarged 'D's with a seventh 6in gun, installed power was doubled and length increased by 100 feet to achieve the additional 3½—4 knots. In consequence, displacement rose by 3,000 tons and cost by £500,000 apiece. To maintain speed in bad weather the 'E's were given a long, high forecastle with a pronounced 'knuckle' which deflected spray and increased lift—a familiar feature in later cruisers.

The after engine room was given a full width protective deck, for, being behind a narrower part of the belt, it had less vertical protection than the other machinery spaces. Also, partial box citadel protection was given to the magazines; otherwise the 'E's were protected much as the 'D's. The boiler rooms were so spaced as to reduce the risk of a single hit causing a total loss of power. *Enterprise* mounted an experimental twin 6in turret forward, similar to the type adopted as secondary armament in the battleships *Nelson* and *Rodney*.

Due to material shortages only three ships were ordered: *Euphrates* was cancelled in November 1918, and the remaining pair were completed at a leisurely pace.

In 1934-35 both ships were fitted with a catapult in place of the aircraft platform: at the same time the mainmast was re-stepped forward of the third funnel, and all three funnels were raised by five feet.

Regarded as freakish ships at the time of their inception, it is interesting how their general characteristics broadly foreshadow the Leanders of ten years later.

Emerald. **Note old style bridge, original low funnels and A & B guns.**

EMERALD

Built by Armstrong, Elswick. Laid down 23.9.1918. Launched 19.5.1920. Completed 14.1.1926. Completed in Chatham. East Indies 1926-33 (China temp. 1927). Refit 1933-34. East Indies 1934-37. Reserve 1937-39. Atlantic escort 1939-40. East Indies 1941-42. Refit, Portsmouth Aug 42-Apr 43. Eastern Fleet 1943-44. Reserve 1945. Scrapped, West of Scotland S/breaking, Troon, 1948.

Battle Honours: Atlantic 1939-40, Normandy 1944.

ENTERPRISE

Built by John Brown, Clydebank. Laid down 23.6.1918. Launched 23.12.1919. Completed 31.3.1926. Completed at Devonport. East Indies 1926-34 (China, temp. 1927). Refit, 1934-35. East Indies 1935-38. Reserve 1938-39. Atlantic escort 1939-40. Home 1940. South Atlantic 1940-41. East Indies 1941-42. Eastern Fleet 1942. Refit, Clyde, Dec 42-Oct 43. Home 1943-44. With *Glasgow* sank 3 German destroyers, *T25, T26 & Z27* in Bay of Biscay 28.12.43. Reserve and trooping 1945. Scrapped, Cashmore, Newport, 1946.

Battle Honours: Atlantic 1939-40. Norway 1940. Biscay 1943. Normandy 1944.

Cancelled 11.1918: *Euphrates* (Fairfield).

Enterprise. Note more modern bridge and twin gun on A position, tripod mast stepped forward of after funnel, and aircraft aft.

CAVENDISH CLASS (5 ships), *Emergency War Programme*

Effingham, Frobisher, Hawkins, Raleigh, Vindictive

Displacement (tons):	9,750 normal, 12,190 deep load.
Dimensions (feet):	565pp, 605oa x 65 x 19¼ deep.
(metres):	172.2pp, 184.4oa x 19.8 x 5.9
Machinery:	4 shaft Brown Curtis (*Hawkins, Vindictive* Parsons) SR geared turbines.
	12 (*Effingham, Frobisher* 10) Yarrow boilers.
	Raleigh: 70,000 SHP = 31 knots, oil 1,480 tons, coal 860 tons.
	Hawkins, Vindictive: 60,000 SHP = 30 knots; oil 1,480 tons, coal 860 tons.
	Effingham, Frobisher: 65,000 SHP = 30½ knots; oil only 2,150 tons.
Protection:	Full length belt 3in-1½in (76mm-38mm). Upper deck 1½in-1in (38mm-25mm) over boiler rooms. Main deck 1½in-1in (38mm-25mm) over machinery.
	Magazines: 1in (25mm) crowns, ½in (13mm) sides. Bulges.
Armament:	7—7.5in, 6—12pdr (3in), 4—3in AA, 4—3pdr, 6—21in TT (2 submerged), beam, 4 above water, fixed).
Complement:	712-749

During the early months of the First World War, the Royal Navy had been hard pressed to round up a relatively small number of German light cruisers. This, and (erroneous) reports that German commerce raiders were to be more heavily armed, prompted the Admiralty to build its first true trade protection cruisers for more than a decade. In June 1915 the DNC was asked to design an 'Improved Birmingham', with a heavier armament and better speed and protection.

In fact, *Cavendish* bore little relation to the Birminghams: the hull, with bulges and sloping sides, was scaled down from that of the 'light battlecruiser' *Courageous*, whilst the general arrangement of armament and protection was closer to that of *Ceres* except for the light 'box' protection to the magazines. The choice of 7.5in guns ensured superiority over German light cruisers and armed raiders, and their shells at 200 lbs. were the largest that could be loaded by hand.

The boilers were intended for dual firing (four coal and six oil) to assist operations in distant waters. However, *Effingham* and *Frobisher* were completed as oil-only burners, and *Hawkins* was so converted in 1929, but with only eight boilers and 55,000 SHP.

Late in 1917, *Cavendish* was earmarked for completion as an aircraft carrier and renamed *Vindictive* in June 1918 to commemorate the old cruiser of Zeebrugge and Ostend fame. Reconverted to a cruiser in 1923-25, she retained a hangar with crane and catapult in place of 'B' gun. Later disarmed and with boilers mutilated, she became Cadet Training Ship, and served as a Repair Ship in the Second World War.

Hawkins completed in 1919, but construction of the other three was not pressed. Magnificent seaboats and the only cruisers in the post-war Fleet specifically intended for trade protection, Britain's desire to retain them was largely responsible for the somewhat artificial Washington Treaty limitations of 8in guns and 10,000 tons.

In 1936-38, *Effingham* was re-armed with nine 6in guns and four (later eight) 4in AA, while the submerged torpedo tubes were replaced by deck mountings. The two after boilers were removed, and all the uptakes trunked into a single funnel. The meagre deck protection, however, was left unaltered.

Ironically, *Effingham* was an early war loss (the second of the class to be wrecked), while the unmodernised *Frobisher* and *Hawkins* served until 1944, mainly on the trade routes.

EFFINGHAM

Built at Portsmouth Dockyard. Laid down 6.4.1917. Launched 8.6.1921. Completed 7.1925. 4 LCS East Indies 1925-32. Reserve 1932-36. Rearmed 1937. America & W.I. 1938-39. 12 CS Atlantic escort and Home Fleet 1940. Wrecked on uncharted rock near Harstad, Norway, 18.5.1940 and sunk by surface forces, 21.5.1940.

Battle Honours: Atlantic 1939-40, Norway 1940.

Frobisher **during WW2 with radar fitted and tripod mainmast.**

FROBISHER

Built at Devonport Dockyard. Laid down 2.8.1916. Launched 20.3.1920. Completed 20.9.1924. 1 LCS Mediterranean 1924-29 (Flagship 1928-29). 2 CS Atlantic 1929-30. Reserve 1930-32 (Flagship, VACR). Cadets' Training Ship 1932-37. Devonport Reserve 1937-39. Harbour service as Cadets' TS, Portsmouth 1939. Rearmed 1939-42. 4 CS Eastern fleet 1942-44. 1 CS Home 1944. Damaged forward by torpedo, 8.8.1944; temporary repairs at Chatham and conversion to TS at Rosyth 1944-45. Cadets' Training Ship 1945-47. Devonport Reserve 1947-49. Broken up, Cashmore, Newport 1949.

Battle Honour: Normandy 1944.

Hawkins **photographed during the early twenties.**

HAWKINS

Built at Chatham Dockyard. Laid down 3.6.1916. Launched 1.10.1917. Completed 23.7.1919. Flagship, 5 LCS China 1919-29. Chatham Refit 1929. 2 CS Atlantic 1929-31. Portsmouth Reserve 1931-32. 4 CS East Indies 1932-35. Portsmouth Reserve 1935-39. Rearmed 1939. South Atlantic 1940-41. East Indies 1941. Portsmouth refit, Dec 1941-May 1942. Eastern fleet 1942-44. 1 CS Home 1944. Paid off, Rosyth, 7.1944—conversion to Training Ship abandoned. Rosyth Reserve 1945. Laid up, Falmouth 1945-47. Target trials, Portsmouth 1947. Broken up by Arnott Young, Dalmuir, 1947.

Battle Honour: Normandy 1944.

RALEIGH

Built by Beardmore, Dalmuir. Laid down 9.12.1915. Launched 28.8.1919. Completed 7.1921. 8 LCS America & W.I. 1921-22 (Flagship 1921). Wrecked in thick fog in Straits of Belleisle, Labrador, 8.8.1922.

VINDICTIVE (ex *Cavendish)*

Built at Harland & Wolff, Belfast. Laid down 29.6.1916. Launched 17.1.1918. Completed 21.9.1918. Completed as aircraft carrier. Grand Fleet 1918-19. Baltic 1919-ran aground and severely damaged. Repairs, Portsmouth 1919-21. Portsmouth Reserve 1921-23 (trooping). Re converted to cruiser, Chatham 1923-25. 5 LCS China 1925-28. 2 CS Atlantic 1928-29. Refit 1929-30. Reserve 1930-36. Converted to training ship 1936-37. Cadets' TS 1937-39. Converted to repair ship 1939-40. South Atlantic 1940-42. Mediterranean 1943-44. Home and Reserve 1945. Broken up by Hughes Bolckow, Blyth, 1946.

Battle Honour: Norway 1940.

Vindictive as completed as an aircraft carrier.

OFFICIAL

Effingham, Aug 1939.

WRIGHT & LOGAN

BRITISH CRUISER DEPLOYMENT, JANUARY 1927

Atlantic Fleet:

2 CS	*Curacoa* (Flag*)*, *Cambrian, Canterbury, Comus.*
Flotillas	*Centaur (Commodore* (D)).

Training:

Portsmouth	Signal School. *Yarmouth.*
	Gunnery Firing Ship. *Champion.*

Reserve & Refit:

Nore	*Caledon, Calliope, Cleopatra, Constance* (all in refit).
Portsmouth	*Weymouth* (Flag of VACR).
Devonport	*Dartmouth, Carysfort, Curlew* (all Reserve).

Mediterranean:

1 CS	*Frobisher* (Flag), *Danae, Dauntless, Delhi, Dragon.*
3 CS	*Cardiff* (Flag), *Calypso, Ceres, Concord.*
Destroyers	*Coventry* (Rear Admiral (D)).

East Indies:

4 CS	*Effingham* (Flag, C-in-C).

Africa:

6 CS	*Birmingham (*Flag, C-in-C), *Lowestoft.*

China:

5 CS	*Hawkins* (Flag, C-in-C), *Caradoc* (temp. from Med.), *Carlisle, Despatch, Durban, Emerald* (temp. from E.I.), *Enterprise* (temp. from E.I.), *Vindictive.*

North America and West Indies:

8 CS	*Calcutta* (Flag, C-in-C), *Cairo, Capetown, Colombo.*

New Zealand Division:

Diomede, Dunedin.

Royal Australian Navy:

Sydney (Commodore commanding HMA Fleet), *Adelaide, Melbourne* (temp. training), *Brisbane* (refit).

1928-49: TREATY LIMITATIONS

Kent, London, Dorsetshire, York, Leander, Amphion and Arethusa classes

At the end of the First World War, all cruisers prior to the Weymouth and Caroline classes were rapidly discarded. Admiral of the Fleet Earl Jellicoe estimated that an absolute minimum of seventy cruisers was necessary for the protection of British seaborne trade, but the Royal Navy had to be content with fifty for most of the inter-war period. The formal dropping of the staff requirement from seventy cruisers to fifty in 1930 only came to terms with what for some years had been the reality. The planning assumption known as the 'Ten Year Rule'—that the Royal Navy would not be involved in a major war for the next ten years—was adopted in 1919 and not dropped until 1933. Until Germany again began to pose a serious threat, the strength of the British Fleet was assessed as that necessary to defeat Japan in the Western Pacific.

The Washington Naval Treaty of 1922 halted a developing naval arms race by agreeing tonnage quotas for capital ships between the major Powers, and by setting an age limit for capital ships of 20 years, before the expiry of which they could not be replaced. The tonnage quotas for Great Britain, the United States and Japan were in the ratios 5:5:3; Britain's acceptance of parity with the US was a recognition of post-war economic and industrial realities. To comply with the Treaty, a whole new generation of giant battleships and battlecruisers projected by each of the major Powers had to be cancelled, and numerous old dreadnoughts were scrapped. Future capital ships were to be limited to 35,000 tons standard, but because of the age limit rules, none could be started before 1932 except for the British *Nelson* and *Rodney*. Cruisers were affected only indirectly by a provision that any ships over 10,000 tons standard, or with larger than 8in guns, would be counted against capital ship quotas. This clause, which enabled Britain to retain the Cavendish class, led unexpectedly to the emergence of a new type of 'treaty cruiser' built right up to these arbitrary limits.

In the wake of the Treaty, the Royal Navy was anxious to build up its cruiser strength to seventy ships, and to replace the numerous 'C' and 'D' classes, designed principally for North Sea operations, with ships more apt for work on the trade routes. The Admiralty had envisaged building forty 10,000 ton cruisers over five years, starting with eight ships in the 1924 Programme. However, the Labour government only authorised five cruisers in 1924, Australia adding two more. Another five year programme was drawn up under the Conservatives in 1925, covering the years 1925-26 to 1929-30. This provided for nine further 'Class A' 10,000 ton cruisers and seven smaller 'Class B' ships of 8,000 tons. Of these, only six 'Class A' and two 'Class B' cruisers were actually built. The third projected 'Class B' ship was built as the 6in gun *Leander*.

Despite severe cutbacks in the programme, its initial vigour gave Britain an early commanding lead in Treaty cruisers. The penalty for having led the field was that the British ships were inferior to some of their later foreign counterparts, particularly in protection. Partly because of this, the Royal Navy never applied the American term 'heavy cruiser' to its Treaty ships. In fact it was reckoned that the 8in gun cruiser had the advantage over modern 6in cruisers only at extreme ranges in good visibility; shorter ranges favoured the 6in ship, with its better rate of fire and superior protection.

It had long been argued in Britain that the smaller cruiser was better suited to the Royal Navy's requirements and more likely to be built in the necessary numbers. Prior to the London Naval Conference of 1930, Britain signalled her intention of abandoning the Treaty type in favour of 6in gun cruisers.

The London Naval Treaty of 1930 set tonnage quotas and age limits for cruisers, destroyers and submarines as the Washington Treaty had done for capital ships. Cruisers were divided into two categories: type A with guns over 6.1in, and type B with guns of 6.1in or under. By the end of 1936 the British Empire was to be limited to 146,800 tons of the larger type, against the United States' 180,000 tons and Japan's 108,400 tons. Quotas for the smaller cruisers were 192,200 tons for Great Britain, 143,500 for the USA and 100,450 for Japan. The Treaty took account of America's desire to continue building type A cruisers, and Britain's preference for the smaller type. Age limits meant that cruisers laid down before 1920 could be replaced once they were 16 years old, whereas more recent ships could not be replaced before they were 20. France and Italy, which were signatories at Washington, refused to be bound by the Treaty of London.

In concrete terms, Britain's quota for Type A cruisers would be fully taken up in the thirteen 'Counties' (including the two Australians) and two 'Yorks'; The Cavendish class would have to be 'demilitarised' or scrapped by 1936. The quota for type B cruisers allowed numbers to remain fairly constant, but as Britain in an unreciprocated gesture had restricted completions to the end of 1936 to 91,000 tons, the quota could only be fully taken up by retaining over-age ships. Consequently, all hopes of maintaining seventy cruisers had to be abandoned, and the old staff requirement was reduced to fifty ships.

The 91,000 ton limit on new cruisers affected the Estimates for the years 1929-30 to 1933-34. The original intention was to build fourteen Leanders, later changed to nine Leanders (including the Amphions) and six Arethusas, and finally to eight Leanders, three Arethusas and two Southamptons.

That the naval treaties between the wars undoubtedly helped restrain rivalries and naval expenditure was all to the good. But economic cutbacks after Washington and an unduly altruistic spirit at London depressed Britain's naval programme too far for safety. In 1936, just three years before a major war, Britain had an elderly fleet, and of her inadequate total of fifty cruisers only twenty-three could be called modern.

THE COUNTIES

Warship design is usually evolutive, such that each successive class can be explained in the light of some previous design. This is not true of the Counties, whose design process needs some special explanation.

Correctly anticipating that the Washington signatories would build right up to Treaty limits, the Admiralty set its own requirements for a so-called 'Treaty cruiser': eight 8in guns in twin turrets, a speed of 33 knots, and high freeboard for good seakeeping. It was estimated that a balanced design with these characteristics would turn out at around 13,000 tons. Obviously, keeping within the 10,000 ton limit would demand the compromise of some military quality—in this case, protection. Dropping speed to 31 knots eased the situation somewhat, but still only about 1,000 tons could be allocated to protection. This was sufficient to give the boiler and engine rooms an armoured deck and bulkheads, and to provide three box citadels for the magazines—but no belt. Robust framing and plating partly made up for the lack of protection, but the absence of side armour drew fierce criticism and invited comparison with the wretched Diadems of 30 years before.

The high freeboard was continued right aft, largely to stiffen the long hull and allowing, incidentally, roomy 8ft deckheads. A large metacentric height meant that the Counties could ship a great deal of water without capsizing, but it also gave them a rather stiff roll.

The 8in gun turrets were 50 tons overweight; it took some years to get them working satisfactorily, and they never achieved their designed rate of fire. Initially there were problems with the torpedoes, which, launched from a height of 27ft, tended to break up or detonate on hitting the water.

Controversial ships, partly because of their unarmoured sides but above all because they were much larger than Britain needed and seemed, on paper at least, a poor return for their large expense, the Royal Navy's eventual abandonment of the Treaty type was greeted with relief and hailed as a return to sanity. However, their fine presence, spacious accommodation, their matchless steaming qualities and weatherliness, earned the Counties an unexpectedly high reputation.

KENT CLASS (5 ships), *1924 Programme and R.A.N.* (2 ships)

Berwick, Cornwall, Cumberland, Kent, Suffolk, Australia, Canberra

Displacement (tons):	9,750 standard, 13,450 full load.
Dimensions (feet):	590pp, 630oa x 68¼ x 16¼
(metres):	179.8pp, 192oa x 20.8 x 5
Machinery:	4 shaft Parsons (*Berwick* and RAN ships Brown Curtis SR geared turbines. 8 Admiralty 3-drum boilers. 80,000 SHP = 31½ knots.
Fuel:	Oil 3,400 tons. Range 3,100/13,300 miles at 31/12 knots.
Protection:	Machinery; deck 1⅜in (35mm), bulkheads 1in (25mm), side plating 1in (25mm)*. Main magazines; crowns 3in-1in (76mm-25mm), sides 4⅜in-1in (111mm-25mm), end 2½in-1in (64mm-25mm). Secondary magazine; crown 2in (51mm), sides 3⅜in (86mm), ends 1½in-½in (38mm-13mm). Steering gear 1½in (38mm) deck.
Armament:	8-8in (4x2), 4—4in AA (4x1, later 4x2), 8-2pdr (2x4), (8—.5in MG(2x4) added 1936-39), 8—21in TT (2x4)—removed from all except *Kent* and RAN vessels 1936-38, 1 aircraft from 1930-31 (later 3 except in *Kent* and RAN vessels).
Complement:	700

Britain's first Treaty cruisers, distinguished from the later Counties by their prominent external bulges. Funnels were raised by 15 feet (18 feet in Australian ships) before completion to overcome smoke problems experienced in *Berwick* and *Cumberland* on trials. By the standards of their day, the Kents had a remarkably strong anti-aircraft armament.

As completed, the class was found to be on average 250 tons inside the Treaty limit, and it was decided to take up some of this margin with increased ammunition stowage and by providing an aircraft, catapult and crane. These modifications were effected in 1930-31, and raised standard displacement to around 9,900 tons.

The Royal Navy ships underwent extensive reconstructions in 1935-38: a narrow 5in belt was added at the waterline behind the bulges; the AA battery was increased, and a large hangar and new aircraft arrangements were added aft. After removal of torpedo tubes and obsolete equipment, displacement had risen to about 10,300 tons—a gentlemen's agreement permitted a 3% 'growth' in Treaty cruisers during reconstruction. Even so, *Cumberland* and *Suffolk* had their hulls cut down aft to stay within limits, while *Kent*, always heavier than her sisters, did not receive a hangar in her refit. *Australia* and *Canberra* were refitted in 1938-40 on similar lines to the *Kent*.

War modifications included the fitting of radar, tripod masts, additional light AA guns, and the removal of aircraft arrangements and hangars. *Australia* was stripped of a lot of tophamper, including 'X' turret, during her 1945 refit; she, and *Cumberland* as a trials ship, were the only Kents to see much post war service.

*All received narrow belt, 5½in (140mm) top—1in (25mm) bottom, 1936-40.

Berwick, **Nov 45, showing end of war fit.**

BERWICK

Built by Fairfield, Govan. Laid down 15.9.1924. Launched 30.3.1926. Completed 15.2.1928. 5 CS China 1928-36. Mediterranean 1936-37. Refit 1937-38. America & W.I. 1938-39. Home 1939-40—intercepted two German blockade runners, *Wolfsburg* and *Uraguay*, which scuttled themselves, 3.1940. Damaged by cruiser gunfire NW of Azores, 25.12.1940—repairs at Portsmouth and Rosyth to 6.1941. Home 1941-45. Trooping to Far East 1945-46. Broken up, Hughes Bolckow, Blyth 1948.

Battle Honours: Atlantic 1939, Norway 1940, Spartivento 1940, Arctic 1941-44.

·*Cornwall,* **in July 1936.**

CORNWALL

Built at Devonport Dockyard. Laid down 9.10.1924. Launched 11.3.1926. Completed 8.5.1928. 5 CS China 1928-36. Chatham Refit 1936-37. 2 CS Home 1938. 5 CS China 1939. South Atlantic 1940-41—sank German raider *Pinguin* in S. Atlantic, 7.5.1941. East Indies 1941-42. With *Dorsetshire*, sunk from bombing by Japanese carrier aircraft W. of Ceylon, Easter Sunday, 5.4.1942. 198 lost.

Cumberland **as trials ship, note torpedo tube and "fish" on stern.**

CUMBERLAND

Built by Vickers Armstrong, Barrow. Laid down 18.10.1924. Launched 16.3.1926. Completed 23.2.1928. 5 CS China 1928-35. Chatham Refit 1935-36. 5 CS China 1936-38. 2 CS Home 1939. South Atlantic 1939-41. Chatham Refit, July-Oct 1941. Home 1941-44 (Arctic convoys). Eastern fleet 1944. 5 CS East Indies 1945. Trooping to Far East 1945-46. Reserve 1946-49. Conversion to Trials Cruiser 1949-51. Gunnery Trials, Home/Mediterranean 1951-59. Broken up, Cashmore, Newport 1959.

Battle Honours: North Africa 1942, Arctic 1942-43, Sabang 1944, Burma 1945.

Kent **with tripod masts—no hangar fitted.**

KENT

Built at Chatham Dockyard. Laid down 15.11.1924. Launched 16.3.1926. Completed 25.6.1928. 5 CS China 1928-36. Chatham Refit 1937-38. 5 CS China 1938-39. 4 CS East Indies 1939-40. Mediterranean 1940. Damaged 9.1940; repairs to 9.1941. 1 CS Home 1941-44. Reserve, Gareloch (flagship) 1945. Chatham Reserve 1946-47. Broken up, W. of Scotland Shipbreaking, Troon, 1948.

Battle Honours: Atlantic 1940, Mediterranean 1940, Arctic 1942-43, Normandy 1944.

SUFFOLK

Built at Portsmouth Dockyard. Laid down 30.9.1924. Launched 16.2.1926. Completed 31.5.1928. 5 CS China 1928-35. Portsmouth Refit 1935-36. 5 CS China 1937-39. Home 1939-40. Bombed off Stavanger 17.4.1940; repairs on Clyde to 2.1941. Home 1941-42. Eastern fleet 1943-44. East Indies 1945. Trooping 1945-46. Broken up, Cashmore, Newport 1948.

Battle Honours: Norway 1940, *Bismarck* Action 1941, Arctic 1941-42, Burma 1945.

Suffolk, in 1942 with hangar, tripod masts and cut down stern.

HMAS *Canberra* **showing bulges**

HMAS *Australia* **arriving at Malta—May 1935.**

AUSTRALIA

Built by John Brown, Clydebank. Laid down 26.8.1925. Launched 17.3.1927. Completed 24.4.1928. Australia 1928-34. Mediterranean 1935-36 (exchanged duties with *Sussex*). Australia 1936-38. Refit 1938-39. Australia 1939-40. East Indies 1941. Australia 1942-45. Badly damaged at Lingayen Gulf, 1.1945; repairs and refit, Devonport and Sydney 1945. Reserve, Sydney 1946-47. Australia 1947-54. Broken up, Ward, Barrow, 1955.

Battle Honours: Coral Sea 1942, Savo Island 1942, Guadalcanal 1942-43, Lingayen Gulf 1945.

CANBERRA

Built by John Brown, Clydebank. Laid down 9.9.1925. Launched 31.3.1927. Completed 10.7.1928. Australia 1928-40. South Atlantic and Australia 1940. East Indies 1941—sank AMC *Coburg* in Indian Ocean, 5.1942. Torpedoed by Japanese surface forces off Savo Island, and finally sunk by destroyer USS *Ellet*, 9.8.1942. 84 lost.

Battle Honour: Savo Island 1942.

LONDON CLASS (4 ships), *1925 Programme and*
DORESETSHIRE CLASS (2 ships), *1926 Programme*

Devonshire, London, Shropshire, Sussex
Dorsetshire, Norfolk

Displacement (tons):	9,750 standard, 13,220 full load (*Dorsetshire* 9,900/13,290).
Dimensions (feet):	595pp, 633oa c 66 x 17
(metres):	181.4pp, 192.9oa x 20.1 x 5.2
Machinery:	4 shaft Parsons SR geared turbines. 8 Admiralty 3-drum boilers. 80,000 SHP = 32¼ knots.
Fuel:	Oil 3,210 tons. Range 2,930/12,500 miles at 31/12 knots.
Protection:	Machinery; deck 1⅜in (35mm), bulkheads 1in (25mm), side plating 1in (25mm). Main magazines; crowns 3in-1in (76mm-25mm), sides 4⅜in-1in (111mm-25mm), ends 2½in-1in (64mm-25mm). Secondary magazine; crown 2in (51mm), sides 3⅜in (86mm), ends 1½in-½in (38mm-13mm). Steering gear 1½in (38mm) deck.
Armament: 1932	8—8in (4x2), 4—4in AA, 8—2pdr (2x4) except *Dorsetshires* 4—2pdr (singles), 8—21in TT (2x4), 1 aircraft.
1939	**8—8in (4x2), 8—4in AA singles except** *Dorsetshire* and, later, *London* (4x2), 16—2pdr (2x8—*Dorsetshires* only), 8—.5in AA (2x4), 8—21in TT (2x4), 1 aircraft.
Complement:	700

Generally similar to the Kents, the Londons had a modified hull form with internal rather than external bulges, giving an extra ½ knot, and the bridge structure was about 15 feet further aft, allowing the forward turrets to fire abaft the beam. Aircraft arrangements were included in the design (though not fitted until 1930-32), and compared with the Kents there were minor differences in protection.

The Dorsetshires were virtually repeat Londons, but with supposedly lightweight Mk. II 8in turrets of the type adopted in *York*, and their main magazine armour was extended to cover the shell rooms. The weight for this additional protection was to be found by careful attention to detail and by using hull plating on the low side of thickness tolerance. Weight calculations were upset by the Mk II turrets turning out much heavier than expected.

Modifications in the 1930s were confined mainly to augmenting the 4in and other AA batteries. Plans were drawn for extensive reconstructions, including new, lighter machinery, but only *London* was taken in hand between 1939-41, and the scale of her refit was cut back. Although her superstructure was completely rebuilt on 'Fiji' lines, internal arrangements were largely unchanged and she retained her original machinery. As with the Kents, a narrow 4½in belt was worked into the *London* abreast the machinery and magazine compartments.

Wartime modifications followed the usual pattern. Aircraft arrangements were removed from all, including *London*, and in 1944-45, 'X' turret was taken out of *Devonshire* and *Sussex*.

After the war, the survivors served on for a few years. *Devonshire*, partially disarmed, replaced *Frobisher* as Cadet Training Ship in 1947.

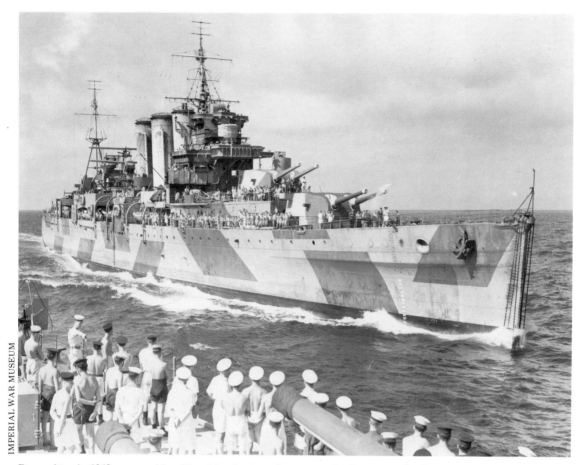

Devonshire, **in 1942, approaching** *Mauritius* **for transfer—note tripod masts and radar.**

DEVONSHIRE

Built at Devonport Dockyard. Laid down 16.3.1926. Launched 22.10.1927. Completed 18.3.1929. 1 CS Mediterranean 1929-32. 5 CS China 1932-33. 1 CS Mediterranean 1933-39. 1 CS Home 1939-41—sank German AMC *Atlantis* in S. Atlantic, 22.11.1941. Eastern fleet 1942-43. Refit, Liverpool, May 1943-Mar 1944 (X turret removed). 1 CS Home 1944-45. Refit 1946-47. Cadets' Training Ship 1947-53. Broken up, Cashmore, Newport 1954.

Battle Honours: Norway 1940, Arctic 1941, Diego Suarez 1942.

LONDON

Built at Portsmouth Dockyard. Laid down 23.2.1926. Launched 14.9.1927. Completed 31.1.1929. 1 CS Mediterranean 1929-39. Reconstructed, Chatham 1939-41. Home and South Atlantic 1941-44—intercepted German supply vessels *Esso Hamburg, Egerland* and *Babitonga* which scuttled themselves, 6.1941. Eastern fleet 1944. 5 CS East Indies 1945-46. Chatham Refit 1946-47. 5 CS Far East 1947-49. Badly damaged by Chinese gunfire trying to rescue HMS *Amethyst* in Yangste river, 21.4.1949 (23 hits, 70 dead, 35 wounded). Paid off, Chatham 1949. Broken up, Ward, Barrow 1950.

Battle Honours: Atlantic 1941, Arctic 1941-43.

London, **Sept 1947, as reconstructed, hull had to be strenthened to cope with extra weight of superstructure.**

SHROPSHIRE

Built by Beardmore, Dalmuir. Laid down 24.2.1927. Launched 5.7.1928. Completed 12.9.1929. 1 CS Mediterranean 1929-39. South Atlantic 1939-40. Red Sea and East Indies 1940-41. Home and South Atlantic 1941-42. Chatham Refit, Nov 1942-June 1943 prior to transfer to Australia (replaced *Canberra*). Australia 1943-48. Laid up, Australia 1948-55. Broken up, Arnott Young, Dalmuir and Troon, 1955.

Battle Honours: Atlantic 1941, Arctic 1941.

Shropshire **in wartime camouflage.**

Sussex in the Mediterranean—where the Counties spent much time prewar.

SUSSEX

Built by Beardmore, Dalmuir. Laid down 24.2.1927. Launched 5.7.1928. Completed 12.9.1929. 19.3.1929. 1 CS Mediterranean 1929-34. Australia 1934-36 (exchanged duties with *Australia*). 1 CS Mediterranean 1936-39. South Atlantic 1939—intercepted German blockade runner *Watussi* which scuttled herself, 2.12.1939. East Indies 1940. Home 1940. Bombed in dock at Greenock, 9.1940 and partially capsized; repairs to 8.1942. Home 1942-43—sank German tanker *Hohenfriedburg*, 26.2.1943. Eastern fleet 1943-44. Sheerness Refit (X turret removed) June 1944-Apr 1945. East Indies 1945-46. Refit 1946-47. 5 CS Far East 1947-49. Paid off 2.2.1949. Sold 1950 and broken up by Arnott Young, Dalmuir, 1955.

Dorsetshire class

DORSETSHIRE

Built at Portsmouth Dockyard. Laid down 21.9.1927. Launched 29.1.1929. Completed 30.9.1930. Atlantic/Home 1930-33. Flagship, 6 CS Africa 1933-35. 5 CS China 1935-39. South Atlantic 1940-41—sank German auxilliary in S. Atlantic, 12.1941. Eastern Fleet 1942. With *Cornwall*, sunk from bombing by Japanese carrier aircraft W. of Ceylon, Easter Sunday, 5.4.1942. 227 lost.

Battle Honours: *Bismarck* Action 1941, Atlantic 1941.

NORFOLK

Built by Fairfield, Govan. Laid down 8.7.1927. Launched 12.12.1928. Completed 30.4.1930. Atlantic/Home 1930-32. America & W.I. 1932-35. Flagship 4 CS East Indies 1935-39. 1 CS Home 1939-43. (Bombed in Scapa Flow, 16.3.1940; repairs on Clyde to 6.1940.) Portsmouth Refit (X turret removed) Jan-Nov 1944. 1 CS Home 1944-45. East Indies 1945-49. Reserve 1949. Broken up, Cashmore, Newport 1950.

Battle Honours: Atlantic 1941, *Bismarck* Action 1941, North Africa 1942, Arctic 1941-43, North Cape 1943, Norway 1945.

Dorsetshire. **She gave *Bismarck* the "coup de grace".**

Norfolk. **X turret removed and tripod masts fitted.**

Cancelled 'Surrey' class (2 ships), *1928 Programme*

Surrey, (Portsmouth Dockyard), *Northumberland* (Devonport Dockyard).

An interesting 10,000 ton cruiser design in which speed was sacrificed for much improved protection. Displacement was 10,000 tons standard, 12,664 tons full load, and dimensions 600ft (oa) x 64ft x 21½ft (182.9m x 19.5m x 6.6m). Armament would have been 8—8in (2x4), 4—4in AA (4X1), 4—3pdr (saluting), 16—2pdr pompoms, 8—21in TT (2x4), and 2 aircraft . 60,000 SHP would have given 30 knots. Protection was on the pattern of the Yorks but generally thicker. They would have resembled *Exeter* in appearance, but with four turrets, and the forecastle deck extended aft to 'X' turret. Neither ship was laid down; both were suspended in August 1929 and cancelled in January 1930 in advance of the London Naval Conference.

YORK CLASS (2 ships)

York (1926 Programme), *Exeter* (1927 Programme)

Displacement (tons):	8,250 *York*, 8,390 *Exeter* standard, 10,500 full load.
Dimensions (feet):	540pp, 575oa x 57 (58 *Exeter*) x 17
(metres):	164.6pp, 175.3oa x 17.4 (17.7) x 5.2
Machinery:	4 shaft Parsons SR geared turbines. 8 Admiralty 3-drum boilers. 80,000 SHP = 32¼ knots.
Fuel:	Oil 1,900 tons. Range 10,000 miles at 14 knots.
Protection:	Machinery; belt 3in (76mm), bulkheads 1in (25mm), deck 1⅜in (35mm). Magazines (3); crowns 2½in (64mm), sides 4in-1in (102mm-25mm), ends 2½in (64mm). Steering gear 1½in (38mm).
Armament:	6—8in (3x2), 4—4in AA, 2—2pdr AA, 6—21in TT (2x3), 1 aircraft.
Complement:	620

Three turret derivatives of the Counties, designated 'Class B' cruisers. By omitting 'X' turret the hull could be shortened by 50 feet, and as high continuous freeboard was not necessary for strength, the forecastle deck terminated amidships. With topweight reduced, beam could be pared by 9 feet, and the Yorks turned out at around 1,750 tons lighter than the Counties. They needed the same machinery as the larger ships for a speed of 32 knots, but bunker capacity was necessarily less.

Weight of armour (970 tons in *York*, 980 tons in *Exeter*) was about the same as in the Counties but better distributed, notably in the provision of a 3in belt to complete the machinery citadel.

Originally *York* was to have had three funnels, making her affinity to the Counties more apparent, but as the leading funnel was rather close to the bridgework, it was trunked back into the second. *York's* bridge was a high pagoda-like structure to give command above the aircraft and catapult, never fitted, but which were to have been carried atop 'B' turret. *Exeter* had a lower, neater box-like bridge structure, and her funnels and masts were stepped without rake to make the estimation of her course more difficult. She was also a foot wider than *York*.

As economical alternatives to the 10,000 ton Counties the Yorks hardly succeeded, for the one-eighth saving in cost was not significant enough. But they were more soundly conceived than the Counties, possessing a better all round balance of military qualities, and Service opinion did not rate the sacrifice of one 8in turret too great a loss.

Despite the promise shown by the Yorks, opinion in Britain swung against the 8in gun cruiser altogether, and the type was abandoned.

York with tall bridge and raked funnels.

YORK

Built by Palmers, Jarrow. Laid down 5.1927. Launched 17.7.1928. Completed 1.5.1930. Atlantic 1930-33. America & W.I. 1934-39. Atlantic escort 1939. Home 1940. Mediterranean 1940-41—sank Italian destroyer *Artigliere* in Sicilian Channel, 12.10.1940. Disabled by torpedo from Italian skiff, 25.3.1941. Attempts to save her were frustrated by enemy aircraft attacks, and she was finally abandoned in Suda Bay, 22.5.1941. Salved in 1952 and scrapped at Bari.

Battle Honours: Atlantic 1939, Norway 1940, Mediterranean 1940-41, Malta Convoys 1941.

EXETER

Built at Devonport Dockyard. Laid down 1.8.1928. Launched 18.7.1929. Completed 23.7.1931. Atlantic 1931-33. America & W.I. 1933-39 (Mediterranean, temp. 1936). South Atlantic 1939—severely damaged in River Plate action. Repairs at Falklands, Dec 1939-Jan 1940, and refitted at Devonport to Mar 1941. 1 CS Home 1941. Eastern fleet 1942. Lost by gunfire of Japanese cruisers *Myoko* and *Ashigara* and destroyers in South Java Sea, 1.3.1942. 54 lost.

Battle Honours: River Plate 1939, Sunda Strait 1942.

Exeter with upright funnels and modern bridge.

LEANDER CLASS (5 ships)

Leander (1929 Programme), *Achilles, Neptune, Orion* (1930 Programme), *Ajax* (1931) Programme).

Displacement (tons):	6,985—7,270 standard, 8,950—9,200 full load.
Dimensions (feet):	522pp, 554½oa x 55¾ (*Leander* 55¼) x 16
(metres):	159.1pp, 169oa x 17 x (16.8) x 4.9
Machinery:	4 shaft Parsons SR geared turbines. 6 Admiralty 3-drum boilers. 72,000 SHP = 32½ knots. Range 10,300 miles at 12 knots.
Fuel:	Oil 1,800 tons.
Protection:	Machinery; belt 4in (102mm), bulkheads 1½in (38mm), upper deck over boiler rooms 1¼in (32mm), lower deck over engine rooms 1¼in (32mm). Magazines (2); crowns 2⅜in-1in (60mm-25mm), sides 3⅞in-1in (98mm-25mm), ends 2½in-1in (64mm-25mm). Steering gear 1½in-1¼in (38mm-32mm).
Armament:	8—6in (4x2), 4—4in AA (later 8—4in AA (4x2)), 12—.5in MG (3x4), 8—21in TT (2x4), 1 aircraft.
Complement:	570

Reduced versions of *Exeter*. The new 6in turrets, with 60 degrees elevation, were based on those adopted as secondary armament in the battleships *Nelson* and *Rodney*. As in the *Exeter*, armour was distributed on the box citadel system mainly around machinery spaces and magazines. The 3in belt was laid on 1in side plating and extended to the upper deck. Transverse subdivision was employed to prevent flooding in the event of shells penetrating unprotected parts of the hull. Boilers were of an improved type, and all the uptakes were trunked into a distinctive large single funnel.

For the first time, welding was employed on more than an experimental basis. Unfettered during construction by the weight monitoring so rigorously applied to the Counties, *Leander* exceeded her design displacement by 135 tons. Closer attention to this aspect, and development of welding technique, led to better results in subsequent ships.

Regarded as good seaboats, the Leanders proved to be rather wet in anything like a heavy sea and a swell. *Leander* as completed was particularly wet amidships, and the boats on the upper deck were prone to sea damage. This was remedied by extending the forecastle plating further aft in all ships and by carrying the boats one deck higher. During the 1930s (later in *Achilles)* the single 4in guns gave way to twin mountings. War modifications followed the usual pattern; 'X' turret was taken out of *Leander* and *Achilles* in 1944-45.

Leander, **July 1933. An early photo showing seaboat in original position.**

LEANDER

Built at Devonport Dockyard. Laid down 8.9.1930. Launched 24.9.1931. Completed 24.3.1933. 2 CS Home 1933-37. Manned by New Zealand Division 1937-43. New Zealand 1937-40. Mediterranean and Red Sea, June-Nov 1940. East Indies and Mediterranean 1940-41—sank Italian AMC *Ramb I* in Indian Ocean, 2.1941. New Zealand 1941-43. Damaged in action with Japanese cruisers at Kula Gulf, 13.7.1943. Repairs at Auckland, Aug-Dec 1943, Boston to 8.1945 and refit at Rosyth and Portsmouth to 3.1946. 1 CS Mediterranean 1946-47. Reserve and target trials 1948-49. Broken up, Hughes Bolckow, Blyth 1950.

Battle Honour: Kula Gulf 1943.

HMNZS *Achilles,* **Aug 1944, X turret removed.**

ACHILLES

Built by Cammell Laird, Birkenhead. Laid down 11.6.1931. Launched 1.9.1932. Completed 6.10.1933. 2 CS Home 1933-36. Manned by New Zealand Division 1936-46. New Zealand 1936-39. South Atlantic 1939. New Zealand 1940-43. Portsmouth Refit, Apr 1943-Mar 1944. (X turret removed). British Pacific Fleet 1944-45. New Zealand 1946. Returned to RN, 9.1946. Reserve 1946-48. Transferred to India 1948 and renamed *Delhi*. Paid off, 1978 and scrapped in India.

Battle Honours: River Plate 1939, Guadalcanal 1942-43, Okinawa 1945.

NEPTUNE

Built at Portsmouth Dockyard. Laid down 24.9.1931. Launched 31.1.1933. Completed 12.2.1934. 2 CS Home 1934-37. 6 CS Africa 1937-39. South Atlantic 1939-40. Mediterranean, East Indies 1940. Home and Mediterranean 1941. Sunk by mine off Tripoli, 19.12.1941. 766 lost.

Battle Honours: Atlantic 1939, Calabria 1940, Mediterranean 1940, *Bismarck* Action 1941, Malta Convoys 1941.

WRIGHT & LOGAN

Orion, **1936/37.**

ORION

Built at Devonport Dockyard. Laid down 26.9.1931. Launched 24.11.1932. Completed 18.1.1934. 2 CS Home 1934-37. 8 CS America & W.I. 1937-40. Mediterranean 1940-41. Damaged in evacuation of Heraclion, 29.5.1941; repairs at Simonstown to 8.1941, Mare Island to 2.1942, Devonport to 4.1942. Mediterranean 1942-44. Home, Apr-Aug 1944. Mediterranean 1944-46. Devonport Refit 1946. Reserve 1947-48. Target trials 1948. Broken up W. of Scotland Shipbreaking, Troon 1949.

Battle Honours: Atlantic 1939, Calabria 1940, Mediterranean 1940-44, Matapan 1941, Greece 1941, Crete 1941, Malta Convoys 1941, Sicily 1943, Salerno 1943, Anzio 1944, Aegean 1944, Normandy 1944, South France 1944.

AJAX

Built by Vickers Armstrong, Barrow. Laid down 7.2.1933. Launched 1.3.1934. Completed 12.4.1935. 8 CS America & W.I. 1935-39. South Atlantic 1939. Repairs after River Plate action, Chatham, Dec 1939-July 1940. Mediterranean 1940-42—sank Italian destroyers *Ariel* and *Airone* east of Malta, and disabled *Artigliere*, later sunk by *York*, 11.10.1940. Repairs, Chatham, May-Oct 1942. Force H 1942-43—damaged 1.1.1943; repaired at New York, Mar-Oct 1943. Mediterranean 1943-48. Paid off, Chatham, 2.1948. Laid up, Falmouth 1948. Broken up, Cashmore, Newport 1949.

Battle Honours: River Plate 1939, Mediterranean 1940-41, Matapan 1941, Greece 1941, Crete 1941, Malta Convoys 1941, Aegean 1944, Normandy 1944, South France 1944.

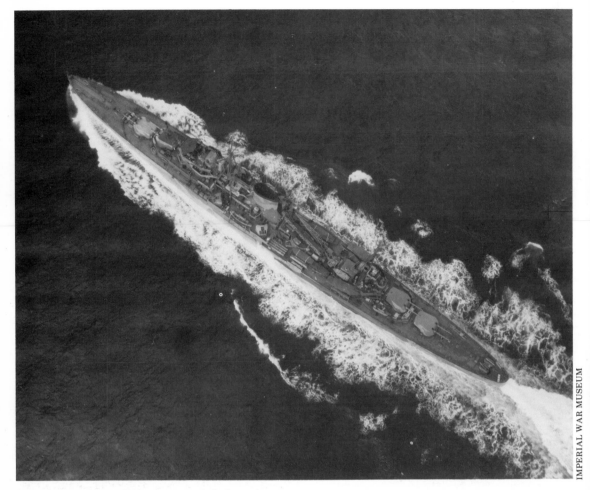

Neptune lost 10 May 1941—there was only 1 survivor.

Ajax leaving Malta, tripod masts and radar fitted.

AMPHION CLASS (3 ships)

Amphion/Perth (1931 Programme), *Apollo/Hobart, Sydney* (1932 Programme)

Displacement (tons):	6,830—7,105 standard, 8,850—9,150 full load.
Dimensions (feet):	530pp, 562¼oa x 56¾ x 15¾
(metres):	161.5pp, 171.4oa x 17.3 x 4.8
Machinery:	4 shaft Parsons SR geared turbines. 4 Admiralty 3-drum boilers. 72,000 SHP = 32½ knots.
Fuel:	Oil 1,800 tons. Range 10,700 miles at 12 knots.
Protection:	Machinery; belt 4in (102mm), bulkheads 1½in (38mm), upper deck over boiler rooms 1¼in (32mm), lower deck over engine rooms 1¼in (32mm). Magazines (2); crowns 2⅜in-1in (60mm-25mm), sides 3⅞in-1in (98mm-25mm, ends 2½in-1in (64mm-25mm). Steering gear 1½in-1¼in (38mm-32mm).
Armament:	8-6in (4x2), 4—4in AA (later 8—4in AA (4x2)), 12—.5in MG (3x4), 8—21in TT (2x4), 1 aircraft.
Complement:	570

Officially described as 'Improved Leanders', their two funnels disclosed a revised arrangement of machinery spaces on the unit system—new to British practice but common in some foreign navies. Instead of all the boilers being in one compartment and all the engines in another, there were four compartments alternating boiler-engine-boiler-engine, and a system of cross connections which ensured that in the event of damage any boiler could feed any turbine. This lengthened machinery spaces by nine feet, requiring additional armour, but the risk of a single hit causing a total loss of power was much reduced. There were only four boilers, of a new, larger type, and as in later classes, the catapult and crane were between the funnels. The Amphions incorporated the extended forecastle plating found necessary in the Leanders, and the 4in AA guns were further aft.

Phaeton was transferred to Australia before completion and renamed *Sydney*; the remaining pair followed her after brief service with the Royal Navy. Before transfer, twin 4in AA guns replaced single mountings in *Apollo* and *Amphion*, but *Sydney* was lost before this modification could be effected.

By the end of the war *Hobart*, the sole survivor of the trio, had had 'X' turret and aircraft removed, allowing the light AA armament to be greatly increased.

Amphion, **in 1938. She later became HMAS** *Perth.*

AMPHION, LATER PERTH

Built at Portsmouth Dockyard. Laid down 26.6.1933. Launched 27.7.1934. Completed 6.7.1936. Flagship, 6 CS Africa 1936-38. Transferred to Australia and renamed *Perth* 6.1939. America and W.I. 1939. Australia 1940. Mediterranean 1941. Australia 1941-42. Torpedoed by Japanese cruisers and destroyers in Sunda Straits and sank, 1.3.1942. 359 lost.

Battle Honours: Atlantic 1939, Matapan 1941, Greece 1941, Crete 1941, Malta Convoys 1941.

APOLLO, LATER HOBART

Built at Devonport Dockyard. Laid down 15.8.1933. Launched 9.10.1934. Completed 13.1.1936. 8 CS America & W.I. 1936-38. Transferred to Australia and renamed *Hobart*, 9.1938. Australia 1938-39. East Indies 1939-40. Red Sea 1940. Mediterranean 1941. Australia 1941-43. Torpedoed by Japanese submarine, 20.7.1943; repairs to early 1945. Australia 1945-47. Reserve 1947-53. Conversion to Training Cruiser commenced at Newcastle, NSW in 1953, but abandoned 1956. Broken up in Japan 1962.

Battle Honours: Mediterranean 1941, Coral Sea 1942, Savo Island 1942, Guadalcanal 1942-43, Kula Gulf 1943.

HMAS *Hobart* **postwar with X turret removed.**

HMAS *Sydney*, **Feb 1941, approaching Freemantle.**

SYDNEY (ex *Phaeton)*

Built by Swan Hunter, Wallsend. Laid down 8.7.1933. Launched 22.9.1934. Completed 24.9.1935. Australia 1935-40. Mediterranean 1940—disabled Italian cruiser *Bartolomeo Colleoni* NW of Crete 19.7.1940, later sunk by destroyers *Hyperion* and *Ilex*. Australia 1941. Sank, and sunk by, German auxiliary cruiser *Kormoran* in E. Indian ocean, 19.11.1941. 645 lost.

Battle Honours: Calabria 1940, Spada 1940, Mediterranean 1940, *Kormoran* 1941.

ARETHUSA CLASS (4 ships)

Arethusa (1931 Programme), *Galatea* (1932 Programme), *Penelope* (1933 Programme)
Aurora (1934 Programme)

Displacement (tons):	5,220 standard, 6,665 full load (5,270/6,715 *Penelope* and *Aurora)*
Dimensions (feet):	480pp, 506oa x 51 x 14
(metres):	146.3pp, 154.2oa x 15.5 x 4.3
Machinery:	4 shaft Parsons SR geared turbines. 4 Admiralty 3-drum boilers. 64,000 SHP = 32¼ knots.
Fuel:	Oil 1,325 tons.
Protection:	Machinery; belt 2¾in (70mm), bulkheads 1in (25mm), upper deck over boilers & fwd. engine room 1in (25mm), lower deck over aft engine room 1in (25mm). Magazines; crowns 2⅜in-1in (60mm-25mm), sides 3⅜in-1in (86mm-25mm), ends 2⅜in-1in (60mm-25mm). Steering gear 1in (25mm).
Armament:	6—6in (3x2), 8—4in AA (4x2), originally 4—4in AA (singles) in *Arethusa* and *Galatea*, 8—.5in MG (2x4), 6—21in TT (2x3), 1 aircraft (except in *Aurora*).
Complement:	500

Designed in parallel with the Amphions, but conceived specifically as small 'fleet cruisers' to replace the old 'C' and 'D' classes at Home and in the Mediterranean. While the Arethusas lacked the range of the bigger 'trade cruiser', they had the acceleration and manoeuvrability to lead destroyers and were small enough for shadowing and screening at night. In many ways they were three-turret diminutives of the Amphions, with the same unit machinery arrangement and similar, though generally thinner, protection. Originally displacement was to have been 5,500 tons standard, but this was reduced by 250 tons to keep within Britain's self-inflicted 91,000 ton limit on new construction. Welding was extensively employed to help save weight.

Penelope and *Aurora* differed in detail from the first pair, principally in having twin 4in AA mountings instead of singles: *Arethusa* and *Galatea* were so modified before the war. *Aurora* had an additional deckhouse for Flag accommodation in place of the catapult.

During the war the light AA armament was considerably increased, partly at the expense of the catapult (or Flag accommodation in *Aurora*), and tripods replaced the pole masts. By 1945 modifications had added 700 tons to the original displacement.

The class served with distinction, particularly in the fiercely contested waters of the Mediterranean.

Arethusa, **1935. Note single 4 inch guns and searchlight.**

ARETHUSA

Built at Chatham Dockyard. Laid down 25.1.1933. Launched 6.3.1934. Completed 23.5.1935. Flagship, 3 CS Mediterranean 1935-40. 2 CS Home 1940. Nore Command, Nov 1940-41—moored close to Tower Bridge as part of London's anti-aircraft defences. 15 CS Mediterranean, Feb-Nov 1942; seriously damaged by aerial torpedo, 18.11.1942; temporary repairs at Alexandria, then Charleston USA to end 1943, and refit, Chatham to Apr 1944. 2 CS Home 1944: received bomb damage in northern waters 24-25 June 1944; repairs on Clyde to Nov 44. 15 CS Mediterranean 1945. Nore Reserve 1945. Transfer to Norway considered but rejected 1946. Target trials 1948. Broken up, Cashmore, Newport 1950.

Battle Honours: Norway 1940-41, Malta Convoys 1941-42, Normandy 1944.

GALATEA

Built by Scotts, Greenock. Laid down 2.6.1933. Launched 9.8.1934. Completed 4.8.1935. Flagship, Rear-Admiral (D) Mediterranean 1935-39. Home 1940-41. Mediterranean 1941. Torpedoed and sunk by German *U557* off Alexandria, 15.12.1941. 470 lost.

Battle Honours: Norway 1940, *Bismarck* Action 1941, Mediterranean 1941.

PENELOPE

Built by Harland & Wolff, Belfast. Laid down 30.5.1934. Launched 15.10.1935. Completed 13.11.1936. 3 CS Mediterranean 1936-39. Home 1940. Grounded off Fleinver, 11.11.1940; repairs to 7.1941. Mediterranean (Force K) 1941-42—with *Aurora* and two destroyers sank an entire Italian convoy of 10 merchantmen and the destroyers *Fulmine* and *Libeccio* in Central Mediterranean, 8.11.1941; again with *Aurora* sank the Italian supply ship *Adriatico*, the tanker *Iridio Mantovani* and the destroyer *Alvise da Mosto*, 1.12.1941. Bombed 26.3.1942; repairs to 11.1942. Mediterranean 1942-44. Torpedoed and sunk by *U410* off Anzio, 18.2.1944. 415 lost.

Battle Honours: Norway 1940, Malta Convoys 1941-42, Mediterranean 1941-43, Sirte 1942, Sicily 1943, Salerno 1943, Aegean 1943, Anzio 1944.

Galatea, 1937.

Aurora, **Dec 1942. The "Silver Phantom". Note tripod masts and director aft.**

AURORA

Built at Portsmouth Dockyard. Laid down 23.7.1935. Launched 20.8.1936. Completed 12.11.1937. Flagship, Rear-Admiral (D) Home 1937-39. 2 CS Home 1939-41—with *Kenya* sank German supply ship *Belchen* in Denmark Strait, 3.6.1941; sank German sloop *Bremse* off Murmansk coast, 2.9.1941. Mediterraean (Force K), Oct-Dec 1941—with *Penelope* and two destroyers sank an entire Italian convoy of 10 merchantment and the destroyers *Fulmine* and *Libeccio* in central Mediterranean, 8.11.1941; again with *Penelope* sank the Italian supply ship *Adriatico*, the tanker *Iridio Mantovani* and the destroyer *Alvise da Mosto*, 1.12.1941. Mined off Tripoli, 19.12.1941; repairs at Malta to 3.1942, Liverpool to 6.1942. Mediterranean 1942-43. Bombed in Aegean, 30.10.1943; repairs at Taranto to 4.1944. Mediterranean 1944-46 (Refit, Malta, June-Oct 1945). Paid off, Portsmouth, 4.1946. Refit 1947, pending transfer. Chinese Nationalist *Chungking,* 1948. Turned Communist 2.1949 and renamed *Tchoung King.* Fired on British forces 1949. Bombed and sunk in Taku harbour, 3.1949. Salved 1951. Renamed *Hsuang Ho.* 1951, *Pei Ching*, 1951, then *Kuang Chou.* Hulked by 1955.

Battle Honours: Norway 1940, *Bismarck* Action 1941, Malta Convoys 1941, Mediterranean 1941-43, North Africa 1942-43, Sicily 1943, Salerno 1943, Aegean 1943-44, South France 1944.

1937-60: REARMAMENT, WAR AND PEACE

Southampton, Gloucester, Edinburgh, Dido, Bellona, Fiji, Ceylon and Swiftsure classes

Britain's return to moderate dimensions with the Leanders was generally followed by the European navies. The USA and Japan, however, built large cruisers armed with 15—6in guns—the Brooklyn and Mogami classes respectively—which were 6in gun versions of earlier Treaty types. The Southamptons were intended as some sort of reply to these ships, but standard displacement had to be held to 9,000 tons so that the first two ships could be built within the London Treaty's 91,000 ton limit on new construction cruisers. Two Arethusas and one Leander were dropped from the programme to make way for them. A further three Southamptons were provided under the 1934 Estimates, and another three of a modified type in 1935. Two enlarged ships, the Edinburghs, were ordered in 1936. Though not themselves part of the Rearmament Programme, the Southamptons set the pattern for the Fijis when rearmament came, and the two classes were regarded on a par with one another.

Hitler came to power in 1933, and Germany again began to look menacing. Somewhat against the sentiments of its people and as quietly as possible, the British Government embarked upon a Rearmament Programme in 1936 which made the Naval Defence Act pale into insignificance. In the four financial years 1936-37 to 1939-40, excluding the War Emergency Estimates, the following programme of construction for the Royal Navy was put in hand:

5 battleships (King George V class)
6 aircraft carriers (Illustrious class)
1 aircraft maintenance ship *(Unicorn)*
13 6in cruisers (2 Edinburgh, 11 Colony)
10 5.25in cruisers (Dido class)
4 fast minelayers (Abdiel class)
49 fleet destroyers

20 escort destroyers
18 submarines
7 sloops
56 corvettes
27 minesweepers
4 patrol vessesl

On the outbreak of war further building was authorised, included another six 5.25in cruisers (*Argonaut* and the Bellonas).

With regard to cruisers, it was urgently desired to boost numbers to 70 ships—the figure proposed by Jellicoe in 1919 but never achieved. To this end, the small Didos were put in hand first. Next came the larger Colonies which were based on the Southamptons, but once again Britain had restricted herself, this time by the London Naval Treaty of 1936, and their displacement had to be limited to 8,000 tons.

Early in the war, emphasis was placed on ships already begun and therefore likely to play an active part in the war. For this reason two repeat Edinburghs programmed for 1940 were dropped, as were four 8in gun cruisers tentatively referred to as the 'Admiral' class.

Cruisers were kept exceptionally busy during the war. Not only were they required for their normal duties with the fleet and on the trade routes, but their usefulness as anti-aircraft vessels led to their being hazarded in confined waters in support of landings and withdrawals by the Army—as, for example, in the evacuation of Crete or at Anzio. This led to losses and to constant scarcity.

Following heavy war losses, twelve cruisers were authorised in 1941-44; eight were the Swiftsures, built to a modified Fiji design, but only three had entered service by the end of 1945. Orders for four much larger ships of a projected Neptune class were never allocated. A fifth ship of the class, *Bellerophon*, originally ordered as one of the Swiftsures, was not laid down.

The Royal Navy began and ended the Second World War with around sixty cruisers: 29 losses (not counting three Australian ships) were balanced by the 29 new ships that entered the Fleet during the war. But many of the ships that survived to 1945 were too old and worn out for further service and were quickly discarded. By 1950 the Royal Navy's cruiser strength had dwindled to 27 ships, all of the Southampton and later classes which make up this section. They had all but vanished before their long delayed younger sisters of the Tiger class arrived in 1959-61 after nearly twenty years gestation.

BRITISH CRUISER DEPLOYMENT, APRIL 1937

Home Fleet:
2 CS   *Southampton* (Flag), *Newcastle*.
Flotillas   *Cairo* (Rear Admiral (D)).

Training:
Portsmouth   Gunnery Firing Ship, *Curacoa*.
Reserve   *Calcutta, Colombo, Coventry, Curlew, Dauntless, Diomede, Durban*.

Major Refit:
              Effingham, Frobisher, Hawkins, Kent, Neptune, Orion.

Mediterranean:
1 CS   *London* (Flag), *Devonshire, Shropshire, Sussex*.
3 CS   *Arethusa, Penelope, Despatch, Delhi*.
Flotillas   *Galatea* (Rear Admiral (D)).

East Indies:
4 CS   *Norfolk* (Flag), *Emerald, Enterprise*.

Africa:
6 CS   *Amphion* (Flag), *Carlisle*.

China:
5 CS   *Dorsetshire* (Flag), *Berwick, Cumberland, Suffolk, Danae, Capetown*.

America and West Indies:
8 CS   *Apollo* (Flag), *York, Dragon*.
              Exeter (Commodore, South America Division), *Ajax*.

New Zealand Division:
              Leander (Flag), *Achilles*.

Royal Australian Navy:
              Australia, Canberra, Sydney, Adelaide (Reserve).

SOUTHAMPTON CLASS (5 ships)

Newcastle, Southampton (1933 Programme), *Birmingham, Glasgow, Sheffield* (1934 Programme)

Displacement (tons):	9,100 standard, 11,350 full load.
Dimensions (feet):	558pp, 591½oa x 61¾ x 17
(metres):	170.1pp, 180.3oa x 18.8 x 5.2
Machinery:	4 shaft Parsons SR geared turbines. 4 Admiralty 3-drum boilers. 72,000 SHP = 32 knots.
Fuel:	Oil 2,075 tons *(Southampton, Newcastle* 1,950). Range 12,100 miles at 12 knots.
Protection:	Main citadel: belt 4½in (114mm), bulkheads 2½in (64mm), upper deck over boilers & fwd. engine room 1½in (38mm), lower deck fore & aft of boiler rooms 1¼in (32mm). Main magazines (2); crowns 2in-1in (51mm-25mm), sides 4½in-1in (114mm-25mm), ends 2½in-1in (64mm-25mm). H.A. magazine; crown 4in (102mm). Steering gear 1½in-1¼in.
Armament: as built	12—6in (4x3), 8—4in AA (4x2), 8—2pdr (2x4), 8—.5in MG (2x4), 6—21in TT (2x3), 2 aircraft.*
Sheffield 1954	9—6in (3x3), 8—4in AA (4x2), 8—2pdr (2x4), 8—40mm AA, 6—21in TT (2x3), no aircraft.
Complement:	750

Although the Leanders represented the Royal Navy's true preference in cruiser dimensions, it became necessary to produce a larger type as some sort of reply to American and Japanese 10,000 ton 6in gun ships. The rakishly handsome Southamptons were the result; and rank among the most successful cruisers ever built. In concept and general arrangement they were triple-turret Amphions, more heavily protected and with the belts extended to cover an extra compartment fore and aft. Aircraft hangars astride the forefunnel formed part of the forward superstucture, causing the bridge level to be raised by one deck. A fixed athwartships catapult was fitted between the funnels, and the cranes served both boatdeck and aircraft. Tripod masts were adopted, as shrouds for pole masts would have masked AA fire.

On completion the *Newcastle* started full power trials in a full gale; shipping no green seas and riding with an easy motion, she established a class reputation for superb weatherly qualitites.

The Southamptons saw arduous war service, mostly with the fleet, in all theatres, but seldom had the opportunity to demonstrate their fine surface action capability. All four survivors were modernized in 1949-52; externally *Glasgow* and *Sheffield* were little altered, but *Birmingham* and *Newcastle* received a lattice foremast and a new round-fronted bridge. *Sheffield* also acquired a lattice foremast in a further modernization in 1956-57.

*A third aircraft could be carried on the catapult.

Newcastle **in WW2, extra AA guns fitted.**

NEWCASTLE (ex *Minotaur*)

Built by Vickers Armstrong, Tyne. Laid down 4.10.34. Launched 23.1.1936. Completed 5.3.1937. 2 CS/18 CS Home 1937-40. South Atlantic 1941. Refit, Boston, USA and Devonport, Sep 1941-Jan 1942. Eastern Fleet 1942. Torpedoed 90 miles NW of Derna, 15.6.1942; repairs at New York and Devonport to 3.1943. Eastern Fleet 1943-44. Flagship, 5 CS East Indies 1944-45. Trooping late 1945. Devonport Refit (X turret removed) 1946-47. 1 CS Mediterranean 1947-50 (Flagship, 1948). Reconstructed, Devonport 1950-52. 5 CS Far East 1952-58 (Flagship, 1953, 1958). Broken up, Shipbreaking Ind., Faslane, 1959.

Battle Honours: Spartivento 1940, Burma 1944-45, Korea 1952-53.

Southampton, **June 1938.**

SOUTHAMPTON (ex *Polyphemus*)

Built by John Brown, Clydebank. Laid down 21.11.34. Launched 10.3.1936. Completed 6.3.1937. Flagship, 2 CS Home 1937-39. Humber Force 1939. 18 CS Home 1939-40. Mediterranean 1940-41—with *Bonaventure* sank Italian TB *Vega* off Pantellaria, 10.1.1941. Scuttled after catching fire in action with German bombing aircraft in Sicilian Narrows, 11.1.1941. 81 lost.

Battle Honours: Norway 1940, Spartivento 1940, Malta Convoys 1941.

BIRMINGHAM

Built at Devonport Dockyard. Laid down 18.7.1935. Launched 1.9.1936. Completed 18.11.1937. Flagship, 5 CS China 1937-40 (Jan). 18 CS Home 1940-41. Flagship, South Atlantic, June 1941-42. 4 CS Eastern fleet, Feb 1942-43. Devonport Refit, Apr-Aug 1943. Eastern fleet 1943, but torpedoed on passage in the Mediterranean, off Cyrenaica, 28.11.1943; repairs at Alexandria and in USA to 1945. 10 CS Home 1945-46. Portsmouth Refit 1946-47. Flagship, 4 CS East Indies 1947-49. Reconstructed, Portsmouth 1950-52. 5 CS Far East 1952-55 (Flagship 1955). South Atlantic 1955. Mediterranean 1956-57. Flag Officer Flotillas, Home 1957-58. Mediterranean 1959. Paid off 12.1959. Broken up, Ward, Inverkeithing 1960.

Battle Honours: Norway 1940, Korea 1952-53.

Birmingham **with round fronted bridge and lattice foremast. The only ship of the class with no knuckle.**

Glasgow in 1953, flying the flag of Admiral Mountbatten.

GLASGOW

Built by Scotts, Greenock. Laid down 16.4.1935. Launched 20.6.1936. Completed 9.9.1937. 2 CS Home 1937-39. Humber Force 1939. 18 CS Home 1939-40. Sank destroyer HMS *Imogen* in collision in thick fog in Pentland Firth, 16.7.1940. Mediterranean, Oct-Dec 1940—torpedoed 3.12.1940 at Suda Bay; repairs at Alexandria and Singapore to 8.1941. Eastern Fleet 1941-42—sank RIN patrol boat *Prabhavati* (mistaken for Japanese submarine) 9.12.1941. Refit, New York and Portsmouth, May-Oct 1942. 10 CS Home 1942-44—with *Enterprise* sank German destroyers *T25*, *T26* and *Z27* in Bay of Biscay, 28.12.1943. Damaged by gunfire off Cherbourg, 25.6.1944. Repairs and refit (X turret removed), June 1944-May 1945. Flagship, 5 CS then 4 CS East Indies 1945-48. Refit, Portsmouth 1948. America & W.I. 1949-50. Refit, Chatham 1951. Flagship, C-in-C, Mediterranean 1952-55. Flag Officer Flotillas, Home 1955-56. Paid off, 11.1956. Broken up, Hughes Bolckow, Blyth 1958.

Battle Honours: Norway 1940, Biscay 1943, Arctic 1943, Normandy 1944.

SHEFFIELD

Built by Vickers Armstrong, Tyne. Laid down 31.1.1935. Launched 23.7.1936. Completed 25.8.1937. 2 CS/18 CS Home 1937-40. Force H based on Gibraltar, Aug 1940-41—forced German tanker *Friedrich Breme* to scuttle herself, 12.6.1941. 10 CS Home 1941-44—sank destroyer *Friedrich Eckholtd* in Barents Sea action, 31.12.1942. Refit, USA, July 1944-May 1945, and Portsmouth (X turret removed) to May 1946. America & W.I. 1946-49 (Flagship 1947-48). Refit 1949-51. Flagship, C-in-C, America & W.I. 1951-52. Flagship, Heavy Squadron, Home 1952-53. Flagship, C-in-C, America & W.I. 1953-54. Home 1955. Refit 1956-57. Home/Mediterranean 1957-59. Refit 1959-60. Reserve Fleet HQ Ship, Portsmouth 1960-66. Broken up, Shipbreaking Industries, Faslane 1967.

Battle Honours: Norway 1940, Spartivento 1940, Atlantic 1941-43, *Bismarck* Action 1941, Mediterranean 1941, Malta Convoys 1941, Arctic 1941-43, North Africa 1942, Barents Sea 1942, Salerno 1943, Biscay 1943, North Cape 1943.

Sheffield on convoy protection duty.

LATER SOUTHAMPTON OR GLOUCESTER CLASS (3 ships),
1935 Programme

Gloucester, Liverpool, Manchester

Displacement (tons):	9,400 standard, 11, 650 full load.
Dimensions (feet):	558pp, 591½oa x 62¼ x 17½
(metres):	170.1pp, 180.3oa x 19 x 5.3
Machinery:	4 shaft Parsons SR geared turbines. 4 Admiralty 3-drum boilers. 82,500 SHP = 32¼ knots.
Fuel:	Oil 2,075 tons. Range 12,100 miles at 12 knots.
Protection:	As in Southamptons except 2in (51mm) between ammunition lobbies and magazines.
Armament: as built	12—6in (4x3), 8—4in AA (4x2), 8—2pdr AA (2x4), 8—.5in MG (2x4), 6—21in TT (2x3), 2 aircraft*
Liverpool 1945	9—6in (3x3), 8—4in AA (4x2), 28—2pdr AA (6x4 & 4x1), 19—20mm AA (6x2 & 7x1), 6—21in TT (2x3), no aircraft.
Complement:	800

Near repeats of the first group. Beam was slightly increased, installed power raised, and gunnery control much improved. They were completed with shelters for the 4in gun crews and a modified bridge structure with a semi-circular front. Turrets were much better protected.

Gloucester and *Manchester* were both war losses. *Gloucester* caught fire and sank after being hit by four bombs in a heavy air attack off Crete. *Manchester*, disabled and listing after a torpedo attack by Italian MAS boats (MTBs) during Operation 'Pedestal', had to be scuttled.

Liverpool was twice seriously damaged by aerial torpedo; first in October 1940 when her bows were blown off by a petrol stowage explosion, and again during Operation 'Harpoon' in June 1942, when a large hole was blown in her starboard side. Consequently, she spent much of the war under repair. By 1945 the usual modifications had been effected, including the removal of 'X' turret and aircraft arrangements. *Liverpool* received no further modernisation after the war and paid off into reserve in 1952.

---

*A third aircraft could be carried on the catapult.

Gloucester, **March 1939, entering Grand Harbour Malta.**

GLOUCESTER

Built at Devonport Dockyard. Laid down 22.9.1936. Launched 19.10.1937. Completed 31.1.1939. 4 CS East Indies 1939-40 (Flagship, C-in-C, 1939). Mediterranean 1940-41—with others attacked 3 Italian destroyers, sinking the *Espero*, 28.6.40: struck by a bomb during Italian air attack 9.7.40, killing Captain and 17 crew. Bombed and sunk by German and Italian aircraft N.W. of Crete, 22.5.1941. 736 lost.

Battle Honours: Calabria 1940, Matapan 1941, Crete 1941, Malta Convoys 1941, Mediterranean 1941.

LIVERPOOL

Built by Fairfield, Govan. Laid down 17.2.1936. Launched 24.3.1937. Completed 2.11.1938. 5 CS China 1938-40. Red Sea and Mediterranean 1940. Torpedoed off Crete, 14.10.1940; repairs in USA to 1942. Home 1942. Mediterranean 1942. Severely damaged by aerial torpedo SW of Sardinia, 14.6.1942. Repairs and refit (X turret removed) at Rosyth, Aug 1943-July 1945. 1 CS Mediterranean 1945-52 (Flagship 1949-50). Portsmouth Reserve 1952. Broken up, McLellan, Bo'ness 1958.

Battle Honours: Calabria 1940, Mediterranean 1940, Arctic 1942, Malta Convoys 1942.

MANCHESTER

Built by Hawthorn Leslie, Hebburn. Laid down 28.3.1936. Launched 12.4.1937. Completed 4.8.1938. 4 CS East Indies 1938-39. 18 CS Home 1939-41. Torpedoed on Malta convoy, 23.7.1941; repairs at Philadelphia to 4.1942. Mediterranean 1942. Torpedoed and sunk by Italian MTBs *MAS 16* and *MAS 22* off Tunisia, 13.8.1942. 150 lost.

Battle Honours: Norway 1940, Spartivento 1940, Arctic 1942, Malta Convoys 1941-42.

Manchester, **29 May 1942.**

Liverpool, **early 1950's with some guns cocooned.**

EDINBURGH CLASS (2 ships), *1936 Programme*

Belfast, Edinburgh

Displacement (tons):	10,260 standard, 12,675 full load.
Dimensions (feet):	579pp, 613½oa x 63¼ x 17¼
(metres):	176.5pp, 187oa x 19.3 x 5.3
Machinery:	4 shaft Parsons SR geared turbines. 4 Admiralty 3-drum boilers. 80,000 SHP = 32½ knots.
Fuel:	Oil 2,250 tons. Range 12,200 miles at 12 knots.
Protection:	Long citadel: belt 4½in (114mm), bulkheads 2½in (64mm), upper deck over boilers & fwd. engine room 1½in (38mm), lower deck fwd. & aft. of boiler rooms 1¼in (32mm). Steering gear 1½in-1¼in (38mm-32mm).
Armament:	12-6in (4x3), 12—4in AA (6x2), 16—2pdr AA (2x8), 8—.5in MG (2x4), 6—21in TT (2x3), 3 aircraft.
Complement:	850

Enlarged versions of the original Southamptons, and Britain's only 6in gun cruisers built right up to the 10,000 ton limit (which in fact they exceeded). Designed to withstand 8in shells, box citadels were abandoned in favour of an extended belt and armoured deck covering the ship's vitals from 'A' to 'Y' turrets. Machinery spaces were shifted aft in the lengthened hull to adjoin the after magazine, forcing the rear turrets to be mounted a deck higher than usual and creating the distinctive gap between the bridge structure and forefunnel. The 4in AA battery was increased by 50%: a curious feature was that the 4in magazines were well forward of their guns, and shells had to be carried aft by a 110 foot conveyer belt from the hoists on the flight deck.

Being larger than the Southamptons, the Edinburghs were even better seaboats, though less handy.

Belfast was severely mined early in the war and almost broke in two. In the course of repairs bulges were added to improve stability, adding 4 feet to her beam, and radar/gunnery control modifications were carried out. By the time she emerged from Devonport Dockyard in late 1942 *Edinburgh* had been lost on an Arctic convoy. In 1944-45 two of *Belfast*'s twin 4in mountings were removed to make way for additional light AA guns, and aircraft arrangements were landed. 'X' turret, however, was retained.

Belfast was extensively modernized in 1955-59. Modifications included lattice masts, a new operations room, a covered bridge, improved gunnery control and better habitability. The mixed light AA battery was replaced by 12—40mm AA guns in twin mounts and torpedo tubes were removed. She became the last Second World War cruiser in commission in the Royal Navy.

Belfast, **as modernised with new bridge, AA guns and lattice masts.**

BELFAST

Built by Harland & Wolff, Belfast. Laid down 10.12.1936. Launched 17.3.1938. Completed 3.8.1939. 2 CS/18 CS Home 1939—captured German liner *Cap Norte*, 9.10.1939. Severely damaged by mine in Firth of Forth, 21.11.1939. Rebuilt, Devonport 1940-Sep 1942. Flagship, 10 CS Home 1942-44. Refit, Aug 1944-May 1945. British Pacific Fleet 1945. 5 CS Far East 1946-47. Reserve 1947-48. 5 CS Far East 1948-52 (Flagship, 1949, 52). Reserve 1952-56. Devonport Refit 1956-59. Far East 1959-62. Flag Officer Flotillas, Home 1962-63. Refit 1963. Reserve 1963-65. Reserve Fleet HQ Ship, Portsmouth 1966-70. Became museum ship in Pool of London, 1971.

Battle Honours: Arctic 1943, North Cape 1943, Normandy 1944, Korea 1950-52.

EDINBURGH

Built by Swan Hunter, Wallsend. Laid down 30.12.1936. Launched 31.3.1938. Completed 6.7.1939. 2 CS/18 CS Home 1939-40. Refit, South Shields, Mar-Oct 1940. Flagship, 18 CS Home 1940-42. Sunk by British forces after being totally disabled by German torpedo attacks in Barents Sea, 2.5.1942. 57 lost.

Battle Honours: Norway 1940-41, *Bismarck* Action 1941, Atlantic 1941, Malta Convoys 1941, Arctic 1941-42.

Edinburgh. **A rare photograph—She was lost in the Barents Sea.**

BRITISH CRUISER DEPLOYMENT, SEPTEMBER 1939

Home Fleet:
18 CS *Sheffield, Edinburgh, Belfast, Newcastle.*
12 CS *Effingham, Emerald, Enterprise, Dunedin, Delhi, Cardiff.*
7 CS *Diomede, Dragon, Caledon, Calyso.*
Flagship (D) *Aurora.*
AA Cruiser *Calcutta.*

Channel Force:
Ceres, Caradoc.
Cairo (AA).

Humber Force:
Southampton, Glasgow.

Mediterranean Fleet:
1 CS *Devonshire, Shropshire, Sussex.*
3 CS *Arethusa, Penelope, Coventry* (AA).
Flagship (D). *Galatea.*

North Atlantic Command (Gibraltar):
Colombo, Capetown.

China:
5 CS *Kent, Cornwall, Birmingham, Dorsetshire.*

South Atlantic Command (Freetown, Sierra Leone):
6 CS *Neptune.*
9 CS *Despatch, Dauntless, Danae, Durban.*

South American Division:
Exeter, Ajax, Cumberland.

America and West Indies:
8 CS *Berwick, Orion, York, Perth.*

East Indies:
4 CS *Gloucester, Liverpool, Manchester.*

Royal Australian Navy:
Canberra, Australia, Sydney, Hobart, Adelaide.

New Zealand:
Leander, Achilles.

Reserve:
Hawkins, Frobisher.

Major Refits:
Suffolk, London, Norfolk, Curlew, Curacoa, Carlisle.

WAR MODIFICATIONS 1939-45

At every refit or overhaul during the war, opportunity was taken to add new items of equipment and armament, always subject to availability. There was little uniformity to the process, and many small differences soon arose between ships of the same class, particularly in light AA armament. Broadly, modifications can be summarised as:

   (a) the addition of varying numbers of single 20mm AA guns, which supplanted the .5in MG's.

   (b) the fitting of radar direction finders (RDF) for warning of attack and gunnery control; tripod masts were fitted to bear the additional weight. Mounting topweight was countered in a variety of ways, depending on the class. These included shipping additional ballast, fuel restrictions in some cases, adjustments to armament, and in most of the later ships:

   (c) the removal of aircraft arrangements, since RDF gave adequate warning of attack and had largely obviated the need for spotter planes. The weight and space thus saved allowed light AA armament to be further increased.

   (d) the removal of 'X' turret from many ships in 1944-45 to permit still more improvements to AA armament and at the same time easing stability problems. By this time the 40mm gun was replacing the 20mm and the 2pdr. There was also a shift away from sheer numbers of AA guns to fewer weapons and better fire control.

Displacements rose inexorably throughout the war; increases of around 10% were not uncommon.

DIDO CLASS (11 ships)

Dido, Euryalus, Naiad, Phoebe, Sirius (1936 Programme)
Bonaventure, Hermione (1937 Programme)
Charybdis, Cleopatra, Scylla (1938 Programme)
Argonaut (1939 War Emergency Programme)

Displacement (tons):	5,600 standard, 6,850 full load.
Dimensions (feet):	485pp, 512oa x 50½ x 14
(metres):	147.8pp, 156.1oa x 15.4 x 4.3
Machinery:	4 shaft Parsons SR geared turbines. 4 Admiralty 3-drum boilers. 62,000 SHP = 32¼ knots.
Fuel:	Oil 1,100 tons. Range 4,240/3,480/1,500 miles at 16/20/30 knots.
Protection:	Belt (boiler and machinery spaces) 3in (76mm), bulkheads 1in (25mm). Forecastle deck, upper deck 1in (25mm). Magazines: platform deck 2in (51mm) longitudinal bulkheads 1½in-1in (38mm-25mm). Steering gear 1in (25mm).
Armament:	*10—5.25in DP (5x2), 8—2pdr AA (2x4), 8—.5in MG (2x4), 6—21in TT (2x3).
Complement:	480

A class of small cruisers, intended to boost numbers as quickly as possible. Derived from the Arethusas, the Didos mounted 10—5.25in dual purpose guns in twin turrets of the type also adopted as secondary armament in the King George V class battleships. On balance, this was superior to the Arethusas' mixture of 6in LA and 4in HA weapons, and the Didos were naturally good anti-aircraft ships. They handled extremely well under way—'just like destroyers'—but were inclined to pitch due to the weight of three turrets forward. Topweight became a severe problem.

The belt enclosed boiler and machinery spaces only, but the protection deck extended forward at forecastle deck level and aft along the main deck to cover both main magazines, which also had a 2in platform deck roof and 1in-1½in longitudinal bulkheads to the sides.

Due to supply difficulties, *Bonaventure*, *Dido* and *Phoebe* were completed minus one turret ('X' in *Bonaventure*, 'Q' in the others), and mounted a 4in starshell gun in lieu as a temporary expedient. *Dido* received her missing turret in 1941, *Bonaventure* was lost in her original state, and *Phoebe* remained a four turret ship. Again because of shortages, *Scylla* and

---

*Reduced to 8—5.25in by 1945 by removal of 'Q' turret from all except *Euryalus* (removed later), *Dido* and *Sirius*. See notes.

Charybdis were completed with a main armament of 8—4.5in DP guns in twin open mountings. *Charybdis* had a 4in starshell gun.

The class earned a very high reputation in the Mediterranean before dispersing later in the war to Home and Far Eastern waters. The four that were lost all fell victim to the torpedo, to which the small cruisers was particularly vulnerable. Rather cramped ships, with too little margin of stability for modernization, the Didos never really found a niche in the post-war fleet, and most passed several years in reserve before finally being scrapped.

Dido. **At Spithead Review (Q turret retained) 1953.**

DIDO

Built by Cammel Laird, Birkenhead. Laid down 20.10.1937. Launched 18.7.1939. Completed 30.9.1940. Home 1940-41. Mediterranean 1941. Bombed off Crete, 29.5.1941; repairs at Brooklyn, USA to 12.1941. Mediterranean 1942-44—with others sank three enemy supply ships off N. Africa, 13.12.1942. Home 1944-47—took surrender of Copenhagen, 9.5.1945. Reserve 1947-56 (Reserve Fleet Flagship Group 1952-53). Broken up, Ward, Barrow 1958.

Battle Honours: Crete 1941, Sirte 1942, Mediterranean 1942-44, Malta Convoys 1942, Sicily 1943, Salerno 1943, Aegean 1943, Anzio 1944, South France 1944, Arctic 1944.

EURYALUS

Built at Chatham Dockyard. Laid down 21.10.1937. Launched 6.6.1939. Completed 30.6.1941. Home 1941. Mediterranean 1941-43—with others sank three enemy supply ships off N. Africa, 13.12.1942. Refit, Clyde, Oct 1943-June1944. Home 1944. 5 CS East Indies 1944-45. British Pacific Fleet 1945-46. 5 CS Far East 1946-47. Mediterranean 1948-53 (replaced *Ajax*). Flagship, C-in-C, South Atlantic 1953-54 (exchanged places with *Bermuda*). Reserve 1954-59. Broken up, Hughes Bolckow, Blyth 1959.

Battle Honours: Malta convoys 1941-42, Mediterranean 1941-43, Sirte 1942, Sicily 1943, Salerno 1943, Okinawa 1945.

Naiad. **Admiral Vian's flagship.**

NAIAD

Built by Hawthorn Leslie, Hebburn. Laid down 26.8.1937. Launched 3.2.1939. Completed 24.7.1940. Home 1940-41. Mediterranean 1941-42. Torpedoed and sunk by German U-boat *U565* south of Crete, 11.3.1942. 77 lost.

Battle Honours: Crete 1941, Mediterranean 1941, Malta Convoys 1941-2.

Phoebe **entering Grand Harbour Malta, 18 October 1948.**

PHOEBE

Built by Fairfield, Govan. Laid down 2.9.1937. Launched 25.3.1939. Completed 30.9.1940. Home 1940-41. Mediterranean 1941. Torpedoed 27.8.1941; repairs at New York to 1942. Mediterranean 1942. Torpedoed off Pointe Noire 23.10.1942; repairs at New York to 7.1943. Mediterranean 1943-44. Eastern Fleet 1944. 5 CS East Indies 1944-45. British Pacific Fleet 1945. Refit 1945-46. Flagship (D) Mediterranean 1946-47. 1 CS Mediterranean 1947-51. Damaged in collision with *Gambia*, 16.10.1950. Paid off 3.1951. Reserve, Nore 1952-53, Portsmouth 1953-55. Broken up, Hughes Bolckow, Blyth 1956.

Battle Honours: Greece 1941, Crete 1941, Malta Convoys 1942, Aegean 1943, Mediterranean 1944, Sabang 1944, Burma 1944-45.

Sirius **at anchor in the Mediterranean—1945.**

SIRIUS

Built at Portsmouth Dockyard. Laid down 6.4.1938. Launched 18.9.1940. Completed 6.5.1942. Home 1942. Mediterranean 1942-43—with others sank four enemy supply ships and a destroyer N. of Tunis, 2.12.1942. Force H 1943. Mediterranean 1944-46 (detached for Normandy landings). Refit 1946. 2 CS Home 1947-49 (laid up 11.47-4.48). Portsmouth Reserve 1949-56—goodwill visit to Trinidad with *Diadem*, 1951. Broken up, Hughes Bolckow, Blyth 1956.

Battle Honours: Arctic 1942, Malta Convoys 1942, Mediterranean 1942, North Africa 1942-43, Sicily 1943, Salerno 1943, Aegean 1943-44, Normandy 1944, South France 1944.

Bonaventure, **as completed—a rare photograph.**

BONAVENTURE

Built by Scotts, Greenock. Laid down 30.8.1937. Launched 19.4.1939. Completed 24.5.1940. Home 1940. Mediterranean 1940-41—with *Southampton* sank Italian TB *Vega* off Pantellaria, 10.1.1941. Torpedoed and sunk by Italian submarine *Ambra* north of Sollum, 31.3.1941. 139 lost.

Battle Honour: Malta convoys 1941.

Hermione

HERMIONE

Built by Alex. Stephen, Govan. Laid down 6.10.1937. Launched 18.5.1939. Completed 25.3.1941. Home 1941. Force H 1941-42—rammed and sank Italian submarine *Tambien* off Tunis, 1.8.1941. Mediterranean 1942. Torpedoed and sunk by German U-boat *U205* north of Sollum, 16.6.1942. 87 lost.

Battle Honours: *Bismarck* Action 1941, Mediterranean 1941, Malta Convoys 1941-42, Diego Suarez 1942.

Charybdis, **Oct 1943—note her 4.5 inch guns.**

CHARYBDIS

Built by Cammell Laird, Birkenhead. Laid down 9.11.1938. Launched 17.9.1940. Completed 3.12.1941. Home and Force H, 1941-42. Home 1943. Torpedoed and sunk by German TBs *T23* and *T27* off N. coast of France, 23.10.1943. 462 lost.

Battle Honours: Malta convoys 1942, North Africa 1942, Salerno 1943, Atlantic 1943, English Channel 1943, Biscay 1943.

CLEOPATRA

Built by Hawthorn Leslie, Hebburn. Laid down 5.1.1939. Launched 27.3.1940. Completed 5.12.1941. Home 1941-42. Mediterranean, Feb 1942-43—with others sank three enemy supply ships off N. Africa, 13.12.1942. Torpedoed by Italian submarine *Dandalo* and badly damaged, 16.7.1943; repairs to 4.1945. 5 CS East Indies 1945-46. Home 1946-51 (laid up 1947-48). Mediterranean 1951-53. Reserve Fleet Flagship Group 1953-56. Broken up, Cashmore, Newport 1958.

Battle Honours: Malta convoys 1942, Sirte 1942, Sicily 1943.

Scylla. **Known as the Toothless Terror with her "reduced" armament.**

SCYLLA

Built by Scotts, Greenock. Laid down 19.4.1939. Launched 24.7.1940. Completed 12.6.1942. Home 1942. Force H 1943. Torpedoed 10.1943; repairs to 4.1944. Home 1944—Flagship of Rear Admiral Sir Philip Vian, Eastern Task Force, at Normandy landings. Badly mined June 1944 and not repaired. Target Ship, Spithead 1944. Disposal list 1948 on account of heavy underwater damage. Broken up, Ward, Barrow 1950.

Battle Honours: North Africa 1942, Arctic 1942-43, Salerno 1943, Atlantic 1943, Biscay 1943, Normandy 1944.

ARGONAUT

Built by Cammel Laird, Birkenhead. Laid down 21.11.1939. Launched 6.9.1941. Completed 8.8.1942. Home 1942 (one Arctic convoy). Mediterranean 1942-43—with others sank four supply ships and a destroyer N. of Tunis, 2.12.1942. Force H 1943. Torpedoed in W. Mediterranean by Italian submarine *Mocenigo*, 14.2.1943—bow and stern blown off. Repairs at Philadelphia to 11.1943, completed in UK early 1944. Home 1944. British Pacific 1945-46. Reserve 1946-55. Broken up, Cashmore, Newport 1955.

Battle Honours: Arctic 1942, North Africa 1942, Mediterranean 1942, Normandy 1944, South France 1944, Aegean 1944, Okinawa 1945.

Argonaut. **Photographed on the Mersey shortly after completion.**

BELLONA CLASS (5 ships), *1939 War Emergency Programme*

Bellona, Black Prince, Diadem, Royalist, Spartan

Displacement (tons):	5,950 standard, 7,200 full load.
Dimensions (feet):	485pp, 512oa x 50½ x 15
(metres):	147.8pp, 156.1oa x 15.4 x 4.6
Machinery:	4 shaft Parsons SR geared turbines. 4 Admiralty 3-drum boilers. 62,000 SHP = 32 knots.
Fuel:	Oil 1,100 tons. Range 4,240/3,480/1,500 miles at 16/20/30 knots.
Protection:	As in Dido.
Armament:	8—5.25in DP (4x2), 12—2pdr AA (3x4), 12—20mm AA (6x2), 6—21in TT (2x3).
Complement:	530

Four turret versions of the original Didos, omitting 'Q' turret and with wartime modifications built in. With lowered bridge and no rake to the funnels and masts, they had a profile quite different from the first groups'. A shortage of 5.25in guns held up construction for six months in 1940-41.

Spartan became the only Dido to succumb to aerial attack when she was struck by a German glider bomb off Anzio.

Bellona and *Black Prince* were loaned to the Royal New Zealand Navy in 1946, replacing *Gambia* and *Leander*. After an extensive refit, *Royalist* relieved *Bellona* in 1956. *Diadem* saw some postwar service with the Royal Navy before her transfer to Pakistan in 1957.

BELLONA

Built by Fairfield, Govan. Laid down 30.11.1939. Launched 29.9.1942. Completed 29.10.1943. 10 CS Home 1943-45. Royal New Zealand Navy 1946-56. New Zealand 1946-52. Took part in NATO exercise 'Mainbrace' in North Sea 1952. Returned to NZ late 1952. Reserve 1952-55. Returned to UK 1955, and RN control April 1956. Reserve 1956-57. Broken up, Ward, Briton Ferry 1959.

Battle Honours: Normandy 1944, Biscay 1944, Norway 1944-45, Arctic 1944-45.

Bellona **in the Bay of Islands, 1946, whilst with the RNZN.**

BLACK PRINCE

Built by Harland & Wolff, Belfast. Laid down 2.11.1939. Launched 27.8.1942. Completed 20.11.1943. Home 1943-44—took part in sinking of German TB *T29* off Ushant, 26.4.1944. Mediterranean 1944. British Pacific Fleet 1945. Royal New Zealand Navy 1946-61. Reserve 1946-52. Refit 1952-53. At Coronation Review of the Fleet, Spithead, June 1953. New Zealand 1953-55—escorted *Gothic* on Royal Tour 1953-54. Reserve 1955-61. Returned to RN control 1961. Scrapped in Japan 1962.

Battle Honours: Normandy 1944, South France 1944, Arctic 1944, English Channel 1944, Aegean 1944, Okinawa 1945.

Diadem **arriving at Portsmouth, December 1945.**

DIADEM

Built by Hawthorn Leslie, Hebburn. Laid down 15.11.1939. Launched 26.8.1942. Completed 6.1.1944. 10 CS Home 1944-45. Damaged by destroyer gunfire, 1.1945; repairs on Tyne to 4.1945. 2 CS Home 1946-50 (temporarily laid up 1948, Flagship 1948). Reserve 1950-56—goodwill visit to Trinidad with *Sirius*, 1951. Sold to Pakistan, 29.2.1956. Refitted, and renamed *Babur*, 5.7.1957. Used for harbour training from 1982, renamed *Jahangir*.

Battle Honours: Arctic 1944-45, Normandy 1944, Biscay 1944, Norway 1945.

Royalist, **after moderisation with new bridge, fire control systems and lattice masts.**

ROYALIST

Built by Scotts, Greenock. Laid down 21.3.1940. Launched 30.5.1942. Completed 10.9.1943. Home 1943-44. Flagship, Escort Carrier Squadron, Mediterranean 1944-45—with destroyer *Teazer* sank two German vessels in Aegean, 15.9.1944. Flagship, 21st Escort Carrier Squadron, East Indies 1945. Reserve 1946-55. Refit 1955-56. Royal New Zealand Navy 1956-66. Returned to RN control 1967. Scrapped in Japan 1968.

Battle Honours: South France 1944, Aegean 1944, Burma 1945.

Spartan **lost to a glider bomb attack.**

SPARTAN

Built by Vickers Armstrong, Barrow. Laid down 21.12.1939. Launched 27.8.1942. Completed 10.8.1943. Home 1943. Mediterranean 1944. Sunk by German glider bomb off Anzio, 29.1.1944. 64 lost.

Battle Honours: Atlantic 1943, Mediterranean 1944, Anzio 1944.

FIJI CLASS (8 ships)

Fiji, Kenya, Mauritius, Nigeria, Trinidad (1937 Programme)
Gambia, Jamaica (1938 Programme), *Bermuda* (1939 Programme)

Displacement (tons):	8,525 standard, 10,450 full load.
Dimensions (feet):	538pp, 555½oa x 62 x 16½
(metres):	164pp, 169.3oa x 18.9 x 5
Machinery:	4 shaft Parsons SR geared turbines. 4 Admiralty 3-drum boilers. 72,500 SHP = 31½ knots.
Fuel:	Oil 1,700 tons. Range 10,200 miles at 12 knots.
Protection:	Long citadel: belt 3½in—3¼in (89mm-83mm), bulkheads 2in-1½in (51mm-38mm), upper deck amidships 2in (51mm), lower deck fore and aft 2in (51mm). Stern belt 1½in (38mm), deck over steering gear 2in-1¼in (51mm-32mm).
Armament: as built;	12—6in (4x3), 8—4in AA (4x2), 8—2pdr AA (2x4), 16—.5in MG (4x4), 6—21in TT (2x3), 2 aircraft.
Gambia **1954;**	9—6in, (3x3), 8—4in AA (4x2), 12—40mm AA Bofors (5x2, 2x1), 6—21in TT (2x3), no aircraft.
Complement:	730

The larger Rearmament Programme cruisers were based on the Southamptons, but design displacement was squeezed to 8,000 tons to comply with the London Naval Treaty of 1936. That the Fijis exceeded this very tight limit by about 500 tons was no bad thing, and hardly mattered as war had broken out before any were completed. Weight was saved principally by a 35 foot reduction in length, achieved by mounting the after pair of boilers transversely. Funnels and masts were stepped without rake.

As in the Edinburghs, box citadels were abandoned in favour of an extended belt and armoured decks enclosing machinery and magazines. Compared with the Southamptons the belt was thinner and deck protection thicker, but total weight of armour was about the same at 1,289 tons.

In spite of the severe restraints under which they were designed, the Colonies earned a high reputation in service. Not as weatherly as the Southamptons, they could maintain their speed in a seaway, though they were very wet at speed in anything but calm weather. Their transom sterns reduced vibration, making the after turrets very steady, and also improved speed and manoeuvrability. However, they were cramped and uncomfortable for a full wartime complement, especially in the tropics, and never made as good flagships as the more spacious Southamptons.

War modifications followed the usual pattern, and 'X' turret was taken out of all except *Gambia* and *Nigeria* in 1944-45. Post-war modernization was fairly minimal, though the class saw extensive service even into the 1960s.

Fiji engaging enemy aircraft during Operation Tiger in 1940.

Mauritius at speed during World War II.

FIJI

Built by John Brown, Clydebank. Laid down 30.3.1938. Launched 31.5.1939. Completed 5.5.1940. Home 1940. Torpedoed in North Atlantic, 1.9.1940; repairs to 3.41. Mediterranean 1941. Bombed and sunk by German and Italian aircraft SW of Crete, 22.5.1941. 241 lost.

Battle Honour: Crete 1941.

KENYA

Built by Alex. Stephen, Govan. Laid down 18.6.1938. Launched 18.8.1939. Completed 27.9.1940. Home 1940-42 (Force H and Malta convoys 1941)—sank German tanker *Kota Pinang*, 3.10.41; helped destroy nine German vessels in Vaagso raid, 29.12.41. Torpedoed during Operation Pedestal, 13.8.42—bow blown off; repairs to 3.43. Eastern Fleet 1943-44. 5 CS East Indies 1944-45. Refit (X turret removed) 1945-46. America & W.I. 1946-47. Reserve 1948-49. Refit 1949. Flagship, C-in-C Far East 1950-51. Flagship, C-in-C East Indies 1952-53. Reserve 1953-54. Refit 1955. Flag Officer Flotillas, Home 1955. Flagship, C-in-C America & W.I. 1956. Home 1956-58. Reserve 1958. Broken up, Shipbreaking Industries, Faslane, 1962.

Battle Honours: Atlantic 1941, *Bismarck* Action 1941, Malta Convoys 1941-42, Arctic 1941-42, Norway 1941, Sabang 1944, Burma 1944-45, Korea 1950-51.

MAURITIUS

Built by Swan Hunter, Wallsend. Laid down 31.3.1938. Launched 19.7.1939. Completed 1.1.1941. Home 1941 (convoys to Freetown). East Indies from 6.1941. Refit early 1942. Eastern Fleet 1942-43. 15 CS Mediterranean 1943-44 (Flagship 1943). 10 CS Home 1944-45—sank two enemy minesweepers and three trawlers between Brest and Lorient, 23.8.44. Refit (X turret removed) Feb 1945-Mar 1946. Flagship 15 CS Mediterranean 1946. 1 CS Mediterranean 1946-48. Refit 1948-49. East Indies 1949-51 (Flagship, C-in-C, 1950-51). Refit 1952-53. Reserve 1953-60. For disposal 1960. Broken up, Ward, Inverkeithing 1965.

Battle Honours: Atlantic 1941, Sicily 1943, Salerno 1943, Mediterranean 1943-44, Anzio 1944, Normandy 1944, Biscay 1944, Norway 1945.

NIGERIA

Built by Vickers Armstrong, Tyne. Laid down 8.2.1938. Launched 18.7.1939. Completed 23.9.1940. Home 1940-42 (Flagship 10 CS 1942). Torpedoed during Operation Pedestal, 8.42; repairs at Charleston to 1.44. Eastern Fleet 1944. 5 CS East Indies 1945. Flagship, C-in-C, South Atlantic 1946-50. Devonport Reserve 1950-54. Purchased by India, 1954. Transferred after extensive refit 1957 and renamed *Mysore*. Paid off 1985.

Battle Honours: Atlantic 1941, Norway 1941, Arctic 1942, Malta Convoys 1942, Sabang 1944, Burma 1944-45.

Keyna in **heavy weather.**

Nigeria **arriving Malta, June 1946.**

TRINIDAD

Built at Devonport Dockyard. Laid down 21.4.1938. Launched 21.3.1940. Completed 14.10.1941. Home 1941-42. Sank German destroyer *Z26* off N. Norway, 29.3.1942, but in same action she was hit by one of her own torpedoes; temporary repairs at Murmansk to 5.42, but the enemy awaited her return to sea. Attacked by German torpedo aircraft in Barents Sea, 14.5.1942 and so badly damaged that she had to be sunk the following day by torpedoes from an escorting destroyer, HMS *Matchless*. 80 lost.

Battle Honour: Arctic 1942.

Trinidad. **A rare photograph taken during her short career.**

Gambia

GAMBIA

Built by Swan Hunter, Wallsend. Laid down 24.7.1939. Launched 30.11.1940. Completed 21.2.1942. Eastern Fleet 1942. East Indies and Eastern Fleet 1943. Refit, Liverpool, June-Sep 1943 prior to transfer to Royal New Zealand Navy, 1943-46. Eastern Fleet 1943-44. British Pacific Fleet 1945. New Zealand 1945-46. Returned to RN July 1946. Devonport Refit (X turret removed) 1946. 5 CS Far East 1946-47. Reserve and refit 1948-49. Mediterranean 1950-51. East Indies 1951-52. Mediterranean 1952-54. East Indies 1955-58 (last Flagship, C-in-C East Indies 1957-58). Home/Mediterranean 1958-59. South Atlantic and Far East 1959-60. Home 1960. Paid off, 12.1960. Portsmouth Reserve 1960-64. Broken up, Ward, Inverkeithing 1968.

Battle Honours: Sabang 1944, Okinawa 1945.

WRIGHT & LOGAN

Jamacia **arriving at Portsmouth, May 1952, in reserve ships colours.**

JAMAICA

Built by Vickers Armstrong, Barrow. Laid down 28.4.1939. Launched 16.11.1940. Completed 29.6.1942. 10 CS Home 1942-44. Refit (X turret removed) 10.4—6.45. 5 CS then 4 CS East Indies 1945-47. Refit, end 1947-48. Temporarily laid up 1948. America & W.I. 1949, loaned to 5 CS Far East 1949-51. Reserve 1951-53 (FOC Reserves 1953). Flag Officer Flotillas, Home 1954 (replaced *Swiftsure*). 1 CS Mediterranean 1954-55. Refit 1955. Mediterranean 1956-57. Home 1957. Reserve 1957. Laid up, Gareloch 1958. Broken up, Arnott Young, Dalmuir 1960 and Troon 1962. Africa

Battle Honours: Arctic 1942-44, North ~~America~~ 1942, Barents Sea 1942, North Cape 1943, Korea 1950.

BERMUDA

Built by John Brown, Clydebank. Laid down 30.11.1939. Launched 11.9.1941. Completed 21.8.1942. 10 CS Home 1942-44. Refit, Glasgow (X turret removed), 6.44—4.45. British Pacific Fleet 1945. Flagship, 5 CS Far East 1946-47. Chatham Refit 1947-48. Sheerness Reserve 1948-50. Devonport Refit 1950. Flagship, C-in-C, South Atlantic 1950-53. Mediterranean 1953-54 (exchanged places with *Euryalus*). Flag Officer Flotillas, Home 1955. Refit, Palmers, Hebburn 1956-57. Home/Mediterranean 1957-60. Refit 1960. Flag Officer Flotillas, Home 1961-62. Reserve 1962. Broken up, Ward, Briton Ferry 1965.

Battle Honours: North Africa 1942, Arctic 1943, Atlantic 1943.

Bermuda, as modified during the later years of her life, c1960.

CEYLON CLASS (3 ships)

Ceylon, Uganda (1938 Programme), *Newfoundland* (1939 Programme)

Displacement (tons):	8,875 standard, 10,850 full load.
Dimensions (feet):	538pp, 555½oa x 62 x 17¼
(metres):	164pp, 169.3oa x 18.9 x 5.3
Machinery:	4 shaft Parsons SR geared turbines. 4 Admiralty 3-drum boilers. 72,500 SHP = 31½ knots.
Fuel:	Oil 1,700 tons. Range 10,200 miles at 12 knots.
Protection:	As in Fiji.
Armament:	9—6in (3x3), 8—4in AA (4x2), 16—2pdr AA (4x4), 20-20mm AA (10x2), 6—21in TT (2x3). No aircraft.
Complement:	730

The last three Colonies were suspended in 1940, and the opportunity was taken to modify their design in the light of war experience. They emerged, in effect, as 'three turret Fijis', sacrificing 'X' turret for a heavier anti-aircraft armament. Aircraft were not carried, and the large hangar spaces were used for offices and additional accommodation.

Owing to manpower shortages, *Uganda* was transferred to the Royal Canadian Navy in 1944, following repairs for bomb damage.

Among the most modern cruisers in the post-war Fleet, *Ceylon* and *Newfoundland* were extensively modernized in the 1950s. Modifications included improvements to AA armament, modernized gunnery control, a new bridge and lattice masts (though *Ceylon* retained her tripod mainmast). Both ships were active with the Royal Navy until their sale to Peru in 1959/60.

Ceylon, **as completed in 1943.**

Uganda. **Photographed in 1944 after refit at Charleston.**

CEYLON

Built by Alex. Stephen, Govan. Laid down 27.4.1939. Launched 30.7.1942. Completed 13.7.1943. 10 CS Home 1943. Eastern Fleet 1943-44. 5 CS East Indies 1945. Refit 1945-47. Reserve 1947-49. Refit 1949-50. Flagship, C-in-C, East Indies 1950, but sent to Korea. 5 CS Far East 1951-52. Flagship, C-in-C, East Indies 1952-54. Refit 1955-56. Mediterranean (temp.) 1956—Suez crisis. Flagship, C-in-C, East Indies 1957. Flag Officer Flotillas, Home 1958. Mediterranean and Far East 1959. Sold to Peru and renamed *Coronel Bolognesi*, 1960. Deleted 1980.

Battle Honours: Sabang 1944, Burma 1945, Korea 1950-52.

NEWFOUNDLAND

Built by Swan Hunter, Wallsend. Laid down 9.11.1939. Launched 19.12.1941. Completed 20.1.1943. 10 CS Home 1943. Flagship, 15 CS Mediterranean 1943. Torpedoed on passage to Malta by Italian submarine *Ascianghi*, 27.3.43; repairs at Boston, USA to 4.44 and on Clyde to 11.44. British Pacific Fleet 1945. Flagship, 5 CS Far East 1946. Refit 1946-47. Harbour Training, Devonport 1947-50. Refit 1951-52. East Indies 1953-55. Flagship, 5 CS Far East 1956—sank Egyptian frigate *Domiat* in Gulf of Suez during Suez crisis, 1.11.1956. Flagship, C-in-C East Indies 1957. 5 CS Far East 1958-59. Paid off, Portsmouth 24.6.1959. Sold to Peru and renamed *Almirante Grau*, 1959. Renamed *Capitan Quinones*, 1973. Deleted 1979.

Battle Honours: Mediterranean 1943, Sicily 1943.

UGANDA

Built by Vickers Armstrong, Tyne. Laid down 20.7.1939. Launched 7.8.1941. Completed 3.1.1943. 10 CS Home 1943. Mediterranean 1943. Bombed 9.43; repairs at Charleston to 10.44. Commissioned in Royal Canadian Navy at Charleston, 21.10.1944. Portsmouth Refit to 6.1945. British Pacific Fleet 1945. Training Cruiser on Canada's East Coast 1946-56 (Refit 1950). Renamed *Quebec*, 1952. For disposal 1959. Broken up, Osaka 1961.

Battle Honours: Sicily 1943, Salerno 1943, Mediterranean 1943, Atlantic 1943.

Newfoundland. **Postwar with lattice masts and modernised AA fire control systems.**

SWIFTSURE CLASS (3 ships, including 1 RCN) *1941 Programme*

*Ontario (*ex *Minotaur), Swiftsure, Superb*

Displacement (tons):	8,800 standard 11,130 *(Minotaur* 11,480) full load.
Dimensions (feet):	538pp, 555½oa x 63 x 17¼
(metres):	164pp, 169.3oa x 19.2 x 5.3
Machinery:	4 shaft Parsons SR geared turbines. 4 Admiralty 3-drum boilers. 72,500 SHP = 31½ knots.
Fuel:	Oil 1,850 tons. Range 8,000/6,000/2,000 miles at 16/20/30 knots.
Protection:	Long citadel: belt 3½in-3¼in (89mm-83mm), bulkheads 2in-1½in (51mm-38mm), upper deck amidships 2in (51mm), lower deck fore and aft 2in (51mm). Stern belt 1½in (38mm), deck over steering gear 2in-1¼in (51mm-32mm).
Armament:	9—6in (3x3), 10-4in AA (5x2), 16—2pdr AA (4x4), 6—40mm AA, 6—21in TT (2x3).
Complement:	855

Second group (*Superb*) as above except:

Displacement (tons):	8,885 standard, 11,560 full load.
Dimensions (feet):	Beam 64 (19.5)
Complement:	867

Based on the Colony design, but incorporating war lessons more fully than was possible in the 'three turret Fijis'. Again, anti-aircraft armament was augmented at the expense of 'X' turret, and gunnery control and direction finding was improved. No aircraft were carried, and eliminating the hangars resulted in a more compact bridge structure. Beam was increased by a foot in *Minotaur* and *Swiftsure* and by two feet in the second group to improve stability.

Of the eight ships ordered, only three were completed to the original design, and of these *Minotaur* was transferred to Canada on completion and renamed *Ontario*. Of the rest, *Bellerophon*(ex *Blake*, ex *Tiger)* and *Hawke* were cancelled in March 1946, while *Tiger* (ex *Bellerophon),* *Defence* (renamed *Lion* in 1957) and *Blake* (ex *Tiger*, ex *Blake*) were laid up incomplete for nine years before construction resumed to a very different design, finally entering service in 1959-61 as the Tiger Class (qv). The name changing in 1945 was meant to ensure that the best names went to the ships most likely to survive the cancellations expected at the end of the war.

Swiftsure and *Superb* were the newest and most up-to-date cruisers in the post war Fleet and they saw extensive service. Much thought was given to modernising them, even to re-arming them on the lines of the Tigers, but limited funds precluded anything so drastic. *Swiftsure's* reconstruction was abandoned in 1960, and in the same year the unmodernised *Superb* went to the breakers.

HMCS *Ontario*, whilst in UK waters for the Coronation Review 1953.

ONTARIO (ex *Minotaur)*

Built by Harland & Wolff, Belfast. Laid down 20.11.1941. Launched 29.7.1943. Completed 25.5.1945. Presented to Royal Canadian Navy on completion and renamed. British Pacific Fleet 1945. Training Cruiser on Canada's West Coast 1946-58 (Refit 1950). Broke up, Osaka 1960.

SWIFTSURE

Built by Vickers Armstrong, Tyne. Laid down 22.9.1941. Launched 4.2.1943. Completed 22.6.1944. 10 CS Home 1944. Flagship, 4 CS British Pacific Fleet 1944-45—Japanese surrender of Hong Kong signed on board, 16.9.1945. Flagship, 4 CS East Indies 1946. Reserve 1946-49. Refit 1949-50. Flagship, 2 CS Home 1950-53. Flag Officer Flotillas, Home 1953. Badly damaged in collision with destroyer HMS *Diamond* 60 miles S. of Iceland, 16.9.1953. Repairs and Nore Reserve 1953-55. Refit, Immingham 1955. Laid up, Gareloch 1955-56. Modernisation commenced at Chatham, 1956 but abandoned 1960. Broken up, Ward, Inverkeithing 1962.

Battle Honour: Okinawa 1945.

SUPERB

Built by Swan Hunter, Wallsend. Laid down 23.6.1942. Launched 31.8.1943. Completed 16.11.1945. 10 CS Home 1945-46—on loan to 15 CS Mediterranean 1946 (Corfu incident). Flagship, 2 CS Home 1946-50. Flagship, C-in-C, America & W.I. 1950-51. Flag Officer Flotillas, Home 1951-53. Flagship, C-in-C, America & W.I. 1953-54. Heavy Squadron, Home 1954. Flagship, C-in-C, America & W.I. 1954-55. Refit 1955-56. Flagship, C-in-C, East Indies 1956-57. Flag Officer Flotillas, Home 1957. Laid up, Gareloch 1957-60. Broken up, Arnott Young, Dalmuir 1960.

Cancelled 3.1946: *Bellerophon* (Vickers Armstrong, Tyne), *Hawke* (Portsmouth—laid down 9.1943: broken up on slip.)

SKYFOTOS

Superb, **June 1953.**

Swiftsure, 29 March 1950, in the Firth of Forth.

Projected 'Neptune' class

Bellerophon, Centurion, Edgar, Mars, Minotaur, Neptune—none ordered.

Much larger than the Swiftsures, with a full load displacement of 18,740 tons and dimensions of 662ft (oa) x 76ft x 24ft (201.8m x 23.2m x 7.3m). Armament would have been 12—6in guns in four American pattern triple turrets, 12—4.5in DP (6x2), 28—40mm AA (14x2), and 16—21in TT (4x4). 108,000 SHP would have given a speed of 32 knots. The design appears to owe much to American experience in the Solomon Islands in 1942-43, particularly reflected in the heavy torpedo armament. They would have been rakish ships, broadly resembling the Southamptons in appearance. The design was abandoned at the end of the war and succeeded by the 'Minotaur' project.

BRITISH CRUISER DEPLOYMENT, JANUARY 1945

Home Fleet:
1 CS *Norfolk* (Flag), *Berwick, Devonshire.*
10 CS *Mauritius, Bellona, Diadem, Dido, (Sussex, Birmingham, Belfast, Glasgow, Bermuda* and *Jamaica* all refitting).

Local Commands:
    Rosyth—Training Squadron: *Dauntless, Diomede, Hawkins.*
    Refitting: *Frobisher, Liverpool.*

    Portsmouth: *Conrad* (refitting), *Scylla* (Reserve).

    Western Approaches: *Cleopatra* (refitting), *Cardiff* (Training).

Reserve Fleet:
    Capetown, Despatch, Emerald, Enterprise.
    Reducing: *Kent.*
    To reduce: *Caledon, Carlisle, Colombo, Dauntless, Diomede.*

Mediterranean Fleet:
15 CS *Ajax, Orion, Aurora, Sirius, Cleopatra* (refitting).
Flagship, Escort Carrier Squadron: *Royalist.* (*Carlisle,* Accommodation Ship).

East Indies:
5 CS *Newcastle* (Flag), *London, Suffolk, Cumberland, Kenya, Nigeria, Euryalus, Phoebe.*

British Pacific Fleet:
4 CS *Swiftsure* (Flag), *Ceylon, Argonaut, Black Prince, Achilles, Gambia* (refitting), *Newfoundland, Uganda.*

South West Pacific:
    Australia (Flag, C-in-C), *Shropshire, Hobart, Adelaide* (Reserve).

Refitting USA:
    Sheffield, Leander.

BRITISH CRUISER DEPLOYMENT, APRIL 1949

Home Fleet:
2 CS *Superb* (Flag), *Diadem, Cleopatra*.

Training:
  Cadet Training Ship *Devonshire*.
  Harbour Training, Devonport *Newfoundland*.

Reserve and Refitting:
*Swiftsure, Ceylon, Kenya, Gambia, Bermuda, Sheffield, Royalist
Argonaut, Dido, Sirius, Cumberland, Sussex*.

Mediterranean Fleet:
1 CS *Liverpool* (Flag), *Phoebe, Euryalus, Newcastle*.

East Indies:
Birmingham, (Flag, C-in-C), *Mauritius, Norfolk*.

South Atlantic:
Nigeria (Flag, C-in-C).

Far East:
5 CS *Belfast*, (Flag), *London*.

America and West Indies:
Glasgow (Flag, C-in-C), *Jamaica*.

Royal New Zealand Navy:
Bellona. (Black Prince in Reserve.)

Royal Australian Navy:
Australia (Flag). *Hobart, Shropshire,* in Reserve.

Royal Canadian Navy:
Ontario. (Uganda in Reserve.)

1959-79: SWAN SONG

Tiger class

During the Second World War, the cruiser found a new role as escort for carrier strike forces. With the speed to keep up with the carriers and the gun power to ward off surface attackers, cruisers had also proved excellent anti-aircraft ships, and had provided aircraft direction facilities both in the fleet and on convoys. As part of the carrier strike force, the cruiser's future seemed assured. But following another revolution in warship design, the fast carrier escorts that emerged in the early 1960s had neither armour nor heavy guns, and relied on guided missiles for their main armament. Of small cruiser size, the Royal Navy called its new County class, oddly, 'guided missile destroyers', while the US Navy preferred 'frigate' for its own ships, reclassifying them as cruisers in 1975. The Soviet Union built broadly similar 'rocket cruisers', though mainly for surface attack. Whatever the new ships were called, they were not cruisers in the conventional sense and did not inherit the cruiser's mantle entirely: aircraft and satellites had largely taken over as the 'eyes of the fleet'; and as for blockade, two wars had shown the vast superiority of the submarine.

However, for ten years after the war, thought was given to a new generation of conventional cruisers. The late-war 'Neptune' design was succeeded by the Minotaur project in 1945-46, on which work continued until about 1951. Designed around new dual-purpose rapid firing 6in and 3in guns, the Minotaurs would have been about 18,400 tons full load, with dimensions of 650ft (oa) x 75ft x 24ft (198.1m x 22.8m x 7.3m), though later versions were slightly smaller. Armament was 10—6in DP (5x2), 6—3in DP (3x2), 20—40mm AA (10x2), 32—20mm AA (16x2), and 16—21in TT (4x4). Four shaft geared turbines developing 100,000 SHP would have given a speed of 32 knots. Possibly influenced by the American Worcester class, they would have been flush decked, with main guns disposed as in the Didos (though latterly there were reservations about shipping 'Q' turret).

The Minotaurs never had a realistic chance of being built. When naval construction resumed in Britain with the 1951 Rearmament Programme, the emphasis was on frigates to counter the growing threat posed by Soviet submarines. However, it was announced in 1951 that the three suspended ships of the Tiger class would be completed with reduced outfits of the Minotaurs' guns.

A series of studies began in the late 1940s for a new class of cruisers planned for the 1960 Estimates, and hence known as the '1960 Cruiser'. These studies were for small, medium and large cruisers, armed with either the new 6in turrets or rapid fire 5in mountings. Some variants incorporated the Seaslug guided missile system, and, unusually for cruisers, a full ASW outfit. All versions had conventional steam power plants, based on those of the Daring class destroyers. But the 1960 Cruiser was abandoned in 1957 and its design team transferred, perhaps prophetically, to the Dreadnought nuclear submarine project. If the cruiser project can be said to have had a successor, it was the big County class destroyer.

Most agreed that the conventional cruiser had had its day. Only Russia built a significant number of cruisers after the Second World War, and even she was turning away from the type by the mid 1950s.

Meanwhile Britain's economy—exhausted by war—was in relative decline, and her empire fading fast. The Royal Navy, overtaken in size by the United States' Navy during the Second World War, was pushed into third place in the 1950s by Russia's naval expansion. Pax Britannica was giving way to Pax Americana.

In 1948, with trooping duties done and war weary ships refitted, the Royal Navy had sixteen cruisers in full commission—under half the pre-war figure. This number fell regularly by one a year into the 1960s, and not even the valuable contribution made by cruisers in the Korean War could halt the decline. The last cruiser on the South Atlantic station was withdrawn in 1954, from America and the West Indies in 1956, from the East Indies in 1958 when that station closed, and from the Far East and Mediterranean in 1963.

Defence. **Laid up for many years in the Gareloch, she was later completed in 1960 as** *Lion.*

The long delayed Tigers, which finally entered service in 1959-61, soon followed their older cousins into reserve—their career an appendix to the cruiser story rather than a new chapter. When *Tiger* paid off in 1966 the conventional cruiser disappeared from the active fleet altogether, but this was not quite the end.

After a decade of being heavily committed East of Suez, the Royal Navy by the early 1970s was concentrated in the North East Atlantic and almost wholly assigned to NATO: apart from a few residual commitments the world role was all but abandoned. This was the Fleet that *Blake* and *Tiger* rejoined after conversion into hybrid 'command' or 'helicopter cruisers'. They were potent anti-submarine platforms and well adapted for leading task groups on global deployments from time to time. Both ships were present at the Silver Jubliee Review of the Fleet in June 1977, but *Tiger* went into Reserve the following year and *Blake* paid off in December 1979: days before in the English Channel she fired the Royal Navy's last 6in gun salvo. The swan song of the cruiser was over. The career of the British cruiser, from the completion of the *Iris*, had lasted a few months longer than a hundred years.

TIGER CLASS (3 ships)

Lion (ex *Defence*), *Tiger* (1941 Programme), *Blake* (1942 Programme)

Displacement (tons):	9,550 standard, 11,700 full load (9,500/12,080 after conversion).
Dimensions (feet):	538pp, 555½oa x 64 x 18 (Length 556½ oa after conversion).
(metres):	164pp, 169.3oa x 19.5 x 5.5 (172.7)
Machinery:	4 shaft Parsons SR geared turbines. 4 Admiralty 3-drum boilers. 80,000 SHP = 31½ knots.
Fuel:	Oil 1,940 tons. Range 6,500/4,000/2,000 miles at 13/20/30 knots.
Protection:	Long citadel: belt 3½in-3¼in (89mm-83mm), bulkheads 2in-1½in (51mm-38mm), upper deck amidships 2in (51mm), lower deck fore and aft 2in (51mm). Stern belt 1½in (38mm), deck over steering gear 2in-1¼in (51mm-32mm).
Armament: as built;	4—6in DP (2x2), 6—3in DP (3x2).
as converted;	2—6in DP (1x2), 2—3in DP (1x2), 2—quad Seacat GWS launchers, 4—Sea King A/S helicopters.
Complement:	716 (later 885).

Laid down as sisters of the *Superb,* suspended at the end of the war, and then redesigned around the rapid-fire 6in and 3in guns originally intended for the abandoned 'Minotaur' project. Work resumed in 1954, and the Tigers finally entered service in 1959-61.

The MK 26 twin 6in turrets had a phenomenal rate of fire—20 rounds per gun per minute—and the Tigers could deliver a greater weight of shell with their four guns than the Southamptons or Fijis had done with twelve. The turrets were troublesome, however, and the ships never enjoyed a very high reputation. Many had doubted the wisdom of completing them, for by 1960 the day of the conventional cruiser was practically over. In service, their demands for technical manpower created manning problems, causing *Blake* to be paid off only two years after commissioning.

Before long, *Blake* and *Tiger* were converted into 'helicopter cruisers'. A large box hangar and raised flight deck for operating four Sea King helicopters replaced the after 6in turret, giving these once handsome ships a bizarre, 'push me pull you' appearance. The 3in guns in the waist gave way to Seacat short-range anti aircraft missile launchers, and they were fitted with extensive command and communications equipment, enabling them to serve as task group flagships. Plans for *Lion*'s conversion (possibly on more radical lines) were cancelled, and she went to the breakers in her original state. *Blake* was the last British cruiser in commission with the Royal Navy, paying off in December 1979.

Lion **arriving in Malta, 1961.**

LION (ex *Defence*)

Built by Scotts, Greenock. Laid down 24.6.1942. Launched 2.9.1944. Completed 20.7.1960.
Completed by Swan Hunter, Wallsend—renamed 1957. Home/Mediterranean
1960-62—departure for Mediterranean in 1961 delayed by repairs for turbine defects. Sales
cruise to South America, late 1961-62. Refit 1962. Home/Far East/Home 1962-64—Flag
Officer Flotillas, Home 1963-64. Devonport Reserve 1964-72. For disposal 1972—stripped at
Rosyth and cannibalised to provide parts for *Tiger*. Broken up, Ward, Inverkeithing 1975.

Tiger

TIGER (ex *Bellerophon*)

Built by John Brown, Clydebank. Laid down 1.10.1941. Launched 25.10.1945. Completed 18.3.1959. Home/Mediterranean 1959-61. Refit 1961. Home/Far East/Home 1961-63. Refit 1963. Flag Officer Flotillas, Home 1964-65. Flagship, 2nd in Command, Home 1965-66. 'Tiger talks' at Gibraltar between Harold Wilson and Ian Smith on future of Rhodesia, 12.1966. Paid off 12.1966. Reserve 1966-68. Conversion to Helicopter Cruiser, Devonport 1968-72. General Sea Service 1972-78—major deployments to Far East 1973, W. Africa and S. America 1977, Far East 1977-78. Flagship, 2nd Flotilla 1974-78. Paid off 4.1978. Portsmouth Reserve 1978-79. For disposal 1980. Sold to Desguaces Varela and broken up in Spain, 1986.

BEFORE . . .

Blake. **Photographed during her only commission as a conventional cruiser.**

BLAKE (ex *Tiger,* ex *Blake)*

Built by Fairfield, Govan. Laid down 17.8.1942. Launched 20.12.1945. Completed 18.3.1961. Home/Mediterranean 1961-63. Reserve 1963-65. Conversion to Helicopter Cruiser, Portsmouth 1965-69. General Sea Service 1969-76—Flag Officers Flotillas, Western Fleet 1969-70. Major deployments to Far East 1970, West Indies and W. Coast of USA late 1971, Far East 1974-75. Flagship, 1st Flotilla 1974-79. Refit 1976-77. General Sea Service 1977-79—major deployment to N. and S. America 1978. Paid off 12.1979. Standby Squadron, Chatham 1980-81. For disposal 1981. Broken up, Shipbreaking (Queenborough) Ltd. Cairnryan 1982.

AND AFTER

Blake. **Photographed during 1970 with her Wessex Mark 3 helicopters.**

APPENDIX I: NOTES ON CRUISER PROTECTION

1. THE PROTECTED CRUISER

A simple and effective form of protection consisted of a full length protective deck at or about the waterline. Normally the deck sloped downwards at the edges to meet the ship's side, and at the bows to reinforce the ram. Additional protection was gained by the custom of having coal bunkers in the ship's side, above the slope of the protective deck. The effect of the deck was to create an impenetratable raft below the waterline containing all the ship's vitals, and able to stay afloat whatever damage the upper part of the hull sustained. Of course, the ship could still fall prey to underwater damage by mine or torpedo, or to explosion caused by fire reaching the magazines.

With or without an armoured belt, the full length protective deck was common to nearly all late Victorian cruisers, and last appeared in the First World War 'Town' classes. By definition, a protected cruiser was one which relied principally for its protection on a full length deck.

A few ships built in the 1880s—the Leander, Scout and Archer classes—had short protective decks, covering only the boiler and machinery spaces. Without the raft effect of the full length deck. these ships relied on internal subdivision of the hull to preserve bouyancy.

2. THE BELTED OR ARMOURED CRUISER

The protective deck was intended to limit damage once a shell had entered the ship. Obviously it was better to keep shells out altogether by armouring the ship's sides. But because the old compound armour was so heavy, it was only possible to provide the early Imperieuse and Orlando class belted cruisers with short, narrow midship belts of dubious value, and complemented anyway by a protective deck. Opinion in Britain swung against the armoured cruiser for several years.

With the advent of lighter, cemented armour, it was possible by the late 1890s to provide the Cressys and subsequent armoured cruisers with a deeper (11ft 6in) belt, running from the bows at least as far aft as the machinery spaces. The belt was thickest amidships, tapering towards bow and stern. Though the full length protective deck was retained in these belted ships, it was thinner than in a protected cruiser.

3. SCOUT CRUISERS

The first, commercially designed Scouts were required to have the equivalent of a light full length protective deck; one pair incorporated a midship belt. The subsequent Boadiceas, however, had only minimal protection, consisting of a partial protective plating over the machinery spaces and a deck over the steering gear. This was the meagre scale of deck protection inherited by the Arethusa class light cruisers, but they were well protected by extensive side armour.

4. LIGHT CRUISERS

Three distinct patterns of protection can be seen in the light cruisers built before and during the First World War. The Bristols and Weymouths of 1909-10 were conventional protected cruisers, with a full length protective deck on the waterline. In the subsequent Chathams and Birminghams the deck was retained but halved in thickness, and the weight saved devoted to a long 2in belt, laid on 1in plating amidships. The Arethusas, 'C's and 'D's similarly had long, extensive belts, but only a partial protective plating over machinery spaces and a deck over the steering gear. Given the extent of their side armour, their almost total lack of horizontal protection was not a weakness in an age before aerial bombing and plunging fire.

Like the Arethusas, 'C's, and 'D's, the much larger 'E's and 'Elizabethans' had extensive belts and limited deck protection, but the 'Elizabethans' also had light and economical 'box' armour around the magazines.

5. CRUISERS AFTER 1918

New conditions after the First World War (aircraft, plunging fire), made a combination of both vertical and horizontal protection essential. However, as all cruisers between the wars were displacement-limited by treaty, protection had to be selectively applied: it was vain to contemplate full length protection decks and extensive belts as in the old armoured cruisers.

The solution adopted in the 'Counties' and most subsequent cruisers was to make three (or four) armoured boxes. The biggest, enclosing the boiler and machinery spaces, had a protective deck as the roof, armoured bulkheads at either end, and an amidships belt as the sides. (The Counties as built had no belt, but a waterline strake of 1in plating.) Smaller armoured boxes within the hull enclosed the magazines, fore and aft of the machinery spaces. In the Edinburgh, Colony, and later classes, the machinery 'box' was extended fore and aft to embrace the magazines as well, so that a single citadel contained all the ship's vitals. The citadel was closed by 'vee' form staggered bulkheads, and its profile was disclosed by the shape of the belt.

All cruisers relied on various forms of internal subdivision to limit flooding in the event of damage. A few (the rebuilt Edgars, the Elizabethans, the 10,000 ton Treaty cruisers and the reconstructed *Belfast*) incorporated anti-torpedo bulges.

A sight never to be repeated . . .

End of an era . . . *Tiger* **is towed away to a Spanish breakers yard, September 1986.**

INDEX

Although her 6″ guns
fell silent long ago, the cruiser,

HMS BELFAST,

last of her kind, is open daily
as a floating museum moored
on the River Thames in
the centre of London.

For details ring 01 407 6434